CW01236881

Jungle Warrior

Britain's Greatest SOE Commander

Richard Duckett

Chiselbury

Copyright © 2025 Duncan Gilmour

Published by Chiselbury Publishing, a division of Woodstock Leasor Limited 14 Devonia Road, London N1 8JH, United Kingdom

www.chiselbury.com

ISBN: 978-1-916556-84-3 (hardback/dustjacket)
ISBN: 978-1-917837-04-0 (hardback/Case laminate cover)
ISBN: 978-1-917837-05-7 (ebook)
A CIP catalogue record for this book is available from the British Library

The moral right of Richard Duckett to be identified as the author of this work is asserted.

This is copyright material and must not be copied, reproduced, transferred, distributed, leased, licensed or publicly performed or used in any way except as specifically permitted by the publishers, as allowed under the terms and conditions under which it was purchased or as strictly permitted by applicable copyright law. Any unauthorised distribution or use of this text may be a direct infringement of the publisher's rights and those responsible may be liable in law accordingly.

Chiselbury Publishing hereby exclude all liability to the extent permitted by law for any errors or omissions in this book and for any loss, damage or expense (whether direct or indirect) suffered by any third party relying on any information contained in this book.

'Edgar was one of the great guerrilla leaders of the last war, one of the greatest, I would say.'

Major Eustace Poles to Geraldine Peacock

'When he came to me and insisted that I must help him to go out and get Gibson back, I thought he was mad, but if loyalty without thought of self is madness, give me madness every time. His stark courage and obstinate persistence got him there and back, when very few would have started.'

General Sir Douglas D. Gracey KCB, KCIE, CBE, MC
Foreword to The Life of a Jungle Walla *1958*

'Peacock himself was quite intolerant of any but his own ideas and was an egoist of the first water.'

Lieutenant Colonel Ritchie Gardiner in a letter to the Official Historian of SOE in the Far East, Charles Cruickshank, December 1981

'I have ever regretted that Edgar, with his great gift for lucid writing, did not produce a book embracing the aspect of the guerrilla fighting in Burma and the creation of his celebrated 'P Force' which grew up by the Chindwin and reached its maturity in the Karen Hills.'

Major Eustace Poles in a letter to Geraldine Peacock

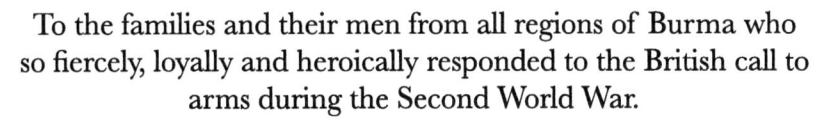

To the families and their men from all regions of Burma who so fiercely, loyally and heroically responded to the British call to arms during the Second World War.

Without them many more lives would have been lost.

Contents

Foreword by General the Lord Richards GCB, CBE, DSO   1
Preface   5
Introduction: 'I am the master of this house'   9

Part I Pre War (1893 to 1939)   17

1. 'Fortunate and powerful'   19
2. 'A wonderful but sometimes aggressive philosophy'   23
3. 'Saviour of the villagers in Burma'   29
4. 'An unknown colonial from those wild places'   32
5. Mrs Sparks, the rector's wife   36
6. 'The dark man in a good government job'   40
7. 'The great Peacock of Burma'   44
8. 'It is the sunshine makes the shadows'   48
9. 'A hard tussle in a 'cock fight''   51
10. 'He had never even tried to flirt with me'   54
11. 'A ship-board affair?'   57
12. 'Tell the old cats you are coming out to be all in all to a wild jungle man'   60
13. 'My darling, you can't come running back this time'   63
14. 'What a wedding day'   66
15. 'I had lived a life time in a very different world'   71
Photos 1   74
16. 'Most of my life is spent in the jungle'   84
17. 'Ghostly nights and weird noises'   87
18. 'Some lovely new frocks'   91
19. 'Quite a civilised life for a change'   95
20. 'A red spot'   99
21. 'So that is why you came home, was it?'   103
22. 'A snake in the grass'   108
23. 'Now don't go raising any objections'   111
24. 'Put old socks over your shoes'   115

Part II The War (to the end of '44)   *119*

25. 'You must come back a colonel'   121
26. 'I can't say I like the news from the Far East'   125
27. 'No one else [...] worshipped the little red gods'   129
28. 'Take care of yourself darling, I love you very much'   135
29. 'Edgar was mysteriously whisked away'   139
30. '2/LT Peacock with all drivers'   142
31. 'A lecturer of considerable ability'   146
32. 'Who knows all those jungles better than I do?'   150
33. 'Our small band of cut-throats'   155
34. 'I am right in the front line as a guerrilla'   159
35. 'A recapitulation'   162
36. 'It is now up to us to justify the confidence placed in us'   166
37. 'Such armed rabble are not merely useless, but may be
    a menace'   170
38. 'A pair of abbreviated bathing trunks'   174
39. 'Our part in the battle for KYAUK KYAW'   177
40. 'Some of us are going to suffer from disease and
    violence from the enemy'   184
41. 'The lower Yu is much too peaceful'   188
42. 'If this is the case our position is serious.'   193
43. 'Big flap and panic'   197
44. 'Edgar and I held a conference'   201
45. 'Give me madness every time'   204
46. 'All ranks are rum drinkers'   212
47. 'Now darling don't panic'   217
48. 'Riddled with malaria'   221

Part III Operation Character And Beyond
(February 1945 to March 1955)   *225*

49. 'Of training in jungle warfare the less said the better'   227
50. 'Bedlam reigned'   231
51. 'I never could understand the hurry'   237
52. 'They told me seven o'clock'   240

53. 'Unswerving loyalty' Part One	245
54. 'Ideal for my purposes'	250
Photos 2	255
55. 'We awaited instructions for offensive operations'	272
56. 'Our equanimity was somewhat shaken'	276
57. 'Unswerving loyalty' Part Two	281
58. 'The Japs were extremely careless at first'	287
59. 'Their greatest achievement'	291
60. 'An extremely trying month for all of us'	295
61. 'A seething furious mass of dense vapour'	299
62. 'We should have been in excellent shape to kill the Japs'	303
63. 'His head was lying a few yards from his body'	307
64. 'I had a large abcess [sic] on my back'	311
65. 'Polite, amenable and meticulous'	315
66. 'I am dog tired'	319
67. 'I am full of eagerness to be home'	323
68. 'An old beret and the uniform of a colonel'	327
69. 'Starting from scratch'	331
70. 'He must be ill in some way'	335
71. 'With God's help I determined to do it'	338
Photos 3	340
72. Jungle Warrior: Britain's Greatest SOE Commander	344
Afterword by General Sir Douglas D. Gracey,	348
Glossary	351
Appendix One	353
Appendix Two	357
Bibliography	359
Books & Articles	362
Websites	365
INDEX	369

List of Maps

Burma	70
Southern Africa	107
January patrol (overview)	179
January patrol (detail)	180
February patrol (detail)	189
February patrol (overview)	190
John Gibson's rescue	209
Operation Character areas	242
Operation Caracter (overview)	249
Operation Character initial march	250
Otter Area	277

Foreword
by
General the Lord Richards GCB, CBE, DSO
Former Chief of Defence Staff

We live in an era in which 'Special Forces' feature prominently: movies, endless books, TV series and even game shows. Understandably we all have a high regard for especially brave and enterprising people who single-mindedly and courageously put their cause and their people before themselves, often at great risk to their own lives. I am a soldier of forty-two years' standing and my passion is military history. I knew of Second World War 'irregulars' including the Long Range Desert Group (LRDG), Army and Royal Marine commandos, Special Operations Executive (SOE) in Europe, the Chindits in Burma, David Stirling and the Special Air Service (SAS) and more. They all merit the high regard in which they are held. It was not, though, until I read this remarkable book that I had a proper understanding of the SOE's operations in Southeast Asia. It stimulated further research on my part. I now think that there is a strong case for claiming that what Force 136 achieved and suffered in the jungles of Burma makes it among, if not the most, daring, demanding and successful of all World War Two Special Forces operations.

The man commanding a key element of Force 136 was Lieutenant Colonel Edgar Peacock DSO, MC and Bar. This compelling book tells his story. The first half establishes the nature of the man, against the backdrop of British colonial life. It is a fascinating tale that in many respects is just as vital a part of Edgar Peacock's story as the pages that go on to describe his military service. Certainly, without it, our understanding of Peacock, his motives, passion for the peoples of Burma

1

FOREWORD

(especially the Karens), and his deep understanding of the jungle, enabling him to operate so successfully in it, would be hazy and incomplete at best. To reprise only his wartime service would beg many questions of what 'maketh the man'. Richard Duckett, much assisted by Peacock's grandson, Duncan Gilmour, answers this very natural question in a sympathetic and engaging manner that is both central to the man but is also historically important. It is an outstanding portrayal of colonial life in India and Burma, in many ways as important as what follows.

But it is the second half of the book that has the reader shaking his or her head in wonderment at the tenacity, determination, raw courage and initiative of Force 136, and particularly of one of its most important commanders. Edgar Peacock is an iron-willed, stubborn, often difficult but hugely courageous officer, who combined an obstreperous morally driven attitude to some of his superiors with a rare devotion to those under his command. He is a quite remarkable man.

Whilst Special Forces will never win a war by themselves, they are a vital part of the Commanding General's military orchestra. Having first been blooded in a mightily brave but failed attempt to reinforce fellow SOE officer Major Hugh Seagrim in 1943/44, Force 136's subsequent tactical achievements and morale-raising exploits without doubt played a crucial role both in the defence of India in 1944 and Fourteenth Army's advance through Burma in 1945. In particular Peacock's unit played a critical role in 20th Indian Infantry Division's advance operations in the Chindwin River area before the Battle for Imphal. Such was his admiration for Peacock and the debt of gratitude that he felt he owed him that the Divisional Commander, General Sir Douglas Gracey, wrote the foreword to Geraldine Peacock's biography of her by now deceased husband, The Life of a Jungle Walla, in 1958.

Although I trained in the jungle of Malaya in the early 1970s, I can barely imagine the physical and mental strains placed on the men of Force 136. The book brings this dimension of their operations into graphic relief. And Peacock had the enormous pressures of command to contend with as well. Today we understand PTSD (Post-Traumatic Stress Disorder) and there are good therapies available for those who suffer from it. But in Peacock's era, except in its most extreme forms, the Army did not recognize the condition. A stiff upper lip was expected and needed. That and the close brotherhood of one's comrades in arms, for only they could properly appreciate what individuals had been through and suffered. My own father, who fought at Imphal, certainly fell into this category, as did many others who served in India and Burma. Peacock was an exceptionally strong-willed character who seemed to relish the role he had been given. Nevertheless what he had done must have affected even him, making his somewhat irascible character and constant questioning of those in authority above him more pronounced. That he was usually right could not have made him any happier at the time. The book covers Edgar's post-war tribulations and associated mental state with much understanding. His long-suffering wife Geraldine bore the brunt of his PTSD, remaining loyal to him until the day he died prematurely at the age of sixty-two, unsurprisingly mentally and physically worn down by his experiences in Force 136.

Jungle Warrior is a splendid book about a very brave and determined man who, literally, gave his all for King and Country. He did this at the expense of much that today many treat as their God-given right. Through a skilful combination of social, military and personal history, Dr Duckett allows us to understand why Lieutenant Colonel Edgar Peacock DSO, MC* did what he did. Though in many ways a man of his times, he was without doubt exceptional by any standards. One cannot help but wonder if successor generations could match his single-minded preparedness to risk all and suffer hugely in pursuit of what he felt was right.

Edgar was in the Royal Artillery. I and the Royal Regiment as a whole are hugely and rightly proud of an immensely courageous officer we are privileged to call a fellow 'Gunner'.

Richards of Herstmonceux
21st October 2024

Preface

Five steps are what it took him to climb into the C47 Dakota aircraft that would transport him some 620 miles to the selected drop zone. The next time his feet touched the ground he would be 370 miles behind enemy lines and on the greatest adventure of his life; one which he had, personally, planned and, arguably, been training for since he was a boy. He had spent so much of his life in the jungles of India and Burma that he felt more at home there, where he roamed freely amongst the wildlife, than he did in 'modern' civilised society.

The C47's engines coughed into life, first starboard then port in turn, and Edgar Peacock's thoughts turned with them to the future. He had been tasked with planning this operation a year ago and ordered to select eighty of his best men to form the core Special Groups. They were supplemented with other special forces men to parachute into the Karen Hills and raise an army of guerrillas to protect the left flank of the British Army as it hurtled southwards to Rangoon, racing both the Japanese and the monsoon. One of his Special Groups was already there but had reported difficulty persuading the Karen to join them. The situation demanded him to arrive in force to tip the balance. This was his time. This was his moment.

Here is a book about a teenage orphan from India who grows up to become Britain's greatest special forces commander.

Through this book, which has been in gestation for nearly fifty years, Lieutenant Colonel Edgar Henry William Peacock DSO MC and Bar will, finally, emerge into public consciousness and take his place, where he belongs, alongside the other great special forces leaders of the Second World War.

Edgar much admired the writings of Rudyard Kipling and had strongly identified with Mowgli as he grew up, spending much of his spare time wandering the forest trails near his home in Lucknow. When he was fifteen, both of his parents and his

Preface

sister died in a cholera epidemic at his home in India, leaving him only with his brothers and an aunt who sent him to the imposing but austere boarding school, La Martinière College, where the emphasis was on sports, academic achievement and self-reliance. Edgar excelled in all three but, after the death of his parents, he found himself more comfortable in his own company than with others. He was perfectly amenable but slightly distant and hard to know, and it was during these years that his adult character formed. In common with many of his peers, his nature was sculpted by duty and allegiance to the Crown but Edgar wrapped around it an unbending will with which he drove himself beyond normal physical limits. Whenever he felt unwell, his remedy was to climb a hill. Weakness was despised, both in himself and in others and, as a leader, he demanded absolute obedience from humans and animals alike. His youngest daughter, Wendy, remembered him as being quick to believe the best in someone but when let down, his opinion changed and could never be recovered. His disapproval was harsh.

Edgar's eldest brother, Charles, had killed himself on the eve of the First World War and the next, Percy, had died in Mesopotamia attempting to relieve the siege of Kut. His nearest brother in age, Gerald, was serving as a doctor elsewhere and Edgar was the sole beneficiary of Percy's hastily made will which amounted to no more than two canvas bags, his regimental sword and 3,000 Rupees. So it was that in the space of no more than six years Edgar had lost all but one member of his family, and he found solace in forests and jungles.

Over several decades of research, I have amassed many records, photographs and testimonies as well as making visits to the places my grandparents lived on the continents of Asia, Africa and Europe. What emerges is the quite extraordinary story of a man long hidden in the thick undergrowth of history. The results of the research are laid before you here. Without it, many of the things that have been discovered would have remained unseen and unfound, but this is a story which, absolutely, needs to be told.

As you will read in the following pages, the Special Operations Executive was an obsessively secret organisation and, at war's end, many valuable records were deliberately destroyed in the name of national security. Others were lost to fire and flood. It is down to the diligent, dogged work of the author and historian Dr. Richard Duckett that those records which remain have been brought to light, examined, recorded and added to the growing pile of evidence. I have also been extremely fortunate to have found and met the granddaughter of Edgar Peacock's closest friend and colleague, Major Eustace Poles. Amanda was kind enough to give me free reign to explore her grandfather's "box of treasures". What Richard Duckett and I discovered there was priceless. Amongst other heart stopping evidence is a contemporary handwritten diary of patrols in the Upper Chindwin during the months leading into the Battle of Imphal, including the dramatic rescue of Captain John Gibson. It is a tale worthy of a Hollywood film and it describes carrying the incapacitated man through jungle covered mountains and crossing very active enemy lines three times within thirty six hours as the Battle for Imphal gathered pace. The diaries also disclosed hitherto unknown information of SOE involvement in that great and decisive battle and I am deeply grateful to the Poles family for their permission to quote from the precious information they have.

In February 1945, Edgar Peacock's greatest of many adventures began and his body of men, known as Peacock Force, formed the nucleus of the first three Special Groups to parachute into the Karen Hills in an operation which was to become the most spectacularly successful guerrilla operation in any theatre of war during World War Two. It has been my absolute privilege to meet some of the indigenous men who served alongside British forces and without whom the reconquest of Burma would have taken a very different shape.

PREFACE

Through my work as a trustee of the superb but niche British charity Help 4 Forgotten Allies, chaired by Sally McLean MBE, I travelled deep into rural Burma meeting and enjoying the company of these very old soldiers. Their loyalty and the genuine friendship they showed (and their families still show) to us is truly humbling and I dedicate this book to them all.

Duncan Gilmour
Grandson of Edgar Peacock
January 2025

Introduction:

'I am the master of this house'

The humidity of the jungle still meant that their clothing was stuck to their bodies, even though they had been lying still for well over three hours now. They had neither seen nor heard anything but the usual jungle sounds on their periphery, and the more immediate buzzing of insects. The mosquito repellent was evidently doing its job though. Having hunted in Southern Africa and across the Indian subcontinent during his fifty-two years, he reflected that this was one of the more comfortable periods of waiting. Waiting. Patience was the hunter's best friend.

There was at least one big difference this time though; he was waiting for his prey with approximately sixty other men, and the prey was not a rogue tiger or an antelope for the pot. This time he was waiting to shoot other men.

The men that he was going to shoot other men with were predominantly Bamar and Karen, some of whom he had only met in recent weeks. Some of them hadn't known how to operate a weapon, let alone how to fight as a guerrilla. Sitting there in his ambush position, he didn't feel nervous, however; most of the men might be untested in combat, and although they had been hastily trained in time to meet the coming enemy, he had confidence in himself and the small group of veterans he had brought with him. They had rehearsed ambush drills with the new recruits, and completed live firing exercises close to their hilltop headquarters, but more importantly, all the men were entirely confident in this jungle environment. It was, after all, their country, as it, also, had been his for eighteen years of his career. As the afternoon wore on, he pushed thoughts of home

Introduction

out of his mind and concentrated on the sounds around him, wise to the fact that the jungle would tell him of their enemy's approach long before he heard them himself. That nobody had fidgeted or made any noise gave him no especial satisfaction for he expected it of the men under his command. He didn't see himself as a hard leader, but his standards had to be met and usually were.

Then it happened. It was almost imperceptible, just a fractional alteration in the rhythm of the peaceful afternoon. There was no flicker of excitement, for he did not enjoy what he knew would happen next; at the same time, there was no fear either. Soon now, the waiting would be over, and a controlled hell would break loose for a short time along a 200 yard stretch of remote road in a remote part of the British Empire.

Just over a year later, the man stripped off his starchy ironed shirt to reveal the huge abscess on his back for the doctor. The physician didn't show any emotion, but he could see that the injury was many months old and hadn't been treated properly. It was difficult to tell exactly what it was, even as a physician who had worked in Africa for a considerable number of years. A tropical ulcer is more usually found beneath the knee and on the feet, rather than on a man's back. Tropical ulcers, also known as Jungle Rot, presented just as this man's wound did. What the doctor did know was that the man had borne the ulcer for a long time, and the best he could do was prescribe some strong antibiotics and hope it cleared up. He wondered how much damage had already been done underneath the wound. If it had been treated with antibiotics early on, it should have healed. Even a decent diet of fresh vegetables, or a course of vitamin supplements, would have helped. The doctor knew that that had not been possible, though. The smelly wound must be very painful, but his patient showed no visible signs of discomfort.

The man was only just home after being away from his family for the greater part of six long years, during which time he had only made it home once to see his wife and two daughters. It was 1946.

One morning that year, the man's wife again forgot to tell the cook to prepare cabbage for his breakfast. Since he had returned, he had wanted green food with every meal. Owning a farm and growing their own vegetables, it should have been fairly straightforward to provide this for her husband, but even before the war he had 'always had queer ideas about food' so there was the thought that this was 'another craze', a bit like the 'Hay Diet' he had tried in the 1930s. The Hay Diet had been so popular in that decade that it was offered on menus when Doctor Hay's adherents went out to dine. On this particular morning, though, the absence of cabbage provoked some fury. The man shouted 'I am the master of this house! Why can't I get a little green food if I want it?' To add to his wife's discomfort, their eldest daughter, Joy, agreed with her father, asking why Daddy couldn't 'have a little green food if he wants it.' The tense atmosphere this created was not an unusual one in the Peacock household; but certainly it was one mimicked in various ways across the world as returning service personnel struggled to adapt to homecoming and the realities of life without war. Reintegrating with loved ones was not easy for many men and their families.

While the long-term damage of his jungle sore may not have killed him, the serious head trauma inflicted during a rebellion in the Burmese jungle in 1932 might have. A life-threatening head wound can cause malignant hypertension, which in turn can cause kidney failure through uraemia. Uraemia was quoted on the man's death certificate as a secondary cause of death, and is consistent with the weight loss dramatically obvious in the last photos taken of the man with his family. Whatever it was that claimed his life at the youngish age of sixty-two on 4 March 1955, it seems to be related in some way to his close lifelong relationship with the jungles of Burma.

Introduction

The man was Edgar Henry William Peacock. At the time he visited the doctor in 1946, he had just celebrated his fifty-third birthday, although his Army records show him as five years younger, apparently born in 1898. Of course, he was not the first person ever to lie about his age in order to ensure that he went to war; Edgar was determined not to miss the second global conflict of his lifetime. Although he had lost a brother in the Great War of 1914–1918, he had still been most put out that his career had been deemed a reserved profession, and that he was therefore not eligible for war service. Instead, Edgar had remained in Burma during the First World War, working in the jungle as Assistant Conservator of Forests. It is lucky he did. If he had 'gone west' like his brother Percy, he wouldn't have worked in the Burmese jungle for eighteen years. Without those eighteen years, he would probably never have been selected for guerrilla operations in Burma with the Special Operations Executive (SOE); then there would have been no book to write about one of the Second World War's best-kept secrets.

There are not a very great many exalted personalities from the war in the Far East, at least relative to the war in Europe and North Africa. Where people are acquainted with names of those who served in the Far East, Orde Wingate of Chindit fame is most commonly mentioned, and possibly 'Mad Mike' Calvert. Some might be familiar with the courageous tale of Hugh Seagrim in Burma, though it is more likely that they know of Freddie Spencer Chapman's exploits in Malaya. These officers are arguably, however, 'in the shadows' when compared to David Stirling and his LRPG (Long Range Patrol Group)/ SAS (Special Air Service) comrades; in recent years the heroines of SOE such as Noor Inayat Khan and Vera Atkins, Odette Sansom and Christine Granville are better known. This is not to criticize or detract from the reputations of these rightly well-remembered people; but it is to place Lieutenant Colonel Edgar Peacock up among them, worthy of the same recognition.

As with all great personalities, it is complicated. When historians look at service records and try and get the measure of their subject, it is easy to see the medals, the Victoria Cross, the Distinguished Service Order, Distinguished Service Medal or the Distinguished Flying Cross, or the military Orders of Empire, or indeed no decorations but a nonetheless distinguished war record, and make a judgement on the personality behind the (mostly) anodyne archival material. Indeed, in the twenty-first century especially, 'hero' status seems to be conferred by most of the press and public upon any and every of the last surviving pensioners of the so-called 'greatest generation', those who served in the Second World War.

The point here is, we need to be careful with our hero worship. History is complicated. A service record, like any historical source, provides a snippet of a life. That snippet is of a few years of a life lived in extraordinary circumstances. The majority of most populations do not join their armed services; thankfully most people will not experience an all-enveloping total war such as the Second World War, so nor will they have to endure the terrors of combat. This means that most people will never fully understand what it means to have been at war, and consequently they will never know for sure how they would have reacted had they been put in that situation. The harsh truth is that, when placed in those extraordinary situations, not everyone behaves in the way we expect a hero to. When those archival files are not so anodyne, they can sometimes reveal secrets and allegations of behaviour with the potential to shock at best, or produce great shame at worst.

History can get complicated, or difficult, or even embarrassing for descendants. It is not always a clear case of Allies 'good', Nazis and Japanese 'bad'. It can be a shock to find out that these very same 'heroes', even close and respected family, may have falsified reports to be awarded that medal; become a morphine addict and stolen the personal morphine from the kit of the men in their team; been openly racist towards

INTRODUCTION

the indigenous population being recruited for guerrilla operations in the country in which they were fighting; or even alleged to have committed crimes against local women. Unfortunately, this all applies to men who served with SOE in Burma. This is why some SOE personnel files still have pages redacted, or remain closed to the public – to avoid embarrassment or harm to the family. Thankfully, nothing even quite as serious as any of this applies to the subject of this biography, but with full access to family documents, memoirs, and oral stories, a remarkable man emerges – just not always for all the right reasons.

If Edgar's service in the Second World War is so remarkable, the question must be asked: why has it taken this long for it to be told? There are a number of reasons which explain this. Firstly, SOE was a top secret organisation and the lengths that they went to in order to remain secret and maintain security even bothered those who belonged to the India Mission at the time. It wasn't until 1983 that an official history of SOE in the Far East, authored by Charles Cruickshank, was published. The files to which he was given exclusive access were only made public in the 1990s, and many of them remain redacted, and still more – particularly the personnel files – continue to be released under the Freedom of Information Act up to today.

Secondly, the extant SOE files are the ones which have survived various purposeful acts and some accidental destruction. We don't know how many files never made it back to the UK; we do know that SIS (Secret Intelligence Service) sat and 'weeded' SOE files after the war, chucking away whatever they thought should go; and there was also a fire, which destroyed another wedge of the archive. The history of SOE is therefore full of the gaps of an incomplete collection.

Thirdly, the focus of most SOE historians is Eurocentric, and that is also where most of the interest lies among the readership of the SOE's secret war. It is only more recently that the Far East has had much of a 'look in'. So much for the 'big picture' reasons.

Fourthly, and on a more personal level, as the final chapters reveal, Edgar and his friend Major Poles did not much endear themselves to many of the staff officers back in India. They were prickly men who were not afraid to speak their minds and this gave them an extra battle to fight after the war when their area of operations was passed over for military honours.

Lastly, Edgar never got around to writing his own experiences for many reasons, as these chapters will show. After he died, Edgar's wife passed all his papers on to a friend and fellow SOE officer from Burma, Captain Ansell. After a considerable time with all the documents, Ansell, too, never got around to writing anything up. It was left to Edgar's wife to have a go, and the result was the book *The Life of a Jungle Walla*, which had a very limited print run in 1958. As the war in Burma has gained greater attention towards the end of the twentieth century, with more general histories of the campaign being written on the back of Louis Allen's hugely important *Burma: The Longest War*, it has only slowly been acknowledged that SOE played an important role in that campaign to the extent that the first comprehensive history of SOE in Burma was only published in 2017, and the first campaign history to really acknowledge and integrate SOE into the strategic narrative only appeared in 2021.[1] For all these reasons, the heroism of most of the individual men of SOE Burma has remained buried until recently, the only exception really being the story of Major Hugh Seagrim – the man who did so much to make Edgar's triumphs in 1945 possible.

---

[1] Richard Duckett, *The Special Operations Executive in Burma: Jungle Warfare and Intelligence Gathering in World War Two* (London: IB Tauris, 2017); Robert Lyman, *A War of Empires: Japan, India, Burma & Britain 1941–1945* (Oxford: Osprey, 2021).

INTRODUCTION

With complete and unfettered access to private papers from Edgar's grandson, and his permission to write Edgar's biography 'warts and all', here is the biography of Lieutenant Colonel Edgar Peacock DSO, MC and Bar. This is the man who was tasked with devising a plan to raise a guerrilla force to rise up in support of the British, a man whose mission was to protect the left flank of General Slim's Fourteenth Army as it raced to Rangoon (now increasingly known as Yangon) in 1945 to reclaim it before the monsoon set in. Having already spent most of the thirteen months from April 1943 to May 1944 behind the lines, in 1945 he spent another nine months living rough in the mountains, forests and jungles of Burma. During that time, the four groups of Operation Character accounted for 11,874 Japanese for a loss of 22 of their own, a ratio of 539 to 1 – a success that his SAS and other Special Forces comrades could only imagine. In mid-April 1945, Lieutenant Colonel Peacock's own group took on a Japanese division with his few hundred hurried and partially trained indigenous personnel and prevented them from regrouping to block the main army's advance. His expertise in the jungle and development of the use of explosives thus helped ensure a strategic victory in Burma in 1945. This is the epitome of what Special Forces are designed to do; in terms of strategic effect and degradation of enemy forces, SOE was more successful in Burma than anywhere else in the entire Second World War. To a very real extent, much of this was down to the initiative, the drive and the unswerving leadership of Lieutenant Colonel Edgar Peacock.

Part I
Pre War (1893 to 1939)

1. 'Fortunate and powerful'

From the year 959 until he died in the year 975, Eadgar the Peaceable was the Anglo-Saxon King of England. The name 'Eadgar' is an amalgamation of two words, 'ead' meaning 'rich' or 'fortune', and 'gar' meaning 'spear'. From that there are a few slight variations on interpretation, but most common seems to be 'wealthy spear' or 'wealthy spearman', and 'fortunate and powerful'. Eadgar's reign earned him the epithet of 'Peaceable' because he was fortunate enough to rule during a hiatus in marauding Viking expeditions, but he is known for ruling England 'with an iron rod'. In some interpretations, it is this controlling nature that meant there was very little internal disorder. He was chronicled not just for his justice and law-making, which contributed to stability during his reign, but also his religious reforms which reinstalled discipline within the monasteries. If that isn't enough to convince opinions of his stature, he was powerful enough to have at least six other kings of the British Isles row him up the River Dee in Chester in a blatant display of his authority.[1]

Like many Anglo-Saxon names, 'Eadgar' disappeared after the Norman invasion until it was revived in the nineteenth century as 'Edgar'. Despite the slight change in spelling, our Edgar seems to have shared many of King Eadgar's characteristics, as well as living up to his name's meaning as 'fortunate and powerful'.

'Fortunate'. Perhaps Edgar can be considered fortunate for working in a reserved profession and thus 'missing' the Great War, but one day in March 1931, Edgar was extremely 'fortunate' to have been wearing, in his daughter's words, 'a particularly robust topi' (pith helmet). According to his wife's memoir, on the morning that a riderless horse brought itself

---

[1] Jessica Brain, 'Edgar the Peaceful', *Historic UK* [online] https://www.historic-uk.com/HistoryUK/HistoryofEngland/Edgar-the-Peaceful/

back into the town, Edgar was 'one of the first to volunteer to round up the rebels in the jungle'. At that time, Edgar was stationed in Maymyo, Burma (Myanmar), where he was Deputy Conservator of Forests. Since just after Christmas 1930, the country was witnessing a peasant revolt known as the Saya San Rebellion. There were concerns for the safety of the horse's missing human since just recently a Forest Officer like Edgar had been murdered in his rest house, and police stations were being raided for weapons, the raiders killing policemen in the process.

Unless there were two occasions where a riderless horse returned itself to Maymyo – which isn't impossible as the Saya San Rebellion was a serious business which gripped the country for the best part of two years – Geraldine might be conflating memories of the rebellion. Edgar nearly lost his life in March; the horse arrived 'with bloodstains' on 17 May.[2] In any case, in March, Edgar must have gone out to round up some rebels, and what happened next even made it into the *Portsmouth Evening Standard*, a local newspaper of limited circulation, thousands of miles away on the south coast of Britain, on Thursday 26 March 1931.[3] Edgar came across a (literal) cartload of belligerent Burmese. According to Geraldine, they were raiding a village for food. She describes them as a 'wild and desperate band of men' who fought back when Edgar tried to accost them with his men. There is no way of knowing if these men were rebels, followers of U Yar Gyaw, also known as Saya San, or just criminals known in Burma as *dacoits*. In any event, there was a sudden attack on Edgar and his party, the main outcome of which seems to be that a man standing on the cart decided to try and cleave Edgar's head in two with his *dah* (known elsewhere as a machete or a short sword, but regularly carried in one form or another by most Burmese men of all ethnicities). Edgar's 'particularly

---

[2] 'Burma Riderless Horse Mystery', *Aberdeen Press and Journal*, 18 May 1931 [online] https://www.newspapers.com/

[3] 'Fighting in Burma', *Portsmouth Evening News*, 26 March 1931 [online] https://www.newspapers.com/

robust topi' took most of the force of the blow, but the *dah* penetrated his skull, causing serious injury and huge loss of blood. The raiders were arrested by Edgar's party, but the danger wasn't over yet. As they approached the police station in Maymyo, they were mistaken for a large band of rebels and they were fired upon by their own police. It doesn't say much for the marksmanship of the authorities – fortunately for Edgar – but they were convinced of their mistake before there were any further casualties and Edgar made it to hospital. He was not expected to live. Nonetheless, Edgar's daughter Wendy wrote in her memoir that the blow to the head 'had a considerable impact on his personality'.

Fast-forward nearly two months, and the riderless horse belonged to someone of much contemporaneous fame. The missing man was forty-eight-year-old Lieutenant Colonel Henry Treise Morshead, DSO. Morshead was an explorer who had mapped much of India, surveyed what is now known to be the world's deepest gorge (the Tsangpo Grand Canyon), and made several attempts at Everest – for which he had had half of three fingers amputated. A search party eventually found Morshead hidden in a bush. He had been shot in the chest at point-blank range and was quite dead. Despite an investigation in which two men were arrested and later released without charge, some mystery still shrouds the circumstances of the colonel's death. In 1982, Morshead's son published a biography of his father, which advanced a few theories about what might have happened, but the case remains unresolved to the extent that Morshead's murder made it into Issue 67 of the magazine *Murder in Mind*, published in 1999.[1]

'Powerful'. There are a few ways in which Edgar's powerful nature will be exemplified throughout this volume, but for now, an anecdote from Squadron Leader Terence O'Brien. O'Brien was the Dakota pilot of 357 RAF Special Duties (SD)

---

[1] Ian Morshead, *The Life and Murder of Henry Morshead: A True Story from the Days of the Raj* (Oleander Press, 1982).

Squadron who flew Edgar and his team into Burma in February 1945. In his book, *The Moonlight War*, O'Brien describes a scene that unfolded before him preparatory to emplaning for their parachute infiltration behind the Japanese lines.[2] Two Special Groups of SOE men were due to be flown in, one led by Edgar, the other by Major Guy Turrall. O'Brien describes Turrall as 'a fearless little man' who didn't defer to rank. He had served with Wingate in both Abyssinia and in Burma as a Chindit in 1943, and now he was going behind the lines again with SOE. The men needed organizing into their 'sticks' for their parachute jump. Edgar had been strapping a map about his body:

> It was fascinating to see the effect of his entry into the straggly crowd of British and Karen parachutists. It was like that of a magnet passed under a paper that holds some iron filings, which swirl around in an instant reaction then stop abruptly in a neat pattern imposed by the magnetic field. Peacock simply moved through the throng and then four compact groups were suddenly standing ahead of the truck, while the other twenty-four men with Turrall were still swirling all about the taxi-track.

---

[2] Terence O'Brien, , *The Moonlight War* (London: Collins, 1987), pp.202-4.

2. 'A wonderful but sometimes aggressive philosophy'

Edgar can be seen as the epitome of 'a child of the Empire'. Even with all the fashionably pejorative connotations that this phrase might evoke in the twentieth century, it should become obvious why this is appropriate for Edgar. Edgar's great-grandfather, born about 1770, went to India and married an Indian in 1794. Their son, Thomas Peacock, is referred to in records as a 'Hindu-Briton' and recent DNA testing has confirmed the Indian connection to Edgar's descendants. Edgar was born in Nagpur, central India, in 1893. It is not known how long Edgar lived in Nagpur, but the rapid development of railway infrastructure and the centrality of Nagpur's location meant that the city had become an important trading centre by the time Edgar arrived. At around the age of fifteen, Edgar and his brothers became orphans. An outbreak of cholera claimed not only their parents but also, according to some family records, a younger sister called Enid, between 1907 and 1908.

It is reckoned that cholera killed around twenty-three million people in India between 1865 and 1947. In 1874, death by cholera was at a low of 0.16 per thousand of the population; in 1906, during the so-called sixth pandemic, it exceeded three per thousand, which translates to an average of 536,000 deaths per annum between 1905 and 1908. In the state of Hyderabad, cholera mortality in 1906 was 85.6 people per 100,000, the fourth highest annual statistic for the years 1904–1948. The worst year was the cholera outbreak of 1948. The city of Hyderabad itself 'has a long history of cholera deaths', with annual peaks in June and July.[1]

---

[1] Serish Nanisetti, 'Epidemic was a seasonal terror in Hyderabad, *The Hindu*, 27 March 2020 [online] https://www.thehindu.com/news/cities/Hyderabad/epidemic-was-a-seasonal-terror-in-hyderabad/article31185071.ece ; R.D. Mehta, 'Cholera in Hyderabad State', *The Indian Medical Gazette*,

Edgar's father, Edward James George Peacock, who died aged sixty-two in 1907, had worked in the postal service in Hyderabad. The postal service was established by the fifth Nizam of Hyderabad, Afzal-ud-Daulah, who reigned from 1857. Hyderabad was the name of the princely state, with the city of the same name as its capital. During the days of the British Raj, princely states continued to be ruled by Indians, making British governance indirect. Indirect rule in a princely state would typically be through a British Resident, who advised and acted as a liaison between the Viceroy and the Indian nobility. In states under direct British rule, a British Governor oversaw administration.

The Nizam of Hyderabad from 1829 to 1857 was Nasir-ud-Daulah. He enjoyed considerable autonomy, apparently having been successful at petitioning the Viceroy to keep the Resident, Sir Charles Metcalfe, at a distance. In 1846, Nasir founded the Hyderabad Medical School, which is known today as the Osmania Medical College. Edgar's grandfather may have been involved with this, as Thomas Peacock is recorded in various documents as having been 'sub assistant surgeon on the Nizam's service' since around 1840. Thomas had been in India from at least 1822 when he married his first wife, Rachell Cummings. Rachell passed away in 1840, and Edgar's father was born to Thomas's second wife, Jane O'Brien Browne, who died in 1855.

For his transition from teenage schoolboy to adulthood, Edgar was therefore raised by his three older brothers, James, Percy and Gerald. As was the custom for children in the Empire, Edgar attended boarding school, but he did not go to England for his education. Since somewhere in the family tree there was a marriage to an Indian or Anglo-Indian, and since India had such a strict social and racial hierarchy, there were specific rules

December 1950 [online] https://www.semanticscholar.org/paper/Cholera-in-Hyderabad-State-Mehta/ 4978da57190724dc9e2a08eb43f282c42d8262dc

to abide by. Anglo-Indians were somewhat in the social wilderness as they were neither one nor the other. As Frank Richards explains in his book *Old Soldier Sahib*:

> But there were drawbacks to these marriages. Just before the battalion left for Burmah I met one of these four men. He had married a half-caste girl who was whiter than he was, and nobody in England would have taken her for an half-caste, or 'half-chat' as the troops in my time contemptuously called them. It was not a term I used myself, any more than I would speak of 'barrack rats,' for the white children. They called themselves Eurasians, a word formed from combining 'European' with 'Asiatic,' but both Europeans and Asiatics despised them. It was a case of the parents eating sour grapes and the children's teeth being set on edge - even unto the second and third generation. This man had been married two years and told me he was now the father of a baby boy, twelve months old, who was a throw-back to his wife's native ancestors. He said gloomily that the child seemed to be getting blacker every day. I told him it was tough luck. 'Tough luck!' he echoed. 'You have no notion how tough it is. I'll tell you candidly that I would not be ashamed to take my wife to Blighty to see my family, but I would be thoroughly ashamed to take my child.[2]

Frank Richards became an orphan in the year that Edgar was born. He enlisted in the Royal Welsh Fusiliers in 1900 and was posted to India two years later. He served in India and Burma until early 1909. Frank's memoir provides many insights into life in India from a soldier's perspective during those years. His description of Eurasians gives some context for the society in

---

[2] Richards, Frank, *Old Soldier Sahib* (Uckfield: Naval & Military Press, 2003, pp.216-17.

'A WONDERFUL BUT SOMETIMES AGGRESSIVE PHILOSOPHY'

which Edgar was raised, a subject his daughter Wendy later explored in her memoir:

> Although no mention was ever made of it in our family, we now know that at some stage one of my father's forebears married an Indian woman, or someone from the Anglo-Indian community. It is interesting that Edgar's father apparently worked for the Post Office and James and Percy for the railways and these were both occupations largely reserved for Anglo-Indians, by which I mean here, mixed race.

We will never know for sure if this heritage contributed to, or was the reason for, Edgar being bullied at boarding school, but in any case his brothers made him fight the bully. Curiously, whether he won or not isn't related, it is assumed. In her memoir, Edgar's eldest daughter, Joy, recounts that her uncles raised Edgar 'very strictly on the Peacock family rules and values' and that if Edgar put a foot wrong he was 'cuffed on the head or worse'. Apparently the Peacock boys were 'strong and tough' but 'respected by all for their moral codes, clean Christian behaviour and excellent manners.'

Even before losing their parents, Edgar and his brothers shared a deep love of the Indian forest and its wildlife. Later on when serving in the Second World War, he took great delight in revisiting the forest he had frequented as a young lad. There are stories of him keeping snakes and birds and a honey bear in his youth, which all seem quite exotic and somewhat magical – like something from a story book rather than real life. The snake Edgar kept was a venomous Indian species, one which required 'milking' on a daily basis. The snake can't have always been kept secure in a tank or a box, for one night Edgar's friend and roommate at La Martinière College, Lucknow, awoke to find it slithering on his bed. Obviously petrified, George Willford screamed at Edgar to 'get the damn thing off me', but Edgar was unmoved, replying that he had milked him 'so if he does bite you it won't hurt much and you certainly won't die'.

The honey bear, also known as a sun bear, was a rescue. Edgar nursed it back to health after finding it injured in the forest. Sun bears are the smallest species of bear, standing up to 120cm tall. Today, they are the second most endangered bear, despite being a popular bear for bile farming. The bile is used to treat bladder and liver conditions in humans, but apparently the Chinese government has recently recommended its use to treat Covid 19.[3] The bears have a life expectancy of about 25 years. It's unknown how long Edgar had his bear, but after it died, Edgar had the skin cured and the fur lay on many household floors while his children were growing up.

When thinking of a fictional character who spoke to birds and surrounded themselves with feathered friends, Snow White may come to mind; or perhaps the original Dr Dolittle with his parrot, duck and owl. Neither of these seem quite the right comparison for Edgar, but his relationship with wild birds is no less enchanting. He and his brothers used to tame birds they found in the jungle, and train them so that they came when whistled for. They would go for walks in the forests with their birds, and the birds would regularly visit the house for something to eat.

The carefree and somewhat Mowgli-esque childhood spent in the forests of India provides a stark contrast to the realities of rigid racial and social hierarchies that Edgar endured at the same time. Maybe that was one of the biggest draws of the jungle, a feeling of freedom from societal scrutiny, and a sense of survival after suffering such a terrific loss during vulnerable teenage years. It is perhaps no wonder that years later, a very

---

[3] Rachel Fobar, 'China promotes bear bile as coronavirus treatment, alarming wildlife advocates', *National Geographic*, 25 March 2020 [online] https://www.nationalgeographic.com/animals/article/chinese-government-promotes-bear-bile-as-coronavirus-covid19-treatment

'A WONDERFUL BUT SOMETIMES AGGRESSIVE PHILOSOPHY'

good friend and comrade in arms would write that Edgar had a 'wonderful but sometimes aggressive philosophy.'[4]

---

[4] Major Eustace Poles, Private Papers.

3. 'Saviour of the villagers in Burma'

The man who walked stoically into the doctor's surgery in 1946 to reveal his suppurating abscess had just returned to Southern Rhodesia. He had been fighting against the Japanese in the forests and jungles of the country now increasingly known as Myanmar. It was a country he was intimately familiar with, however, for Edgar first arrived there, aged 21, in July 1914. It was just before the 'mother country' declared war on Germany on 4 August, beginning Britain's belligerence in World War One. Back then Burma was administered by the British Empire as a state of India. Edgar had arrived to take up his first posting with the British Overseas Forestry Service having just graduated from the Forest Research Institute College in Dehra Dun, northeast India. His official job title was 'Extra Assistant Conservator of Forests'.

At Dehra Dun, Edgar had been trained for his career in arboriculture at one of the pioneering schools of scientific forestry. The institute had originally been established in 1878, but in 1906 it was rebranded as the Imperial Indian Forest College. It is still going today as the Forest Research Institute and has managed to retain its prestigious reputation through the decades since Edgar's time there.

The school was founded by Sir Dietrich Brandis, the man acknowledged as the 'father of systematic forest management in the British Empire' in an obituary which appeared in the journal *Nature* in 1907.[1] This idea of 'Scientific Forestry' was all about sustainable forest management. In practical terms it meant working out how much timber could be extracted annually from the forests across the Empire without chopping it all down and being left with no timber industry. A second main aim was all about minimizing environmental

---

[1] W. Schlich, 'Sir Dietrich Brandis, K.C.I.E., F.R.S.' *Nature* 76, 131–132 (1907) [online] https://www.nature.com/articles/076131a0

damage, for example ensuring soil was kept healthy and didn't get washed away once the protection afforded by the trees had been removed. Edgar's job as Extra Assistant Conservator of Forests was, therefore, to spend long periods of time in remote areas of the Burmese jungle surveying and measuring trees, and interacting with the various indigenous inhabitants of Burma.

Not everyone appreciated this new colonial encroachment upon their forests. In part, it was friction with the authorities over forest access, cultivation and timber extraction which led to widespread rebellion across Burma between 1930 and 1932. Of course, it was during that rebellion that Edgar nearly lost his life. On the one hand, then, we have Edgar as a prominent symbol of colonial authority as a conservator and game warden of Burma and its forests, enforcing the new rules of scientific forest management; on the other hand, interaction with local populations led to him being described as a 'saviour of the villagers in Burma'. This was largely due to the fact that Edgar dealt with man-eating tigers or marauding elephants when they threatened rural life, as well as settling disputes between bickering villagers. A man can be many things to many people, but what this apparent paradox indicates is the multi-faceted and complex nature of colonial relationships.

Maybe Edgar was able to navigate his relationships with the people of Burma better than someone who had just arrived off the boat fresh from 'Blighty' with some recently passed colonial service exam results tucked in his back pocket. Due to his heritage and his life in India, and his deep love of his environment and all the creatures in it, it appears that he was able to build quite a reputation for himself in the eight years between his arrival in 1914 and 1922, when family sources record that he organized a Royal Hunt for the visiting Prince of Wales.

While there is scanty evidence in family records detailing specifics of his time in Burma compared to after his fiancée arrived in April 1924, knowing what these ten years of his working life entailed, it is obvious that they become a vital part of Edgar's story. His trajectory as an officer during the Second World War, when he was again to become 'saviour of the villagers in Burma', was almost all based on his extended time as a 'Jungle Walla' between 1914 and 1932.

4. 'An unknown colonial from those wild places'

Even though he was born thousands of miles away in India, events in South Africa before Edgar was born were to have a significant influence on his life. Some time in 1867, Erasmus Jacobs, the fifteen-year-old son of a poor Afrikaner farming family, was innocently playing on the banks of the Orange River in South Africa. He returned home that day with a glittery pebble about the size of a walnut. That 'pebble' has subsequently been named the 'Eureka Diamond'. Weighing in at 21.25 carats, this was the diamond that prompted the so-called 'Mineral Revolution' in South Africa, totally altering the course of history in this region forever. Europeans flocked to the diamond fields, claims were pegged out, industrial-scale mining began, and the town known as Kimberley was established. Very soon Kimberley became home to (what was then) the largest man-made hole on the planet, and the scene of much misery for many Africans. It also prompted a territorial dispute between Boer and Briton; on whose territory did the diamond mines belong?

Approximately twenty years before Erasmus Jacobs found the Eureka Diamond, in 1846, four Irish brothers had left the 'Emerald Isle' to sail for South Africa. The eldest of these four boys went on to become the Surveyor General of the territory known as Griqualand West. In his job as Surveyor General, Francis Orpen played an important part in resolving the territorial dispute so that the Kimberley diamond fields became British territory.

One of the most famous men known for making his fortune at Kimberley is the arch-imperialist, Cecil John Rhodes. Later, Rhodes made even more money on the South African goldfields; Rhodes became so rich that the University of Oxford has a college and a scholarship named after him. In the 2020s, Rhodes continues to hit the headlines as arguments about maintaining his Oxford college with its statue, and his scholarship, rumble on. With his wealth made in South Africa, Rhodes also funded expeditions to the north of the Transvaal goldfields, which ultimately ended up with two countries being named after him – Southern and Northern Rhodesia, respectively Zimbabwe and Zambia today. The addition of Southern Rhodesia to the territories of the British Empire later provided a home for Edgar and his family. Similar to Rhodes, Orpen the Surveyor would one day have an important role in shaping the life of Edgar Peacock.

Francis Orpen was the father of Alicia Frances Charlotte Orpen. Born in 1858, Alicia Orpen was destined to become Edgar's mother-in-law from 1924. During the 1930s, Alicia and Edgar worked together in England, despite Alicia being in her seventies by then. It was not an easy time, as will become clear, but it was also a time which resulted in some far-reaching decisions being made, as well as setting the path for Edgar's somewhat problematic married life.

Constance Mary Geraldine Godwin, the daughter of Alicia and the Very Reverend Dr Robert Herbert Godwin, was born in Umtata, South Africa, on 3 August 1890. Known by her third name, Geraldine, or more affectionately as 'Wee-o' to her close family, the story of how she and Edgar came to be married is yet another extraordinary tale within Edgar's rather extraordinary life.

Edgar did not get to ask Geraldine's father for his daughter's hand in marriage; in fact, Edgar did not even meet Reverend Godwin. Godwin was the Provost of St John's Cathedral in Umtata, in the area of South Africa now known as the Transkei in the Eastern Cape. At this time, the district was known as Kaffraria, or Kaffirland, perhaps reflecting the racial attitudes of the time. Reverend Godwin originally went to South Africa because of health issues, believing the climate would be better for him. It seems he did get better, and the decision was made to return to Britain, but his health reversed and so he was sent back out to South Africa for a second time, which is when he took up his post in Umtata, and where Geraldine was born.

In 1893, the same year in which Edgar was born, the Reverend Godwin again returned to Britain, ahead of his young family in order to look after his ageing mother. Alicia and their three children joined him around two years later in 1895 once he had found work and could support them. The family of five were living in Feltham, where Godwin worked at the Spelthorne St Mary Sanatorium for middle and upper class women who had drug and alcohol addictions. Run by the Anglican Community of St Mary the Virgin, it was here during a 7.00 am service that Godwin had a stroke in 1898 which left him incapacitated for the rest of his life. Geraldine remembered her dad's life hanging in the balance for six weeks, he being unable to talk to or even recognize his family.

The Community of St Mary the Virgin had been founded in Wantage, near Oxford, by the Reverend William Butler in 1848. The Rector of Wantage in 1898, Canon Houblon, invited the family to come and stay in Wantage so that Godwin might continue to recover. With her husband in convalescent care, Alicia now had to start earning an income to look after the family, and initially she was employed by the Sisterhood as a housekeeper. This only lasted a term though, because hearing how well Alicia looked after her boarding students, all the other pupils wanted to stay there too. Thus feeling undermined, the acrimonious Sisters simply asked Alicia to go, so the family moved out. There ended their time in what Geraldine described as 'Paradise, the best house and garden we had since coming to England.' The religious fraternity in which Geraldine's Reverend father had ensconced the family seems to have been terribly inconsistent in their care of the Godwins.

Needing an income, Alicia now started off by passing a dressmakers' exam, but she found 'it did not pay' because 'people ran up accounts and only settled them when they liked' so she decided to sit a Sanitary Inspectors' exam. She passed this too, but 'only to find I was too near the age limit for that to be any good'. Reverend Godwin was moved to the Anglican 'Homes of St Barnabas', still suffering the effects of his stroke, leaving Alicia to leaf through the job advertisements in the *Church Times*. She noticed an offer to work in charge of a laundry in Margate, Kent. The laundry was apparently owned by a rector's wife, which no doubt added to the facade of legitimacy from being advertised in a Christian publication. It seems that people in these times were no less unscrupulous than the fraudsters and tricksters of today, but in any event, an unknowing Alicia, with Edgar's future wife now not yet ten years old, packed up and moved to Kent after having been interviewed in London. Schoolboy Edgar, growing up in the Raj, would have had absolutely no idea that the foundations of what would eventually become such an intense period of his adult life were being played out far away in England – at the same time as Queen Victoria, Empress of India since 1876, was succeeded by her son, King Edward VII.

For Alicia, her situation in England at the turn of the twentieth century was not unlike Edgar's marginalization in India. Socially, she was regarded as 'an unknown colonial from those wild places overseas'. As a woman, with three children, it must have been terribly hard to survive, even without the scammers and fraudsters she came up against. But by the time her husband, the Reverend Godwin, died in St Barnabas' care home in January 1913, she was the owner of her own empire – a very successful laundry business based in East Grinstead.

5. Mrs Sparks, the rector's wife

The year Alicia left South Africa in 1895, a close associate of Cecil John Rhodes took a party of 500 or so British South Africa Company troopers over the border from the new country called Rhodesia into the Boer Republic of the Transvaal. The Mineral Revolution caused by young Erasmus finding his diamond had been stimulated in 1886 when gold was found on the Witwatersrand. The subsequent gold rush, which led to the founding of Johannesburg, created a population of mine workers known disparagingly by the Boer government as 'Uitlanders', or 'outsiders'. Paul Johannes Kruger, President of the Boer state, after whom Johannesburg is named, refused to give citizen's rights to this foreign legion of fortune hunters. The British South Africa Company troopers who rode into the Transvaal at the end of 1895 were expecting to bolster a rebellion by the Uitlanders against the Kruger government in an attempt to gain their rights. No rebellion was forthcoming, however, and the troopers, led by Dr Leander Starr Jameson, were ambushed and captured by the Boers.

The gold deposits in the Transvaal were the largest in the world, and there was no way the British Empire could allow the status of London as the financial centre of the globe to be threatened. The Empire needed the gold to assure Britain's future as the '*Pax Britannica*' came under increased pressure from newly united Germany and an ambitious America where the West had been 'won'. Alicia had left all her family behind in South Africa, and just as her husband suffered his stroke and life became difficult in Britain for the Godwin family, so war broke out in 1899 between Briton and Boer in South Africa. Ultimately it was a war about the ownership of the goldfields, something that had been avoided for settling ownership of the diamond mines; more publicly, the war was justified as the morally correct thing to do to ensure the rights of the Uitlanders.

Although there is no record of Orpen casualties, and two of Alicia's brothers did saddle up to fight, it appears that there was no familial loss of life due to the war. It came quite close, though. In her memoir, Geraldine recounts how a party of Boers came and surrounded the family farm and told them 'to clear out before sunset if they didn't want to be shot.' They cleared out, 'while the Boers jeered at them', but after the war ended with the signing of the Treaty of Vereeniging on 31 May 1902, the family moved back into their home 'and remained there until their deaths.'

The Treaty of Vereeniging finally led to the formation of the Union of South Africa in 1910. While South Africa's future was thus determined during these eight years, the Godwins struggled to determine theirs in England. There is no doubt that Alicia and Geraldine sorely missed the freedom and open spaces of South Africa, and the fresh air; but they couldn't go back leaving their husband/father in the Anglican care home. In any case, the three Godwin children had to go to school, and this was a time when it was the 'done thing' to send the children of Empire to Britain for their education. Their schooling was paid for by aunts and uncles, but nothing further seems to have been forthcoming in terms of helping Alicia to survive. The stories of her hardship at the hands of unscrupulous and audacious Edwardians is quite astonishing, even by today's standards:

The woman who answered the door to Alicia was drunk. Maybe she also needed to be admitted to the Spelthorne St Mary sanatorium for those with sobriety issues. She peered at the family who had just arrived in Margate through dark eyes set deep in her skull and found it easy to continue the lie with which she had ensnared this gullible colonial woman. For their part, the family all looked confused. Their cabbie had just assured them that he had brought them to the correct address, in the correct part of town, but there was no rectory, and the inebriated woman with the sly face didn't look at all like the wife of a respected clergyman. The house was in a dilapidated state and situated in a slummy part of the town.

The 'rector's wife' had already managed to get £350 out of the new laundry manageress; people were so trusting in the Christian community. It had been a genius idea to advertise there. She felt only the success of victory as she led the woman and her kids up a narrow wooden staircase to the one room she was giving them for lodgings. The disgust on her new tenant's face was plain to see, but so was the resignation as she became more fully cognisant of her predicament. Having handed over all her savings, there was nothing else for it. Inebriated as she was, though, the trickster did not fail to notice that despite the grim acceptance of her new life, this new woman had a steely determination, making her wonder just how long she would be able to hold her and her children as hostages to fortune.

In fact, she didn't have to wonder too long, for the children were soon packed off to boarding school. The middle child, the girl, clearly didn't want to go, but surely if there was money for boarding school, there was the potential for extorting yet more funds. The trickster had five other women in the building, all of whom had been daft enough to part with large sums of money in return for a stake in the laundry business, somewhere to live and the promise of a weekly wage of £3. It wouldn't be long before a man joined their ranks, another colonial type from somewhere in Africa, from whom she had already secured £500. She didn't worry that the man and this latest woman might find a common interest having come from Africa, and might work together against her, nor did she worry about the man's father apparently being a lawyer. The scam was working well and there was no reason to believe it wouldn't continue to do so.

When Mr Barrat arrived from Africa, Mrs Sparks announced that he was now in charge of the laundry, just as she had announced the mother as the new manageress not many days before. Rather than causing her any bother, it actually worked out quite well for Mrs Sparks the rector's wife, in the very short term at least. The colonials did befriend each other, and soon Mr Barrat's lawyer father was able to convince Alicia to pack up and leave, freeing up space in the house that much quicker, ready for the next victim. It had become obvious that there was no more money to extort despite wherever the school fees were coming from, so she was content to let them go.

Mrs Sparks was not the only source of skulduggery which Edgar's future mother-in-law faced in the fight to raise her family – as if being female and an 'unknown colonial' didn't present enough difficulty. Before her laundry business was finally established, while the suffragettes fought for female civil liberties in the years leading up to the Great War, the Godwin family fought to survive. Though the odds were against her, Alicia's fortitude and hardiness, forged through being at the frontier of Empire through the *fin de siècle*, saw her through. But Alicia was never to return to those frontiers, or indeed see her family in South Africa ever again, even though she lived until 1945. More adventures in the Empire, however, lay in wait for Geraldine, the middle child of Alicia and the Reverend, their little 'Wee-o'.

6. 'The dark man in a good government job'

It was pouring with rain. Rain meant no customers, so the young lady selling her handmade leather goods was frustrated and bored. Other stallholders at the exhibition looked equally bored, standing idle waiting for the weather to ease off. At length, it appeared that something was going on at the other end of the hall, as lots of sellers were gathered around something, or someone. Curiosity and boredom combined, and soon the leather craftswoman found herself queuing to have her fortune read. The rain continued to pour, and no customers appeared, so it was something to do to while away the time. When it was eventually her turn, the fortune-teller's words were very specific. She would meet a dark man on a ship who worked in a very good government position. There would be another voyage on a ship, across the Indian Ocean, and she would marry this man. How absurd, she thought. At nearly thirty years of age, she was almost 'on the shelf'. She thought no more about it, as the rain continued to fall and she packed up her wares to go home.

As far as she was concerned she was destined to become an 'old maid'; she already had a dog for companionship, and was used to taking long, lonely bike rides. Apart from long but not so lonely walks with the dog, she kept herself busy in her studio doing her art, weaving baskets, making leather goods, sewing, and doing woodwork. Selling her wares at exhibitions and fairs like the one where the fortune-teller had told her the outlandish prediction of her taking overseas voyages was a nice distraction, and provided some pocket money. It was a little bit odd, though, that on a trip to the cinema with her brother and his friends, instead of finding a suitor, the film hinted at a future similar to the one foreseen by the fortune-teller. The story was all about a boy, born in India, and a girl, in England, but not *born* there. They finally met and were married.

Jungle Warrior

Some time in the summer of 1921, the girl's mother surprised her with a bright idea. Money was no longer tight, and it was a long time since she had been able to give her daughter a real treat. The war years had been hard, especially when one of her brothers had gone missing at the Battle of the Somme; he was never seen again. A relative was due to return to South Africa, so it was arranged that she would travel back with her second cousin, Constance Godwin, and have an adventure back in the land of her birth. And what an adventure it was! The ship's manifest, available in the National Archives, shows that she sailed aboard the *Dunluce Castle*, leaving in September 1921. She enjoyed a splendid voyage out, with deck games and lovely food, and a dance – but no dark man in a good government job swept her off her feet.

After a wonderful time delighting in the sights of Cape Town, she journeyed by train for miles and miles into the interior, visiting farms in the Great Karoo. She marvelled at the isolation from other people, living so far from civilization that they had to be self-supporting. It's fair to say that love was found in South Africa, but it was a love of the country, and a strong desire to return one day was firmly wedged in her heart. All too soon it was time for the boat to take her back to grey and busy England. Once again, no 'dark man in a good government job' made himself known to her. She stepped off the boat onto the docks in Southampton perhaps a little deflated, and returned to her life as an 'old maid'. Something was different, though. Africa had worked some magic on her soul, and that thirst to return needed to be slaked.

After a few months back in England, the girl found an advert for a dream job in an art magazine. The Alexandra Hospital in Cape Town was in need of an art teacher for occupational therapy. She applied at once, for Cape Town was the very place she had fallen in love with on her recent adventure. A very quick reply to her application requested an

'THE DARK MAN IN A GOOD GOVERNMENT JOB'

interview in London. There was nothing for it but to go, not that she thought she stood any chance of being successful.

Feeling all the normal nervous anxiety of the recruitment process, she saw another applicant exit from their interview and of course told herself that this short, dark girl would obviously get the job. Her own interview followed, and it was so short – if pleasant – that her prediction that her previous rival had already stolen the show was reinforced. Once again, though, there was nothing for it but to return home and wait to see what happened.

A day or two later, a letter arrived, obviously from London, and quite certainly, she felt, it would tell her that she had been unsuccessful. The exhilaration and relief and joy of reading otherwise surged through her body, but very quickly it was tampered down by the realization that she would have to leave her mother. What had she done? The letter even said that she would have to teach cane basket making, which she had never learnt. Had she really been so rash as to apply for a job on the other side of the world based on the whim of having holidayed there?

There was a month before she was due to sail south once again, but before that she hurried north to the city of Leicester to take a course in basket making. It was all such a rush, so the day soon came when she would leave home for the three years of her contract; and then it hit her. Panic! It suddenly all seemed too much for her to face, and her courage was all gone. Although she was approaching thirty-two years old, just like many children before her and many yet to leave the family home, she turned to her mother holding back her tears and asked 'Oh, what have I done?'

On 10 October 1922, her surviving Great War veteran brother, Harold, saw her on to the *Walmer Castle* at Southampton. Her mother had stayed at home, too sad to face the goodbye. As the departure bells clanged and rope chains rattled, she might have wondered if she was going to meet the 'dark man in a good government job', but if she did it was amidst all the sadness and consciously applied facade of fortitude at leaving on a new adventure, thousands of miles away in the land of her birth.

7. 'The great Peacock of Burma'

Meanwhile, as he approached thirty years of age, the 'dark man in a good government job' had emerged from the jungles of Burma and travelled to England for his first ever 'home' visit. Before making this trip 'home' to a country far, far away – that had never been home – Edgar may have been intimately involved in something quite royal.

In an age where the coronation of King Charles III raises mixed emotions and trophy hunting is almost universally reviled, family memoirs tell us that Edgar was asked to arrange a Royal Hunt in Burma for the future King of the British Empire, Prince Edward, the Prince of Wales. It is unclear who this request came from, but most probably it came from the Lieutenant Governor of Burma, Sir Reginald Henry Craddock. Edgar was given three weeks to go and find a suitable area for the hunt, and to make sure he was familiar with it. Craddock's successor from December 1922 was Sir Harcourt Butler. Butler is noted in Geraldine's biography of her husband as having personally asked for Edgar to arrange a hunt for him in 1923 based upon how well the Royal Hunt had played out.

The request for Edgar's services as an expert on the jungles of Burma arrived almost at the same time that Prince Edward left Portsmouth on his Royal Tour on 26 October 1921. The Prince was due to be away from London for eight months or so, and he ended up travelling around 41,000 miles in that time. Although it was nearly three years since the armistice silenced the Great War guns, this tour of the Empire's eastern colonies, and particularly India, was supposed to be an expression of thanks for the loyalty shown by Indians to the British Empire. It was also meant to bolster failing colonial relationships during a period of rising nationalism; Gandhi had returned to India from South Africa in 1915, and in 1920 his first national *Satyagraha* (non-violent protest) posed a new and

JUNGLE WARRIOR

different threat to the integrity of the Raj. We can only wonder what Edgar made of Gandhi's 'Truth Force' (the literal definition of *Satyagraha*) from hundreds of miles away in a country still administered as an Indian state by the colonial authorities. Yet, there he was, specifically asked for as the man to organise a Royal Hunt in Burma.

The problem is, there seems to be no trace of Edgar's part in the Prince of Wales's short tour of Burma; he was only there for nine days of his eight months abroad, arriving in Rangoon on 2 January 1922. The Prince apparently 'regretted he could not stay much longer', concentrating his time in the big Indian provinces taking part in big hunts which are well photographed.[1] There are many photos of dead tigers and the Prince riding on elephants, but there are none for Burma. This doesn't necessarily mean it didn't happen, for the family stories have to have had some basis to start with. What it does show, similar to the confusion around the details of Edgar's near-death experience at the hands of some Burmese thieves, is the difficulty of untangling the threads of family memories and memoirs when there is very little evidence to consult.

The question that perhaps needs to be asked, then, is how did Edgar get himself so well known; how had he earned a reputation for himself that meant those at the top of the colonial hierarchy knew to ask him to organize hunts for both themselves and possibly also for the next King of the British Empire? He had, after all, gone to Burma to be a conservator of the forests, and the Forest Department was also responsible for the protection of wild birds and animals. In this respect, Burma appears to have been well ahead of other areas of Empire –

---

[1] *The Prince of Wales' Eastern Book: A Pictorial Record of the Voyages of H.M.S. 'Renown' 1921-1922* (London: Hodder & Stoughton, 1922). Available online (no page numbers) https://commons.wikimedia.org/wiki/File:The_Prince_of_Wales%27_Eastern_book,_a_pictorial_record_of_the_voyages_of_H._M.S._%22Renown%22,_1921-1922_(IA_cu31924098820289).pdf

45

'THE GREAT PEACOCK OF BURMA'

including India – in its laws to protect the natural world by creating sanctuaries for wildlife in an effort to prevent extinction of both flora and fauna.

Similar to other areas of the Empire, though, where the natural world and human safety collided, control measures were permitted. An earlier chapter described Edgar as the 'saviour of villagers in Burma'. Part of the reason for this is because he had shown great skill in protecting villagers and their livestock from marauding tigers. Edgar had shot his first buck at just eight years old, and he continued to hunt throughout his life, but in these years in Burma during and just after the Great War, he earned himself a reputation as 'The Great Peacock of Burma' by adding thirty tigers to his name. In her biography of her husband, Geraldine quoted Sir Harcourt Butler's account of hunting a tiger with Edgar at length, but one line will suffice here: 'Peacock has a great reputation as a Shikari, and he clearly has earned it.' The word 'Shikari' comes from Persian and Urdu, and means 'big game hunter'.

While his hunting skills alone might have been enough to get him noticed, Edgar was also busy earning a reputation by other means; besides the proverbial sword, Edgar was also very active with the pen (and his camera). His preoccupation in his role as Game Warden in Burma was the preservation of animals rather than the gratuitous slaughter and trophy hunting often associated with the days of Empire. It is obvious that Edgar had a great respect for the natural world, so the honour of being asked to organize a Royal Hunt must have conflicted with his commitment to preservation of wildlife, even if he did not object to 'sportsman like hunting'.

This was the Edgar who emerged from Burma after his first eight years of Forestry Service. A man with a reputation, but a man with morals; a man approaching thirty years of age, but a man with no wife; a man who had money to invest, but a man who spent long spells far away from civilization. Edgar set off on his way 'home' in 1922 with the intention of taking care of these latter two points; in Britain he hoped to find a bride, and on the way back to Burma he planned to stop off in South Africa to have a look at an estate where he had made an investment in oranges.

8. 'It is the sunshine makes the shadows'

The cacophony of sound as the boat prepared to depart Southampton docks, topped off by a loud blast from the funnel of the *Walmer Castle*, did nothing but make the young woman's heart sink right down into her shoes. Still, she had managed to wave gaily to her brother as he had descended the gang plank to reach the shores that she would surely not set foot on again for at least the next three years. Quite why she felt so bereft she did not know. She was off to a job she had worked hard to secure, in a city she loved, in the land of her birth. She should have been happy to be finally making her way in life, and there was always the merest of chances that the words of the fortune-teller might come true. This positive thought was, nonetheless, outweighed at this moment of departure. Her depression was compounded by the knowledge that no 'dark man in a good government job' had presented himself to her on her previous two voyages. It was more likely that the fortune-teller had either made a mistake, or was a fraud.

As the ship slowly glided out to sea, she made her way into the dining saloon for the first time. Before she sat down, she noticed a sign above the bar which said 'It is the sunshine makes the shadows', which seemed to epitomize where she was in her own life. She felt too sick to eat, but managed a few sips of her tea and she allowed herself to wallow in her thoughts. The British always seem to regard tea as having some sort of magic restorative powers whether feeling tired, melancholic or just plain depressed. So it was now for the woman, sipping her brew. As the tea slowly worked its way into her system, she gradually became increasingly aware of being in public, and was suddenly more interested in her surroundings than the indulgence of her anxieties.

Spotting a table of three persons, two men and a female, she wondered at the possible permutations of relationship that might bind them. Were they all siblings? Was she married to one of them? Was the handsome one who appeared to be the youngest of the party the married one? At that moment, though, the restorative powers of the magic tea failed her. Suddenly feeling quite nauseous, she managed to be sick over the side of the boat, with the handsome young man watching. Feeling not a little embarrassed, and entirely self-conscious, there was nothing for it but to disappear to her cabin and lie down. Would being sick preclude any advances that the handsome man might have made? It seemed so as the days went by and they never spoke. Finding herself wondering whether he was supposed to be the man of the fortune-teller's prophecy, she realized she had not completely given up on the idea of finding love on a boat.

Sitting with his older brother and his sister-in-law, the man was enjoying his first bite to eat on his voyage down to South Africa. He was happy to be leaving the busy, crowded and depressing place that he had been led to believe was 'home'. He had not felt at all at home in Britain, and looked forward to his return to warmer climates and the familiarity of being his own master in the more remote parts of the Empire. This feeling of impatience to get back to his own private wilderness was acutely accentuated by his brother's choice of wife. Just as she had made his life somewhat excruciating on land, so she proceeded to do so at sea. Over and over again, the man found that he was having to suppress his nature as a born fighter, affecting the stoicism and stiff upper lip that was as synonymously British as the tea he was drinking.

Gerald's wife, Irene, had taken it upon herself to mother her husband's brother. Maybe it was because they were orphans and she felt some kind of duty of care to look after the two men that she thought it best to control their lives so closely, or maybe it was just her personality. Either way, the man had been relieved to have at least some of his trip away from her misguided ministrations. He had made it up to Scotland, and it wasn't just being away from the clutches of his sister-in-law that had made the trip so memorable. Of course, the sparsely populated highlands had appealed to his nature, but he had also come within an ace of achieving one of the main goals of his trip 'home' – getting engaged to be married. Without *his* chaperone, the man had been able to take many pleasant outings with a charming young heiress in the city of Edinburgh. They had been staying in the same hotel, where she was chaperoned by her aunt. He had been very attracted to the lady in question, and had had the intention of asking for her hand one afternoon, but just at the very moment he was about to pop the question, she suffered an urgent call of nature – and the chance never presented itself again. How would he ever manage to meet someone on this final stretch of his leave, as he headed back home to Burma? His sister-in-law was determined to continue to restrict his social interactions, and to intervene presumably to vet anyone he – or his brother – spoke to.

As he sat there feeling the weeks of frustration, shoving his resentment of Irene once again as deep into his boots as he could, they were distracted by a woman being sick over the side of the boat. It was the same woman from whom he had caught a few furtive glances across the saloon over the last half an hour or so. Looking away from her, he also noted the signage above the bar: 'It is the sunshine makes the shadows.'

9. 'A hard tussle in a 'cock fight"

It had all happened in a sudden impulse of sympathy for the handsome man, who she now had a name for. Edgar. She also knew the relationship between Edgar and his companions: it turned out that the older man was Edgar's brother, who was a doctor. The doctor was married to the stern-looking woman who accompanied them.

Edgar had been wrestling another man on the deck of the ship. There were other sports such as tennis to keep the passengers amused, but this deck sport was an altogether more serious test of individual stamina and strength. Edgar's opponent had been a good match, and the contest had gone on for some time before Edgar had eventually won. Victory had come at the price of elbows rubbed raw by the deck of the boat, although from what she could make out, it didn't appear to worry him in the least. But it was the elbows which had provided her with her opening the morning after the hard tussle.

He wasn't going to capitulate or show any weakness, because he knew she was watching. She was good-looking, and unlike many of the other young women on the boat who he had spoken to, she was obviously not engaged or on her way to meet a man. He felt the pain in his elbows as they scraped along the hard wooden deck, but it only goaded him on to greater exertion. His opponent was good, but Edgar knew he was wearing him down. If Edgar's own elbows were suffering, his adversary must be enduring the same. Confident that his rival would break, and with the patience of a hunter who enjoys the hardship of the chase, he allowed himself a slight smile of enjoyment. It wouldn't be long now. He felt more stinging in his elbows as he parried what he guessed was the final all-out attempt by his challenger to end the competition, and then it was all over as Edgar pinned him. Amidst the claps of the crowd the two men got to their feet, both smiling, and shook hands.

'A HARD TUSSLE IN A 'COCK FIGHT''

The onlookers quickly dispersed to find their next source of entertainment, and Edgar did not see the girl again until the next morning. It was an awkward exchange; they were both very shy, but she had somehow plucked up the courage to ask him how his wounds were. He told her that he was travelling with his brother who was able to see to his abrasions as he was a doctor. Before she had gone, he had at least asked for her name. It was Geraldine.

Later that day, Geraldine was walking around the deck with one of the travelling brides-to-be when she spotted Edgar sitting down right beside where they were to pass by. He was with his brother and sister-in-law. The young bride's voice seemed to recede in volume as Geraldine and Edgar locked eyes. As she passed, Geraldine was sure that he had given her an appealing look, an imploring look, a look asking for help. How strange, she thought, not quite understanding why he would look at her in that way. Had she read the situation wrongly? Coming back to reality, the bride-to-be was still talking, and as her voice audibly merged back into her consciousness, Geraldine was obliged to acknowledge and tune back into their conversation. Odd feelings about the handsome Edgar persisted on the periphery of her mind as she struggled not to be rude and give the lucky lady the courtesy expected of a deck companion.

The next time they spoke was at a deck tennis tournament. Irene was a champion tennis player, having won the British Indian Singles Championship every year between 1915 and 1920, and had just won the South African Singles before coming to England to compete at Wimbledon in 1922 and making it into the semi-finals. Edgar's brother, Gerald, could hold his own, so they made a formidable pairing. Perhaps unsurprisingly, therefore, they won the *Walmer Castle's* little tournament. More importantly, while they played, it gave Edgar and Geraldine a chance to talk without interference. Thus unrestrained, Edgar told Geraldine how he had to have such forbearance for his sister-in-law if he wasn't to be estranged from his brother. To Geraldine, it all seemed very strange and sinister, and she couldn't understand how Irene had such a hold over the two Peacock men.

As the final days of the voyage rapidly approached, Edgar told Geraldine about his life in Burma and his interest in hunting big game, and why he was on his way to South Africa now, before returning to his jungle job. He was going to check on an investment he had made in a company called Zebediela. Zebediela, he said, was a huge estate that produced oranges. He wanted to purchase some land nearby, with a view to settling on it when he retired from the forestry service.

Gerald & Irene Peacock, with whom Edgar travelled south to Cape Town on SS Walmer Castle

10. 'He had never even tried to flirt with me'

Geraldine decided she would go to the fancy dress dance after all. She hoped she might see Edgar, and it was one of the last of the entertainments put on by the Union Castle liner before docking in Cape Town. But what to go as? She decided to pay a visit to the ship's carpenter to see if he could help her. She had to be persuasive, but she got round the carpenter in the end and he provided her with a load of his wood shavings. Back in her cabin, she used her artistic skills to fashion a wig of long curls, and attached the rest of her haul of shavings to her dress. Looking at herself in the mirror, she was pleased with the result; she left her cabin and went to the dance as 'Chips'.

Arriving in the ballroom, it wasn't hard to find Edgar, despite his disguise. Who else could be over six foot tall and dressed like a Burman? She was thrilled when he asked her to join his party for supper, and hugely relieved to find that he had somehow broken loose from familial oversight. Perhaps they might even dance together! She was not all that keen on dancing, not having had much practice, but that is what young people who were interested in each other were supposed to do at these sorts of evenings. It turned out she needn't have worried, though, for dancing was not his particular form of amusement any more than it was hers. She was both shy and nervous, and worried that it would show. She was, after all, the girl who had thrown up over the railings of the boat not too long ago.

Again, she needn't have worried, for she soon realized that he was just as shy as she was; a lack of dancing skill was not all they had in common, and they often trod on each other's toes. At the end of the evening, she thought he might attempt something a bit more forward...

Edgar hoped that she would come, and she did. She had somehow managed to procure a most brilliantly made wig fashioned out of wood shavings. He was impressed to find out that she had made it herself after persuading the carpenter to part with some of his debris. He was relieved when he was rewarded with a 'yes' after asking her if she would like to join him for supper. Perhaps she was interested in him, it was hard to tell. He wasn't very good at reading the signals, and he wasn't sure that she was sending any in a hopefully romantic way. By now they had spoken more than a few times, and played some tennis together, and he liked her company. The voyage was coming to an end, though, and he knew that if he returned to Burma without having made an offer of marriage to someone, he stood little chance of finding anyone while working in the remote reaches of the Burmese forests. At almost thirty years old, he wasn't getting any younger, and another eight years in the jungle would take him up to almost forty.

He enjoyed her company over dinner, and as he loosened up a little after a beer or two, he plucked up enough courage to ask her to dance. Anyone watching them must have had a little giggle to themselves, as they were probably the most uncoordinated couple on the dance floor, regularly tripping on each other's feet. To her credit she persevered, as did he, and it was fun rather than completely awkward.

As the evening came to a close – ship's rules were lights out by 22:30 – it occurred to him that perhaps he should make some kind of effort to do more than simply say 'goodnight', but it was all very public. As it was they thanked each other for an enjoyable evening and went their separate ways.

With just two days of the journey left, she found herself up on a busy deck. She fell into conversation with Edgar, and they watched the moon reflecting on the surface of the sea as the *Walmer Castle* continued to carry them inexorably south towards Cape Town. She supposed she must have been paying him very close attention, for all of a sudden she realized they were all alone. Somehow the deck had cleared, everyone had gone below, so she turned to do the same.

'HE HAD NEVER EVEN TRIED TO FLIRT WITH ME'

'Don't go!'

She was stunned for a moment by the urgency in his voice, but then he rapidly continued: 'We shall be landing in a day or two now, and I don't want to lose sight of you. Will you marry me?'

Now she was completely stunned. Had she heard him correctly? This wasn't how it happened in the novels she had read. She was completely unprepared. He had never – so far as she could tell – even tried to flirt with her. And in this particular moment, the moment when she might have expected it most, he still made no effort to kiss her or even take her hand. Her mind was racing, it was all so... out of the blue. Not really knowing what she replied, she found herself back in her cabin. Looking at herself in the mirror, she said out loud: ' I believe you have just had a proposal of marriage, my girl! Can such a thing have happened to me? Just when I have got the best job I have ever had yet.'

Despite the shock of it all, sleep came easily, and tomorrow was another day.

11. 'A ship-board affair?'

Was it all a dream? Had he really proposed to her? What would the day bring? Excited to find out, hoping to meet Edgar, Geraldine got up on this Sunday morning and went up on deck. There he was!

He greeted her as he would any other passenger. Confusion reigned in her head but, being a Sunday, there was only one place for them to go, and that was to the ship's service. After church, they sat on the deck together and looked through Edgar's collection of poems by Kipling.

Geraldine thought it was romantic, but in truth, she had no experience of being in love and wasn't sure how she was supposed to feel. She thought that Edgar should be more demonstrative, but since he still made no attempt at any romantic physical gesture, she presumed that he was showing her the utmost respect by not taking any liberties. Still, she was shocked to realize he had not told his brother and sister-in-law. Was she engaged? Was this an odd 'ship-board affair' or was it real and going to last? The next day would bring them into docks on the Victoria and Albert waterfront beneath the majestic Table Mountain. The voyage would be over and they were going to go their separate ways.

This was evidently going through both their minds; how was *this* – whatever *this* was – going to work?

Edgar asked for Geraldine's address. He said, 'I want to buy you a ring, but all my money has been used up while on leave, so will you accept this ivory bangle to wear, till I return to Burma, where I shall immediately sell a valuable trophy of mine, a rhino horn which is sought after by the Burmese for medicinal purposes? They pay well, and I shall be able to send you at least £30 and you can buy a good ring for that amount.'

In a sudden flood of empathy, Geraldine felt sorry for his embarrassment at not having any means to buy a decent ring there and then; she felt overwhelmed at the thought of owning something so expensive as £30; but most of all she just wanted some affection, not an expensive ring, so she replied, 'Surely something cheaper would do.'

Disembarkation at Cape Town was as expected. The newly betrothed couple did not manage to see each other, and Geraldine was hastily taken off to her new place of employment, having been met on the dock. Mixed feelings and bewilderment at the events of the last few days needed to be controlled as she began her new job and settled into unfamiliar rhythms as an occupational therapist.

She feared that Edgar might have forgotten her, that it was just an odd ship-board affair after all, but then some post arrived from him. There was a photo of Edgar, taken professionally in Johannesburg, as well as his special volume of Kipling poems, and an invitation to lunch in Cape Town at 'Cartwrights' to celebrate their engagement. But it was when she noticed what he had written in the flyleaf of the Kipling volume that there was joy in her heart:

'Oh, I have seen my true love's eyes
To stand with Adam in Eden's glade
And run in the woods of paradise.'

Dinner at 'Cartwrights' was awkward, for Irene clearly considered their relationship to be a ship-board affair. She made it obvious that she thought Geraldine was too old for Edgar, since she was almost three years his senior at 32. The atmosphere thus unpleasant, Edgar must have made the decision not to let his brother's wife ruin their nascent relationship, and determined on proving this wasn't just another floating fling and that it could withstand the challenges of life on land.

Finally, at the gates before the Alexandra Hospital for the mentally ill, Edgar acknowledged that he had never even kissed her yet, and so he did so, full on the mouth.

12. 'Tell the old cats you are coming out to be all in all to a wild jungle man'

In the twenty-first century, almost exactly 100 years since Edgar and Geraldine were courting in Cape Town, the urgency to find a potential spouse and propose marriage in such a way is almost unimaginable. It seems it was not so unusual then, however; the Burma policeman, Bill Tydd, reminisced about how 'Shipboard romances started to flourish in no time' on his voyage to Britain on his first period of leave in 1933.[1] While he never made it to Cornwall to pick up where his onboard courting had left off, he proposed to another girl within four days of meeting her in London. Just as Edgar and Geraldine then spent the next year apart, so Bill too returned to Burma to await his fiancée's arrival six months later.

Edgar had stayed in Cape Town a little while, however, and Geraldine describes meeting him between her shifts at the hospital, walking together in a 'lovely park', and going out for an Indian meal where Edgar impressed her by speaking in Urdu to the staff. All too soon he disappeared off to the Transvaal, to see about his investment in oranges and to purchase some land on which to build the marital home. While he was gone, he wrote Geraldine 'such lovely, glowing letters', but when he returned briefly to Cape Town he was 'inarticulate and undemonstrative'. Maybe he was thinking about what would happen next, as he boarded his boat taking him back to Burma. In any case they said their goodbyes, and Edgar promised to send the money for Geraldine to buy herself a ring. He also suggested she leave her hospital job and go back to Britain to wait for his summons. 'Bells clanged, steam belched forth in a bellow of sound from the funnel, and the steamer slowly glided away, and Edgar had gone.'

---

[1] Bill Tydd, *Peacock Dreams* (London: BACSA, 1986), pp.81-82.

Making a decision that she would regret in retrospect, Geraldine broke her contract at the Alexandra Hospital and left Cape Town. She had been in South Africa for six months. Edgar had been true to his word, however, and Geraldine was now sporting a shiny new engagement ring as she sailed up the Atlantic.

Alicia was glad to have her daughter home and excited to hear all about Edgar and their engagement. They got to work on preparing and making Geraldine's trousseau, her 'little bundle' of bride's clothing and things that she would take to her married life.

When they weren't preparing for Geraldine's Big Day, some days were 'enlivened' attending or hosting tea parties 'with the old ladies and their sour daughters'. Rather than being happy for Geraldine, it seems she took some flak. One of the 'sour daughters' said: 'So you have managed to get off at last, have you? Your mother will not find it easy to let you go to someone she has never seen.' Another asked what Geraldine knew of Edgar's life in Burma, while others started prying by writing to people they knew in Burma to see what they could find out about Edgar. The answers all came back positive, so they were unable to gossip further, at least in respect of Edgar's reputation and character. After Geraldine told Edgar about the excitement their engagement had caused, he replied: 'Tell the old cats you are coming out to be all in all to a wild jungle man.'

After a year at home in Britain, Edgar finally wrote to say that he was at a good station in the town of Pyinmana, and that everything was ready for Geraldine to come and join him. Geraldine was eager to get going, but first she had to buy a pair of dogs; Edgar had asked that she bring two bull terriers out to Burma with her.

Dogs found and purchased, trousseau packed, Alicia saw her daughter on to the train in London, and Harold once again saw the not so little Wee-o onto the boat that would be her home

'TELL THE OLD CATS YOU ARE COMING...'

for a month at sea. It was March 1924, and very soon Edgar would have a wife, and Geraldine would become a Peacock, funnily enough in a country whose national bird is, well, a peacock...

13. 'My darling, you can't come running back this time'

Before getting on the boat, she had had another wobble, a 'sudden panic of insecurity', but Alicia had kissed her daughter tenderly and hugged her 'in a last, long embrace.' There had been tears, and a run-in with a train guard who had done that thing that people in positions of authority seem to like doing: he had told Geraldine that she wasn't allowed the dogs in her compartment on the train but that he was going to let her.

Cruising across the Indian Ocean to her wedding, the sea suddenly turned a muddy brown, and stayed that way for miles, and 'the heat was terrific'. She was approaching Rangoon; she was approaching married life; she was going to spend the best part of the next decade 'as all in all to a wild jungle man' in the forests of Burma. It was a wild jungle man who she had not seen for over a year, and had in any case only known a few weeks at best.

Then, there he was, 'looking so different in a white suit and a topee', as her ship finally brought her into Rangoon docks.

With all the sensations of being in a new land and the associated assaults on all their senses, her two bull terriers nearly pulled her over in their eagerness to be off the boat. Geraldine was just as impatient to disembark and finally be reunited with Edgar, but unlike the bull terriers, she could not be so obviously excited in public without provoking gossip and embarrassing Edgar. As it was, their reunion 'was not as [she] had imagined, but rather strained [she] thought, but [she] knew he was self conscious and shy in public.'

What about Edgar? How must he have been feeling at this moment? He had sailed off from Cape Town over a year ago, and had even met someone onboard the ship travelling back to Burma. Years later he told Geraldine that if he hadn't already agreed to marry her, then he would have proposed to this other woman he had met. Where we have the insight into Geraldine's feelings, we have nothing for Edgar, so can only speculate and wonder at what was going through his mind in these incredible moments of their lives.

There was no time to waste at the docks, however. Geraldine and Edgar were due to be married in Rangoon Cathedral at 15:30 that afternoon. She was soon whisked off the quay and taken to a large department store where Edgar said:

'Buy whatever you think will be necessary for the house.' He then vanished.

Geraldine, 'bewildered' by the 'magnificence' of the store, feeling all discombobulated at being in a new country, slightly unsettled by the lack of romantic reunion that she had harboured in her imagination, not knowing what the house looked like or how it was already furnished, faced her first challenge of her new life. What should she buy? How much money was she able to spend? Without much time to think, a store assistant 'bore down' on her, 'rubbing his hands in anticipation.'

'Can I help you, madame?' he asked.

'I have only just arrived in this country,' she said, 'and my husband has left me to buy something useful for the house up country. What do you suggest?'

'He produced an ice box.'

It seemed like a fantastic idea. Rangoon was sweltering, 'the temperature was then about the same as a good hot baking oven.'

Little did she realize that, where she was going – up country – there would be no ice to put in the box. Edgar was not very impressed, but nor did he have the courage to take it back to the shop and exchange it. Rather depressingly, Geraldine paints a picture of this ice box following them across Burma over the years; 'a useless white elephant, and a constant reminder of my incompetence.'

As her mum had kissed her and held her in that embrace before relinquishing her daughter to her future she had said, 'My darling, you can't come running back this time.' Geraldine was a strong woman, and she was not going to go running back. She was in a beautiful new land, and she was committed to it – and her man.

14. 'What a wedding day'

It wasn't only the awkward reunion and the ice box that had thrown Geraldine off balance the day she finally arrived in Rangoon. Descending the gang plank to the quay, fairly dragged along by her eager bull terriers, Edgar had said that she should hand them over to a person dressed in something like a silk skirt, a neatly embroidered jacket, and with a colourful scarf tied around their hair. Assuming said person was a female, Geraldine had replied with the question:

'But can she manage both, they are very strong, you know?'

Edgar had 'replied in a frigid voice':

'That is not a woman'.

Being new to the country, Geraldine hadn't known that Burmese men wear longyis (pronounced 'long gee'), and that this was a man called Maung Thein.

Still off balance and smarting from the mortification of the ice box purchase, the next stop after the department store was a large hotel. Walking around Rangoon nearly a century later, looking at all the relics of the colonial era, we can only wonder which building it might have been; indeed, if it even still exists. Rangoon is a city full of its colonial ghosts, with any imposing Victorian buildings that remain only hinting at their previous majesty in the throes of their neglect. Wonderful architectural facades are alive with green as nature reclaims its place, reminding us that once this place was a jungle. It is a very green city, with desperate dereliction sitting right beside sultry splendour, with a curious mix of the old and the new, of colonial and indigenous, all wrapped in the turgid heat of a boisterous city. For all the mystery and melancholia that the city provokes, there is something missing that most Southeast Asian cities are all filled with, but which certainly isn't missed here: since 2003 there have been no motorbikes in Yangon (Rangoon's modern name).

As she made her way from the docks to the hotel where Edgar had arranged a room for her, Geraldine would have seen Rangoon in all its splendour before the destruction wrought upon it by the Second World War. Perhaps we could say that she saw the city at the peak of its 'imperial glory'. It was forty years on from the Third Anglo-Burmese War of 1886 which overthrew the Konbaung Dynasty and made all of Burma part of the British Raj, and when Rangoon had become the colonial capital of Burma. It is even now still referred to as the 'Garden City of the East', or Myanmar's 'Garden City'.

Somewhere in the Garden City, at the 'large' hotel, Edgar sent Geraldine up to her room to rest, and to 'change and be ready for the wedding at half past three.'

Finding it difficult to relax alone in her room and 'in strange surroundings', Geraldine unpacked her wedding dress and put it on. It was a two-piece white satin brocade, matched with white hat, shoes and gloves. Still 'depressed' about the 'stupid mistake over the ice box', Geraldine was struggling with the climate too as she dressed herself: 'The terrific heat made me feel I was nearer Hell then [sic] Heaven. I craved a little love and sympathy'. Wouldn't it have been nice if Edgar could have arranged for some female friends, or partners of friends, to be there to cheer her up and encourage her ahead of their appointment at the cathedral?

'What a wedding day', she thought, 'all alone in a strange country with no one to care what I look like.'

She finished dressing and then, as she descended the great staircase of the hotel, she recognized some men from the boat who were having drinks at the hotel bar. They turned to stare at Geraldine in her silk two-piece with her matching white shoes, gloves and hat; now they knew why she had sailed to

'WHAT A WEDDING DAY'

Burma. Edgar was waiting for her dressed in a grey suit, and very soon they were making their way to the cathedral.

Rangoon Cathedral is still there today, although it did not come through the Second World War unscathed. The foundation stone was laid by the Viceroy of India at the time, Lord Dufferin, when construction began in 1886. The architect was Robert Chisholm, who designed many of the government and colonial buildings across the Raj between 1865 and 1902 (when he returned to Britain). The Indo-Saracenic style which he pioneered drew on Mughal influence, and can be seen in Britain in buildings such as the Brighton Pavilion. It took eight years to build, so the cathedral was thirty years old when it hosted Edgar and Geraldine that afternoon.

Edgar's grandson bemoans the fact that he can't ever recall seeing a wedding photo, which is odd considering Edgar was such a keen photographer. Indeed, the family archive is a treasure trove of days gone by, as the selection within these pages testifies. Geraldine herself wrote in her private memoir that the wedding was 'just a quiet affair, with Edgar's two friends to give us support.' Later on, she wrote 'of the ceremony I remember very little'.

The story of the cathedral and its significance to the Peacocks does not start and finish with the wedding just described. In November 2017, a special Remembrance Sunday service was held in Holy Trinity Cathedral on the Bogyoke Aung San Road. Its purpose was to unveil a memorial to Major Hugh Seagrim. Edgar's only grandson and his wife were there, along with as many Chin and Karen war veterans as could make it. One Karen veteran present that day, Saw Berney, remembered Edgar, having served with him during 1945.

Edgar could never have known in April 1924, as the world finally seemed to settle down after the Great War, that there would be another global conflict just fifteen years later. He couldn't know that, during that conflict, he would be in

JUNGLE WARRIOR

command of *the* most successful wartime operation of a very secret organisation known as the Special Operations Executive. Nor would he have known that the man who sacrificed his life for the Karen people of Burma, and who made Edgar's operation possible, would have a memorial stone unveiled in the wall of the cathedral just mere metres away from where he and Geraldine made their vows. Nor would he have known that the grandson of the Viceroy who laid the stone to commence the building of that same cathedral would lose his life in Burma serving in that very same organisation, the Special Operations Executive. And nor could he know that his friend, Fred Bodeker, witness at his wedding that day, would also join SOE and serve alongside the Viceroy's grandson.[1]

'What a wedding day.'

---

[1] Captain Basil Sheridan Hamilton-Temple-Blackwood, 4th Marquis of Dufferin: The Marquis was killed in action in Burma on 25 March 1945. He was serving as officer commanding No.2 Indian Field Broadcasting Unit (IFBU). The IFBUs were responsible for SOE's political and psychological warfare. See National Archives HS 9/454/9 for the Marquis; HS 9/171/4 for Captain Fred Bodeker. For immediate access to short biographies of most of the men who served in Burma, see Richard Duckett, 'The men of SOE Burma' [online] https://soeinburma.com/the-men-of-soe-burma/

INDIA
Kohima
CHINA
BANGLA-
DESH
Imphal
Tamu
Yuwa
Mawlaik
Lashio
Mandalay
BURMA
Akyab
Loikaw
LAOS
Toungoo
Mawchi
Bago
Rangoon
Bay of
Bengal
Moulmein
Bassein
THAILAND
Andaman Sea
Tenasserim
Mergui
Gulf of
Thailand
Victoria Point

15. 'I had lived a life time in a very different world'

Afterwards, they went for a wedding tea, where there were more of Edgar's friends 'who were waiting to wish us good luck.' But, just as she had been 'hurried' off the boat, and just as she had been 'whisked' away to the cathedral, it wasn't long before Geraldine found herself on a train leaving 'for up country'. The train was an overnighter, and they had a 'very large compartment to [them]selves'. Despite living in South Africa until she was five, and her subsequent travels back in the land of her birth from Cape Town into the Great Karoo, Geraldine wrote that she 'never had any experience of sleeping on a train'. She 'never thought of undressing' but it need not have mattered, for Edgar said:

'It will be best to wait till we get home, darling.' In her naivety, she 'didn't really know what he meant.'

The distance from Rangoon to Pyinmana, is approximately 233 miles by road and nearly a five-hour journey in 2023. This distance is comparable to what would have taken Geraldine far into the Great Karoo when she visited those remote farms which she marvelled at in South Africa back in 1920. Today, no trains are available for either of these destinations.

Mr and Mrs Peacock did not arrive at their destination until the early morning. There was still a bit more travelling to go, however, and while Edgar was absolutely used to it, Geraldine found herself on 'a hard wooden seated and uncomfortable four wheeler, drawn buy [sic] one horse'.

Along the way, the groom teased his bride by pointing at shed-like buildings made of bamboo with no doors and saying:

'That is my house over there.'

'I HAD LIVED A LIFE TIME IN A VERY DIFFERENT WORLD'

Luckily, and much to her relief, none of them were, and suddenly the uncomfortable 'Garry' turned into a 'long drive' and a splendid 'large wooden bungalow' presented itself to the newly weds. There were shutters on the windows and a large verandah, called a stoep in South Africa, which surrounded the house. There were cane chairs which looked like they needed sitting in and lots of pots containing 'ferns and palms, which gave it a cool and exotic appearance.'

'Welcome to your new home,' Edgar said, as he kissed her on the threshold.

After the whirlwind of the last twenty-four hours that kiss must have meant so much.

It was breakfast time and the table was being set by an Indian boy who gazed 'at the new Mem-Sahib in wonder'. Realizing she was very hungry, Geraldine wondered what would be served for the first meal of the day in her new surroundings. As her eye swept around the house she noted it was (of course) a bachelor dwelling, 'sadly lacking the touch of a feminine hand.' She at once made a note to change the tablecloth with another from her trousseau.

Edgar had to go to work. 'Make yourself at home', he said, and off he went. Geraldine went to explore upstairs, apparently feeling like Goldilocks. She found 'a large room with a very hard, wooden, native made bed in it, with an equally hard mattress.' Opening her trousseau, she made the bed up with sheets from home. 'It was far too hot to even look at a blanket.' Trying out the bed, she found it was 'awful', but it had to do.

The bathroom was a very simple affair. A small room contained a tin bath, a large earthenware jar of cold water, and a commode in the corner. This simplicity should not have come as much of a surprise. Many homes in Britain still had outhouses into the 1970s, some fifty years after Geraldine made herself at home in Burma. Nonetheless, as the evening drew in, it seemed to Geraldine that she 'had lived a life time in a very different world'.

Edgar returned from work for their first night together in their home as a married couple. It seems amazing to us now that even in the 1950s and 1960s, parents often never discussed certain things like menstruation or sex with their children. For her part, Geraldine, at thirty-four, knew very little about 'the physical side of marriage'. Consequently, her abiding memory of that night is of Edgar pacing up and down 'in great agitation', finding it hard to believe that Geraldine's mother had allowed her daughter to 'remain so ignorant'. At this time, her mother's last words were actually ringing in her ears – 'you can't come running back this time.' 'I felt between the devil and the deep blue sea' she wrote. But she finally managed to calm Edgar, stop him walking up and down, and to get him to come to bed: 'and so ended that very long day.'

PHOTOS 1

Edgar's future wife, Geraldine in 1906, aged 16

Geraldine Peacock in 1922, aged 32. Taken shortly after Edgar and Geraldine met on board ship bound for Cape Town, South Africa.

Photos 1

Edgar Peacock in 1922, aged 29. Edgar had this photograph taken in Johannesburg, weeks after meeting Geraldine on board ship.

A memento of their meeting on board the Walmer Castle. Geraldine treasured this card for her whole life.

Geraldine Peacock in 1924, aged 34

Photos 1

The house in Pyinmana in early 1925. A far cry from jungle living!

Geraldine writes of this photo taken in 1924: "This was my first camp after my marriage and my only honeymoon".

Edgar Peacock inspecting logging operations in Burma circa 1925

PHOTOS 1

Edgar Peacock was involved with training and welfare of elephants. He later used them, when available, for transporting stores behind enemy lines.

The imposing house in Mawlaik Where Joy Peacock was born and close to the area where Edgar Peacock operated with P Force in 1943/44

JUNGLE WARRIOR

(Above and below): Joy Peacock age 2yrs 6 mths on a jungle tour near Tamu, where P Force was based in 1944

PHOTOS 1

The Peacocks on leave in England in 1932. Alicia Godwin (mother of Geraldine), Joy, Edgar & Geraldine Peacock

JUNGLE WARRIOR

Edgar Peacock with his eldest child, Joy, on a camp in the Jungle circa 1931. Edgar was called 'the saviour of the villagers' for keeping rogue tigers and elephants at bay.

16. 'Most of my life is spent in the jungle'

Before setting out into the jungle with Edgar on tour, the dogs Geraldine had brought out from Britain had to be tested for discipline. Peter responded to Edgar's commands well, and was considered satisfactory for the journey ahead. Not so, Tilly. Tilly was a stubborn bitch, and though Edgar called her, she repeatedly turned tail and ran away. Edgar lost his patience and said:

'She must be broken in or we will have endless bother with her in the jungle.'

Using methods which probably make most of us wince in the twenty-first century, Edgar proceeded to 'break her in'. Having called for a stick, each time Tilly didn't do as she was told, Edgar beat her. She got such a thrashing that there were raised marks all over her back. Geraldine was scared by this hard streak in her husband. She thought that Tilly 'needed a little love and sympathy'; like Geraldine herself, Tilly was new to the country and its ways and so could have done with a more gentle approach.

In his own environment, Edgar was a different character to the shy young man Geraldine had met on the boat. He was comfortable in command of his workers and servants, and everything ran 'most efficiently'. It is not too hard to see how this would translate very well into a wartime setting, fighting the Japanese far behind the front lines. But this was twenty years away in the future, when Edgar should have been too old to be considered for service.

On their six- to eight-week long treks through the jungle, the day started with cups of tea before the dawn. Elephants would be loaded up with all their supplies and tents, their bells jingling as belongings were made secure. There was a lot of equipment; the tents were large and comfortable, with everything necessary to make life as normal as possible. On her first trip, since she had not been 'proved' on long jungle treks, Edgar provided his bride with a horse for what was, to all intents and purposes, their honeymoon. Geraldine considered the horse to be a 'great concession' as everyone else always had to walk the trails with Edgar. In any event, some of the paths were so steep that Geraldine found it far less terrifying to walk rather than remain on horseback. Edgar apparently wasn't too happy that she asked the new trainee forestry employee who accompanied them, also on his first trip, to lead her horse on some of the more precipitous paths. In the future, she chose to march too.

After around ten miles or so, the procedure was to call a halt and take tiffin. The word 'tiffin' evolved in India during the nineteenth century until it became a common term. Quite simply, tiffin is the word used for any light meal during the hot hours of the day, between breakfast and dinner. Once the halt was called, the cook would get tiffin on and the tents would go up, and with each person doing their job the camp was soon established. By the time tiffin had been consumed, the heat of the day would have descended, so elephants were let loose and everyone tried to find the coolest spot they could until it was tea time. After tea, Edgar always took his rifle and went to find something for the pot. Deer or fowl, he always supplied the camp with something. Geraldine very soon came to admire his skill as a hunter and marksman – both for the pot and to help out the local villagers who often came and asked for help with a rogue elephant or an over-inquisitive tiger.

Their second jungle tour was without the young apprentice fresh from the mother country. Geraldine 'thoroughly enjoyed it'. She had quickly come to love the majesty of the jungle canopy, like a great cathedral above their heads. Edgar began to teach her some jungle skills, how to shoot green pigeon, and how to call up a deer by blowing on a folded leaf. To Geraldine it was all so very interesting and romantic – until she went down with dengue fever.

'Most of my life is spent in the jungle'

Dengue fever, also known as 'break-bone fever' because of how it attacks the joints and causes muscle spasms, is a mosquito-borne virus. It is not usually fatal, but it is extremely uncomfortable in severe cases. Geraldine had a 'bad attack' of it, and had to take to her bed. Despite his wife's predicament, Edgar left the camp to go for his customary stroll with his gun and the dogs. To his mind, since he could do nothing for her, there was no need to stay with her. She sobbed as he left.

Geraldine did not respond to the normal treatment of quinine and aspirin, so a doctor became necessary. The journey back to civilization was made on a bullock cart, loaned from the nearest village. The trip was horribly uncomfortable, only for the doctor at the end of it to say that the worst of the fever was over – fortunately. It must have been quite scary for Geraldine, but Edgar seems to have taken it all in his stride. She had, after all, chosen to be 'all in all to a wild jungle man'.

17. 'Ghostly nights and weird noises'

The bull terrier bitch never became the obedient dog that the 'severe thrashings' were supposed to produce. As soon as a gun was fired, she would run off through the undergrowth to the first village she could find, and hide underneath a house. Edgar therefore considered Tilly to be 'quite useless', but she did produce a litter of ten pups. Not long after, Edgar and Geraldine learned they were expecting their own addition to their household too.

While the arrival of a baby was in the not too distant future, in the immediate future, Edgar and Geraldine had to leave the jungle bungalow in Pyinmana for a new Forestry Service posting hundreds of miles away. Just as nobody could have foretold that Edgar and Geraldine's wedding in Rangoon Cathedral would become intimately woven into their future family history, nobody could have known in 1925 the importance of Edgar's posting to Mawlaik. This posting to the remote northeast of Burma on the Upper Chindwin River was in many ways a game changer for the fortunes of SOE's India Mission in 1943–1944.

With a baby on its way, the jungle life that Geraldine had grown accustomed to and enjoyed so much changed. She no longer accompanied Edgar on the long treks that lasted weeks; rather she stayed home in the big house in Mawlaik, alone.

They had spent ten days on a steamer to get them to Mawlaik, a town Geraldine described as an 'outlandish place'. There were apparently just five other people living there, which meant there wasn't much competition for the tennis courts or much of a crowd which could gather in the club. Their new house was double-storeyed and made of brick rather than timber and bamboo, with plenty of large rooms 'and many doors and windows.' Even so, having arrived in the hottest part

'GHOSTLY NIGHTS AND WEIRD NOISES'

of the year, the days and nights were unbearably warm before the rainy season.

When the rains finally broke and the wind ripped trees up in the garden, it was no less terrifying for the lonely, pregnant Geraldine than the hot weather had been when insects and lizards made strange sounds all around the house. One such creature, which Geraldine called a 'Tuctoo' and described as a 'miniature crocodile', caused particular distress. They would scuttle around the walls and shout 'tuctoo' seven times before falling with a loud 'plop' to the floor and scuttling away again. The 'tuctoo' is actually the tokay gecko, and its markings are quite crocodilish! Since 2019 it has been on the CITES list of endangered species. It is described as having 'a large repertoire of powerful vocalisations, which can be heard several dozen meters [sic] away'.[1] Growing ever larger with their child, rattling around on her own in a large house far up country, Geraldine did not enjoy the 'nervous tension of ghostly nights and weird noises.'

It took ten days by boat to get down to Mandalay where the baby was to be born. Edgar accompanied Geraldine to the hospital, but was unable to stay as he had to get back to work. He asked the matron to send a telegram every day to update him on how Geraldine was doing, but didn't quite get the reply he was after: 'My dear man, I will do my best, but it is not usual to wire to husbands till the baby arrives.' For her part, Geraldine was 'secretly terrified', admitting in her private memoir that she had no idea how babies arrived in the world: 'The only comfort was that babies were always being born, so it must happen somehow, and I supposed that was why one went to hospital.' Again, a century later, it seems incredible that anyone could make it into their thirties and not know the basics of childbirth.

---

[1] 'Tokay Gecko', *Managing Exotic Reptiles on Caribbean Islands* (MERCI Project) [online] https://www.merci-project.com/en/tokay-gecko/

Joy Peacock was born on 20 July 1925. Geraldine was so excited to see Edgar again, and for him to meet their precious little bundle, 'but when he did arrive he hardly showed any interest in her. He had wanted a boy, and probably felt disappointed.' He was, however, very concerned about his wife, and whether she would be able to make the journey back up to the house in Mawlaik. Leaving the hospital and boarding the flat-bottomed steamer once again, Geraldine felt the weight of the responsibility of motherhood, and was acutely aware of her naivety in such matters. Geraldine and Joy had an ayah, though, which must have been a massive reassurance for Geraldine, who was often alone for weeks when Edgar went off on his tours. Those 'ghostly nights and weird noises' were not quite so unbearable now since they were spent with her daughter who was such 'a comfort and a blessing'.

Over the next eighteen months, life for Edgar progressed in a cycle of jungle tours and periods at home with his family. Joy remembers playing in the garden with all its colourful flowers and creepers, where her mother taught her to walk and 'to know and love the two bull-terriers and their puppies.' She remembers the house being very busy with visitors; seemingly important men in dinner attire or uniform, accompanied by their wives in 'stylish long dresses'. Guests sat at a long table for a dozen people, waited on by Burmese servers dressed in white suits with white gloves, delivering various dishes made by a Burmese cook who had his kitchen separate to the main house, as was customary. During the day, mahouts often brought their forestry elephants to the back of the garden for Edgar to inspect.

Then, at eighteen months old, Joy was taken on her first jungle tour with her mother and father. This created a bit of a stir, for not only did the other wives seldom foray into the wild places with their jungle men, but nobody took their infants with them. No 'proper ayah' would apparently 'dream of it' either, so one of the servants' wives was brought along instead. It sounds like it was a happy time, for Geraldine wrote:

'GHOSTLY NIGHTS AND WEIRD NOISES'

Many were the exciting adventures we had in the jungle. Touring all day in a native dugout boat, on fast flowing streams in Crocodile infested rivers. All day for several days on a native raft with a small hut built on it for shade, camping at night on the banks of some lonely stream. Following long lonely trails into the heart of the jungle, and safely in camp, hearing a tiger roar as it seeks its prey, or a herd of elephants stamping and breaking branches rather too near to our tent to be pleasant. Marching up hill and down dale, and arriving at last at a Rest house, too tired to care what dangerous reptiles or poisonous insects are lurking inside, for the Rest houses are left deserted for months on end till a Forest Officer turns up in the course of his duties to spend the night.

Much later, these same rest houses would first be filled with civilians and soldiers fleeing an invading army, desperate to escape to India; and in turn filled with the troops of the pursuing army of Imperial Japan as they prepared for their march on Delhi.

18. 'Some lovely new frocks'

In 1928, when Joy was almost three, it was time for some home leave, and for Alicia to meet her grandchild. Geraldine and Joy went ahead of Edgar, who remained in Burma. There is no sense of it in any of the memoirs, but the Burma of 1926–27, forty years after the Third Anglo-Burmese War had annexed all of the country to Britain, was a rather unsettled place. According to the Government Report on the Administration of Burma 1926–27, there was 'a noticeable increase in crime' in 1926.[1] The number of crimes reported went up, there were more sentences and convicts had to be released and put to work to make space in the prisons. They were mostly put to work improving communications, building roads and making tracks, maintaining canals and improving irrigation. As more and more land came under cultivation, effective irrigation was critical to the production of rice, cotton and tobacco.

The water situation was not helped in 1926 with late rains and then floods; Geraldine did make mention of the Chindwin being in full spate, more like a sea than a river. A cyclone also hit Akyab on the west coast of Burma, causing significant damage and flooding. The municipal authorities started construction of a reservoir to resolve Rangoon's acute problem with a secure, clean water supply; in 1926 there was an outbreak of cholera and over 6000 people died. This was an unusually high number of victims, added to which infant mortality took its toll, with one in three babies dying that year. It wasn't just humans dying of disease in Burma in 1926 either; around 40,000 head of plough oxen and cattle died of rinderpest.

---

[1] Report on the Administration of Burma 1926 - 1927 (Superintendent, Government Printing & Stationery, Rangoon, 1928) [online] https://www.myanmar-law-library.org/law-library/legal-journal/reports-on-the-administration-of-british-burma/nouvel-article-no-402.html

Although no link to these problems was made in the government report, it was noted that 'Politics have invaded the villages, manifesting their effect in movements of resistance to the collection of taxes.' This seems to have applied only to central Burma; in the frontier areas, for example in the Chin Hills, an increase in tax met barely any resistance. The frontier areas, however, had other issues which the colonial authorities were working hard to eradicate; two expeditions into the Naga Hills aimed to put an end to human sacrifice. Approximately eighty-one chiefs and headmen pledged to end the practice, handing over weapons and human remains associated with their custom. In the Kachin Hills, a Durbar was held in which it was made clear that slavery was unacceptable, and over 3000 slaves were 'redeemed'. At first there had been some resistance from the Kachins. Military columns were attacked and the loss of Captain E.M. West and two others is recorded. In response, however, 'punitive measures were taken and there was no further opposition.' There was also an effort to put an end to slavery in the Hukawng Valley area, around 400 miles north of where Edgar and Geraldine were living in Mawlaik.

In Edgar's forestry business, a further 300 square miles of new reserves were created and forest revenue was the highest on record. Teak bounced back in the international market after a bit of a slump, but even so, more reserved woods other than teak were harvested than in previous years. Mostly the emphasis was on protection and regeneration, and a number of surveys were carried out mapping many tens of thousands of square miles across the country. Both the maps and the lines of communication being made in this year would prove to be of particular importance to Edgar and SOE a couple of decades later.

At the Bawdwin Silver and Lead Mine, a facility that SOE targeted in its scorched earth policy in 1942, tragedy struck when a landslide killed forty-nine people as they slept. Sadly, landslides in Myanmar's jade mines have also been a fairly regular feature in the news recently with hundreds dying in 2019, 2020 and 2021.

Leaving all this behind for the time being, Geraldine and Joy made their way across the oceans and seas to Britain. Edgar had seen his family onto the boat in Rangoon before heading back up country. At two years old, Joy was mobile, and it sounds as though Geraldine had a tough journey back, even buying some reins to prevent her falling overboard. In both her private memoir and her published biography, Geraldine wrote about being 'on the verge of a nervous breakdown' by the time she arrived in Southampton. She appears to have been in enough of a state that both her mother and the doctor tried to advise her not to return to Burma! This was not an idea that Geraldine was prepared to entertain for a moment.

Finding her clothes out of date with the latest fashions, Geraldine took Joy into London and went shopping, and she also bought a Fiat car and learned to drive as she had been instructed to by Edgar. The car probably added to her nervous state as it 'would stop in the most awkward places. One would have to get out and wind her up in front with a long handle.' She sprained her wrist cranking the car, and had to go back to the doctor who didn't want her to go back to Burma.

One morning, some post arrived 'addressed to Edgar in a woman's hand.' Curiosity didn't quite overrule privacy, and since it was the morning of the day Edgar was due to finally arrive in Britain, she pocketed the letter and drove the Fiat down to meet him at the docks. She finally found him helping a pregnant lady with her belongings. After a kiss, she gave him the letter and was soon 'feeling rather ashamed of her suspicious thoughts.' The letter was from a missionary girl Edgar had met on the ship, and he had planned to meet her and others, with Geraldine, in London; 'he wanted to show me off to them, he said.'

Edgar soon mastered the Fiat, and, leaving Joy with her grandmother, Edgar and Geraldine drove off to tour Cornwall, via London, where they met up with the missionary girl and the other friends made on the boat. Despite discovering that there was, of course, no threat posed by the letter writer, Geraldine admits she was not especially cordial, to the extent that their tour of Cornwall was somewhat blighted in the days afterwards. Nonetheless, just like the countless swarms of people who have followed after them, both Edgar and Geraldine were 'greatly struck' by the beauty of Cornwall with its rugged coasts and charming little villages.

Before getting the boat back to Burma, there was time for a trip to the seaside with Alicia. Once again, Geraldine admits to getting a touch of the green-eyed monster when Edgar went swimming in the sea with another married woman. Geraldine had never learned to swim, so she was confined to the shore feeling 'jealous and neglected.' After the seaside, there was a trip to London together for a day's shopping, and Edgar spoiled Geraldine by buying her 'some lovely new frocks.' She very much enjoyed his attention and his help in selecting London's 'latest creations' for her to take back overseas.

Alicia still tried to keep Geraldine from returning to Burma, but she was resolute and soon it was time for another boat. Edgar had been posted to the southern tail of Burma, far from the house of 'ghostly nights and weird noises' in Mawlaik. The delights of the tropical beaches of the Mergui Archipelago were to be their next new home. And it was on this return that the 'politics [which] have invaded the villages' were soon to catch up with the Peacocks of Burma.

19. 'Quite a civilised life for a change'

On arrival in Rangoon, the Peacocks were met at the quay by their cook from Mawlaik, and his wife, who had been Joy's ayah. They were 'anxious' to go with Edgar and Geraldine to Mergui, and Edgar and Geraldine were glad to have them. It was not unusual for Burmese house staff to stay with a family for as long as they stayed in Burma. Having assembled more of their staff, the journey to Mergui was made in baking heat onboard a small cargo boat.

Mergui, now known as Myeik, is located far down the southern tail of Burma, over 500 miles from Yangon by road; in 2017 a new ferry service advertised the journey as ten hours in duration. After capture by the Burmese from its Thai rulers in 1765, Mergui was annexed to Britain in 1826 after the First Anglo-Burmese War. The region has a tropical climate, and is known for its beautiful beaches and islands on the Andaman Sea. The author of the popular 'Biggles' series of novels, Captain W.E. Jones, had his protagonist fly over the region in *Biggles Delivers the Goods*: 'To the right, the horizon was defined by a long dark stain that was the forest-clad hinterland of Lower Burma. Below the aircraft, like a string of green beads dropped carelessly on blue velvet, were the islands of the archipelago, lonely, untouched by civilisation'. Tourism brochures today still market the area as 'one of the most sumptuous and unspoilt segments of Southeast Asia.'[1]

Evidently, Edgar was on tour 'a great deal' – even fellow officers in government employment joked about how they never found him at home – and similar to before, Geraldine and Joy were able to accompany him sometimes. Part of Edgar's remit was to explore the limestone caves on the islands and Geraldine found these tours 'most interesting.' These caves are still visited

---

[1] 'About Myanmar', *Sampan Travel* [online] https://www.sampantravel.com/about-myanmar/

'QUITE A CIVILISED LIFE FOR A CHANGE'

by people who harvest the nests of the birds which populate them. The nests are made from the saliva of the birds, and are harvested to be made into a soup for Chinese culinary delight. In traditional Chinese medicine, the gelatinous soup is said to relieve digestive problems, clear the skin, and act as an aphrodisiac. Nutritionally, however, it is reckoned that one egg has the same value as 26 soups. The nests command a high price in restaurants that serve them; in 1929–30 when Edgar and Geraldine and Joy were there, the colonial government was paid 'large sums of money' by people who were involved in the swiftlet nest trade. Nearly 100 years later, there is still a brisk legal and illegal trade in bird-spit nests.

During the Second World War, SOE sent Operation Corton to the Mergui Archipelago. Perhaps surprisingly, they don't seem to have approached Edgar for his specialist and intimate knowledge of the area formed during his posting there just over a decade before. The SOE operation was tasked with setting up a wireless transmitter (W/T) on the island and acting as a relay station; to collect intelligence from the mainland and also information about local boat activity; to report enemy air and sea activity and, lastly, to look into the possibility of establishing caches of stores for future operations. The personnel for the operation, codenamed Corton, were Captain. K.E. Green, Lieutenant. A.M. McNab, three Anglo-Burmese other ranks (ORs) and two W/T operators (one British and one Indian). Corton I was launched on 31 January 1944 and ran until the night of 5/6 April. Corton II ran from 5/6 April through to 14 October 1944.

According to Captain Green, malaria was 'the main cause of the failure of this operation', but it seems the disease was just one of their many difficulties. There is a whole section of the report dedicated to 'weather', which might be described as a typically British topic of conversation, but here it brought obvious difficulties and discomfort. The diary entry for July provides some idea of conditions, and when to consider a visit to Mergui:

> July 1 – 31 – Nothing occurred during July of any importance. It rained for 27 days without stopping and it was impossible to have any lookouts or patrols during this month.[2]

Despite the hardships endured by the Corton team some years later, Edgar and Geraldine enjoyed their time in Mergui. Geraldine wrote that they 'were just getting accustomed to this interesting part of the world when we were transferred to Maymyo, a hill station. It would certainly be a very pleasant change from the terrific heat of the Mergui Archipelago.'

Like Simla in India, Maymyo in Burma was the more temperate retreat of the colonial government during the hot months of the year. Maymyo, now known as Pyin Oo Lwin, is described by Leslie Glass in his book *The Changing of the Kings:*

> Up in Maymyo were the Governor's summer residence, official villas, with passable efforts at English gardens, a swimming pool, carefully cut rides through the woods, a number of forest firm holiday chummeries, a British battalion, a Burma Rifles battalion, and a well-appointed club with tennis courts and polo ground.[3]

Upon arrival after a somewhat scary journey up to 4000 feet in a zigzagging train, Edgar and Geraldine found they had been posted to 'a large and pleasant house and garden not far from a beautiful club with lovely tennis courts and plenty of other social activities'. Edgar went out touring as usual, and Geraldine continued to accompany him from time to time, though she seems to have appreciated her now 'quite civilised life' in Maymyo. That civilized life was about to undergo a bit of

[2] Richard Duckett, 'Monkey Nuts Are Rotten', *SOE in Burma* [online] https://soeinburma.com/2018/02/16/monkey-nuts-are-rotten/
[3] Leslie Glass, *The Changing of the Kings* (London: Peter Owen, 1985), p.74.

a shock when a Forest Officer was murdered in his rest house and his guns were stolen. Out on tour themselves, the rumour was confirmed as true upon their return to Maymyo. The Saya San Rebellion had reached Maymyo, and that March of 1931 was when Edgar ended up fighting for his life in hospital having had a *dah* split his skull open. At the same time, Alicia was 'constantly writing and begging' her daughter to come home. She needed help with the laundry business. Surrounded by violence in Burma and facing pressure from home, Geraldine was wondering anxiously about her future when an opportunity for another spot of clairvoyance presented itself.

20. 'A red spot'

The ladies in Maymyo were talking about a very clever Indian fortune-teller. Wondering once more about her future, and having had a fairly accurate prediction before, Geraldine decided to check out the old man's skills. One day, the Indian man turned up at the house. She was made to sit on the floor, and to stare into his eyes. Anticipation soon turned to shock as a wrinkled hand made its way down her top to her breast, while the other hand began to climb up her leg. At the same time, she heard herself being told that if there was a red spot on her chest as well as under her skirt, then there was a message for her future. That future prediction was never told, for she tore her 'eyes away from his ugly face and the spell was broken.' Jumping to her feet, she shouted at the man to clear off, 'shaking with fright' as he demanded a bottle of whisky in payment for his services. There was no one else at home, and there was no whisky either. Thinking and acting fast, she wrote a note asking the local shopkeeper to provide the bearer of the note with a bottle; she just wanted him out of the house. Realizing she had been conned, minutes later Geraldine drove to the store to prevent her note from being honoured, but alas, she was too late. Both the man and the whisky had 'vanished into the thronging bazaar.' Surely he can't have been the same fortune-teller that the ladies had been discussing! She never did find out, but nor was she given any idea of what the next few years had in store for her family.

The last place that Edgar, Geraldine and little Joy were posted together in Burma was Moulmein. Now called Mawlamyine, this was Geraldine's least favourite posting. The house was said to be haunted and the jungles around Moulmein 'were very rough.' Incidentally, stories of hauntings in Burma seem to have been quite common in these times. Bill Tydd devoted chapter four of his memoir to 'The Haunting', relating how they put a young visiting Irish police officer in a barrack room that nobody used because it was said to be haunted; it was also said that the Irish were 'more susceptible to the unusual'. The Irish officer did not have a good night.[1] During the retreat from Burma in 1942, while working for SOE, Captain Jack Barnard was guarding a bridge over the N'Sop Hka River which he had been told was often visited by a ghostly female apparition. Jack wrote in his memoir that 'many years after the event, I am fully convinced that Dennis and I saw a ghost on the N'Sop Hka bridge.'[2] There is one more ghost story to come, towards the end of this book, which concerns Edgar directly.

Edgar didn't like leaving his pregnant wife behind and so when a voluntary redundancy programme was offered by the Forestry Service, Edgar decided to apply with a view to relocating his family to Britain. The jungle man was about to become manager of a laundry business. Eighteen years of a career in forestry and as a Game Warden was almost at an end. Geraldine was apprehensive of Edgar leaving his jungle environs, and nor did she relish the thought of leaving a life she had 'grown to love [...] so much.' Nonetheless, and against Geraldine's better judgement, it was agreed that she would go on ahead of Edgar once again. As she boarded the boat with Joy for yet another voyage, Geraldine 'felt that life would never be quite the same again' and was 'full of forebodings.'

The decision to retire early from the Forestry Service seems to have been prompted by a few simultaneous developments: as a result of governmental retrenchment, the post which Edgar held of Game Warden of Burma was to be abolished, which would have, necessarily, resulted in him becoming more deskbound, a situation he undoubtedly found unappealing; the Saya San Rebellion and the consequent threat to life which nearly claimed Edgar; the Moulmein posting which was their least favourite of all the places they lived in Burma;

---

[1] Bill Tydd, Peacock Dreams (London: BACSA, 1986), pp.14-15.
[2] Jack Barnard MC, *The Hump* (London: Four Square, 1966), pp.37-9

learning that they were expecting a second child; and the fact that Joy was six years old. Europeans were not allowed to keep their children in Burma from that age according to government rules and regulations. For families in colonial service, this was '[o]ne of the great drawbacks, probably the greatest for most of us' because of the 'inevitable separation' that must follow.[3] The climate and a 'lack of educational facilities' meant most children went to Britain to start their schooling. If the letters from Geraldine's mother had not assured Edgar of a job in England, at the very least, Joy would have had to be packed off to boarding school.

Before Edgar left Burma to take up his position as manager of the Phoenix Laundry in East Grinstead, he went off on a last tour as Game Warden, this time to the Dawna Mountains in Lower Burma. The mountains rise up to around 6000 feet and are situated northeast of Moulmein, close to the border with Thailand. He was desperately keen to find out if the rumour was true that a rare species of mammal that looks like a cross between a deer and a goat could be found in these mountains. The creature in question, a goral, is sometimes described as a 'goat-antelope' and has four species; the Himalayan goral; long-tailed goral; red goral; and the Chinese goral. It seems the species Edgar wanted to find was 'Naemorhedus griseus', which is commonly called the Chinese goral. There was also rumour of serow and Fea's muntjac in the area. The former is also a goat-like antelope and until recently it was classified in the same genus as the goral; the latter is a rare species of barking deer and is currently an endangered species.

The local Karen hunters assured Edgar that the animals made their home in the Dawna Range, but that to get anywhere near them the ground would be terribly difficult. Not put off, Edgar set off with a blanket and basic rations to try and reach the source of a chaung where the local hunter said they might find

---

[3] Bill Tydd, Peacock Dreams (London: BACSA, 1986), p.24.

'A RED SPOT'

the sought-after game.[4] Edgar managed to find, and shoot, both a serow and a goral, after a few hard days in the mountains. He was happy with two out of three. A few days later he emerged from the Dawna Range and retired from the Forestry Service. It was February 1932, and he was just short of his fortieth birthday.

Thousands of miles away in England, while Edgar was proving the existence of rare species of goat-antelopes (and reducing them by one each) in the Dawna Range, Geraldine was struggling with a strange family environment. Edgar did not know what awaited him, but Geraldine had been right to feel her foreboding.

---

[4] Chaungs are a prolific part of the Burmese landscape. In the dry season, they are empty, but in the monsoon season they become raging torrents of water.

21. 'So that is why you came home, was it?'

The laundry empire that Edgar was due to take over had been hard won. Mrs Sparks the rector's wife wasn't the only person of questionable morals who had tested Alicia's resolve, and her determination to survive. One employer, who really didn't know what they were doing, allowed Alicia to get the laundry system up and running properly before firing her when she and Harold got measles. Alicia was turfed out of her home in such a weak condition that 'she feared she might collapse on the journey, so she tied a luggage label on to Harold, showing his destination.' The next laundry job was no better; after Alicia got the business up and running, the owners expected larger profits so they gave Alicia a week's notice and told the employees that she 'had made away with all the profits.' After two years establishing the business for the sum of £1 a week, Alicia 'was back where she had started'; jobless and homeless.

She found a small home to rent, and there was a knock on the door one day and Alicia was asked if she wanted to buy two workman's cottages for £75.00. The plan was to live in one, and start a laundry in the other cottage. Having no money, Alicia was convinced to take a loan by the Sisters in a nearby convent. They recommended a man by the name of Turner. 'The loan was arranged and the business bought, and she was told not to worry, but just to pay back the loan, little by little whenever it was convenient.' What Alicia didn't know until some years after the purchase in 1905 was that the usurious Mr Turner was charging a handsome interest. By this time, however, and with all her experience, Alicia was turning a good profit, so she was able to pay off the 'considerable sum' owed. By 1932, when Edgar caught up with Geraldine to take it on, the Phoenix Laundry in East Grinstead had gone from strength to strength; indeed it was still going into the 1970s.

'SO THAT IS WHY YOU CAME HOME, WAS IT?'

For Edgar and Geraldine, having given up their exciting life in Burma, this was a huge change. The transition was always going to be tough, but there's no way either Edgar or Geraldine could have expected what transpired, and in the various family memoirs the bitter aftertaste of those times is still tangible.

Edgar and Geraldine's first daughter, Joy, remembered walking down a country lane at about six years old and noticing her mother crying. She did not know it then, but 'in the adult world there were great troubles.' After Edgar finally arrived in East Grinstead, it was only to be told that the position of manager of the Phoenix Laundry was no longer open to him. Joy writes of how she only 'learned, many years later, of the intricacies of the game played with greed and jealousy' by close family which had such consequences for Edgar's family. Even before Edgar arrived, there was discussion of giving the job to another man who was supposed to already have experience as a laundry manager. Edgar therefore arrived into a somewhat tense situation.

For her part, Geraldine blamed herself; 'I was terribly upset at the crisis I had brought about.' Whether right or wrong in her introspection, what caused Geraldine to think this way was precipitated by the behaviour of her brother who had asked her the loaded question when she had arrived: 'So that is why you came home, was it?' Desperate to prove she had not come home with any ulterior motives to consume the family's wealth, Geraldine had suggested to the laundry committee that they should take on the trained manager so that she and Edgar could move to South Africa and build their farm on the land Edgar had bought. Up to this point, Geraldine did not feel that she had been welcomed home: 'No one appeared kindly or delighted that I had come, and because I was to have a baby, I appeared to be looked on with suspicion at a business meeting I had to attend, and was accused of 'trailing a red herring'. Such was the situation into which Edgar arrived.

As his daughter wrote, 'understandably' Edgar 'felt great anger, disillusion and amazement at finding himself suddenly with no work or place for him and his family.' The stress of the situation can only have been added to with the imminent arrival of their second child, but instead of embracing his wife, Edgar came to blame Geraldine too, 'he saw her as the cause for every difficulty and bitter disappointment he was having.' Meanwhile, Edgar's mother-in-law, who, it seems, had been outmanoeuvred by her own board of business, felt 'very upset' about the whole situation and was at pains to put things right as far as possible. To that end, she tried to help Edgar find another job, and find a new home for the four in Tunbridge Wells – their second daughter, Wendy, having been born on 13 July 1932.

During all this, Edgar might have thought that he was not living up to the 'fortunate' element of his name, which could be why he decided to flex his 'powerful' side. Even before they moved to Tunbridge Wells, he became 'more and more cold and aloof', and took a bedroom for himself. His wife described him as departing 'into his own private wilderness', completely shutting Geraldine out. Geraldine was allowed no part in either choosing the new house or any of the furnishings that were supposed to make it a home. Consequently, she felt like a visitor in her own home, amplified by the fact that she had a bedroom for herself and the baby, Edgar having once again taken his own bedroom elsewhere in the house.

Before they even moved into the Tunbridge house, the 'experienced' manager proved to be a flop. It had taken approximately two months after Edgar had been usurped to find this out. In a somewhat audacious manner, Edgar was then re-offered the manager's position. Surprisingly, given all that had happened, Edgar agreed. This did not bring any rapprochement to the marriage, however, and Geraldine described the next six months of her life as 'very miserable'. She was alone all day at home, and since Edgar retreated to 'his own private jungle' when he returned home, there was nothing for her to do but

'SO THAT IS WHY YOU CAME HOME, WAS IT?'

hope for forgiveness 'although for what, I really do not know'. Something had to change, and it was not long before it did.

Edgar 'was not seeing eye to eye' with his mother-in-law, and so the Phoenix Laundry lost its second manager within seven months. The house in Tunbridge Wells and its contents were all auctioned off, wife and children were sent to live with his mother-in-law, and Edgar sailed for South Africa. He would send for his family when he was ready for them. It was 10 February 1934. Adolf Hitler had been Chancellor of Germany for just over a year. Leaving the family storm in England, Edgar was also sailing away from the gathering storm in Europe.

ANGOLA
Ondjiva
Oshakati
Tsumeb
Grootfontein
Rundu
Otjiwarongo
S.W. AFRICA
Okahandja
WINDHOEK
Rehoboth
Mariental
Keetmanshoop
Swakopmund
Walvis baai
Lüderitz
ATLANTIC
OCEAN
Cape Town
Port Elizabeth
SOUTH AFRICA
Kimberley
Bloemfontein
LESOTHO
Durban
Mafeking
GABORONE
BOTSWANA
Okavango
Delta
Francistown
Serowe
Livingstone
Seshke
Mazabuka
Choma
Lake
Kariba
Gatooma
S. RHODESIA
Bulawayo
Gwelo
Gwanda
SALISBURY
Marandellas
Umtali
Fern Valley
Fort Victoria
Zebedelia
Pietersburg
Kleinwonder
PRETORIA
Johannesburg
SWAZILAND
LOURENCO MARQUES
João Belo
Vila Trigo de Morais
Inhambane
Vilankulo
MOZAMBIQUE
Beira
Dondo
Vila Pery
Tete
Quelimane
Mocuba
António Enes
INDIAN
OCEAN

22. 'A snake in the grass'

Thirteen months later, on 5 March 1935, Edgar's family sailed to Lourenco Marques onboard the *City of Exeter* to join him in South Africa. Hitler was, by now, the Führer, having added the presidency to his chancellorship the year before. While the Peacocks sailed to join Edgar that March, Hitler was busy dismantling the Treaty of Versailles by creating the Luftwaffe and then openly declaring a programme of German rearmament. These actions by the Nazi regime had all been encouraged by observing the impotence of the League of Nations, and correctly reading the general lack of enthusiasm among the European Great Powers for war so soon after the peace treaty of June 1919. Japanese expansion in 1931 had included the invasion of Manchuria, not long after which they had simply walked out of the League of Nations in March 1933. In Italy, Mussolini began preparations for a second war with Abyssinia, hoping to erase the ignominy of Italian defeat at Adowa (now Adwa) in 1896 and build a new Italian Empire to emulate the Romans.

How much the Peacocks knew or were concerned by any of these clouds of another global war gathering around them is not mentioned in any of the family archives. What is known is that Geraldine was excited for a new start, and to be reunited with her husband in a country she loved. England was cold and snowy that March, and as she left for warmer climes, Geraldine hoped that the cold of England was not the only cold she was leaving behind. She remembers a popular song playing on the wireless in a restaurant before they boarded the boat, called 'A Snake in the Grass'. She 'thought it rather appropriate, and wondered what snake had been in my grass.'

The Portuguese adventurer Lourenco Marques had his name given to the port city on the east coast of Africa to which Geraldine and her two daughters were sailing. Lourenco had explored what became the colony of Mozambique in 1544.

Located in what was still in 1935 Portuguese East Africa, the port was the closest to the northern part of South Africa where Edgar had set up house. Edgar's three girls disembarked after their long journey from Southampton, but it was a crushing reunion for his wife, for Geraldine wrote: 'I thought Edgar would be delighted to see us, and to see what a beautiful little girl his baby had turned into, but he appeared quite unmoved by her charms [...] I sensed too that I was still unforgiven'. This hard character of Edgar's is perhaps difficult to comprehend, but Joy, who was close to her father, explained it thus: 'Over the years, I learned that my father always found it almost impossible not to change a good view of a person, when he suddenly saw a new bad view of them, he just could not help his feelings change completely.'

From the port of Lourenco Marques to their new home in Pietersburg was a distance of over 500km, if the same roads were taken then as now. Pietersburg is now called Polokwane, and is 320km northeast of Johannesburg in Limpopo Province. It took the Peacocks around a week to travel there in Edgar's big truck. They finally arrived at the land which Edgar had bought so many years before, and which Geraldine 'had been waiting all these years to see.' It was a 'Paradise', and Edgar had not been idle in the months they had been separated. He had built a house from scratch, even making his own bricks on site with the help of local labourers. Three bedrooms were finished, with 'a dining room-cum-sitting room' too. Still to come was a large lounge, a hall, and a stoep to surround the house. The house was called *Kleinwonder*, and was set beside a lake with views of the mountains, some 36 miles from Pietersburg – and right next door to the Zebediela Orange Estates.

Geraldine could see and appreciate immediately just how much hard work Edgar had put into creating their new home. If only that new home, *Kleinwonder*, could have lived up to its name and provided a 'little wonder' for the adult part of the Peacock family to share. Even bearing in mind that Edgar still has no voice in this part of his life, his wife's unpublished memoir makes for seriously depressing reading, and is by any standard an immensely frank and candid account of how she endured life in 'Paradise':

> It was crying at the moon to ask for a perfect relationship with another, while we remained as we were. But how to snap out of it? I didn't know, and his black moods made me feel nervous and afraid of him. I kept out of his way, keeping myself busy, while he, when work was done, would sit brooding on the stoep. How I longed with a terrible ache to go to him and talk and be pleasant and admire the lovely view together, but I was afraid because he showed no signs of wanting me. So in due course we would each go off to our lonely beds, and I would wonder why I was being punished like this, and did the punishment fit the crime? For it was more than I could bear. And how long was it to last?

Over the next three years up to 1939, three of the four in the family were seriously ill and could have died. Edgar went down with malaria; Geraldine got appendicitis; Joy, away at boarding school in Pretoria, was hospitalized for weeks with double pneumonia. Apart from a glimmer of normality while in Pretoria to look after Joy, the answer to Geraldine's question about 'how long was it to last' was a definite three years at least – three long years until the next big change of life for the Peacocks. Of course, in that year, 1939, life changed dramatically for those back in Britain as well. The clouds had gathered and so were no longer merely threatening. A Second World War for Europe followed the Sino-Japanese War, which was already nearly two years old after the Marco Polo Bridge 'incident' in 1937. Although South Africa was far from the battlefields of Europe and Asia, Geraldine's battle on the 'Home Front' continued.

23. 'Now don't go raising any objections'

After the last governess had been taken ill and then declined to come back to the tense Peacock household, Edgar had disappeared for about three weeks. He had left quite suddenly, and he returned just as suddenly, as far as his family were concerned. His youngest daughter, Wendy, wrote that her dad was convinced he had found the 'Promised Land', a land which was 'thriving' with its new self-governing status; a land where tobacco and maize were abundant and lucrative cash crops, and livestock, flourished in a more temperate environment. Edgar had been to Southern Rhodesia.

Southern Rhodesia is now called Zimbabwe. Zimbabwe is landlocked, bordered by South Africa, Botswana to the west, Zambia and Malawi to the north, and Mozambique to the east. Despite this geographical isolation from the sea, Southern Rhodesia was described as the most prosperous African country south of the Sahara, so perhaps there was something to Edgar's belief in a 'Promised Land'. Upon his sudden arrival back home at *Kleinwonder*, he announced that the family were going to up sticks and live in Southern Rhodesia. 'Now don't go raising any objections', he apparently said to Geraldine, when her face registered this shock announcement. She didn't object: she hoped for a new start, together, without the snake in the grass.

In a matter of days, the family had packed the essentials for a new home from *Kleinwonder* onto Edgar's truck and were making their way north in the hope of a more prosperous future. They were following in the footsteps of Mzilikazi, who, exactly 100 years before, had made his way to this same Promised Land. Mzilikazi was a defector from the Zulu Kingdom and, having abandoned King Shaka, he eventually established Matabeleland in modern day Zimbabwe by 1840. Just like the Zulus, Matabele society was organized on a military basis. Huge pride was taken in belonging to specific regiments known as *'impis'*. After

Mzilikazi, King Lobengula became the Matabele King, and it was Lobengula and his *impis* who had fought the troopers of Cecil Rhodes' British South Africa Company (BSAC) in 1893, as a new wave of settlers fought for the Promised Land. In the 1890s, it was hoped that the goldfields recently found in the Transvaal might be replicated in the north. This notion was encouraged by the discovery of traces of gold in the ruins of Great Zimbabwe, an ancient city that some speculated must have been built by the Phoenicians as it was far too advanced – in their opinion – to be anything other than European in origin.

Although no gold deposits to rival South Africa's Witwatersrand have ever been discovered in Zimbabwe, other treasure seekers have tried – unsuccessfully – to track down a massive haul of diamonds said to be hidden somewhere north of the Matabele capital of Bulawayo. Lobengula had become King in 1868, the year after fifteen-year-old Erasmus Jacobs had found the Eureka Diamond when playing just beyond his stoep. In those early days of diamond mining in Kimberley, there hadn't been the controls that were later savagely emplaced to prevent any of the African labourers from returning home with a diamond or two. Lobengula had sent many of his subjects to work in Kimberley, and when they returned, they are said to have each brought their King a stone. Thus, over the years, Lobengula is thought to have accumulated a hoard of precious diamonds. It was said that he enjoyed being greased in tallow from head to foot, and having his treasured stones stuck all over his body; in other stories, he is said to have done the same with gold sovereigns that his subjects had similarly brought back to him.

After his *impis* had been mown down by an early use of a new invention, the Maxim machine gun, Lobengula fled north pursued by the BSAC's troopers. Spears wielded by much greater numbers of men had been no match for the machine gun. Lobengula travelled, so legend goes, in an ox wagon with all his kingly wealth, including the gold sovereigns and diamonds.[1] He gave orders that he would be sealed in a cave with his wagon, and that the entrance to the cave would be expertly camouflaged. In other orders, the men who sealed the cave and so knew of the entombed King's location were to be murdered by those Matabele they returned to, so that nobody alive knew the King's final resting place. In an alternative telling of the tale, Lobengula's wealth was buried in a hole before the Matabele Wars began in 1893, and there were no survivors who knew the whereabouts of the treasure. Whatever the truth, according to a *Sydney Morning Herald* article of August 1954, 'Lobengula's riches are now well and truly lost. But that they exist is not seriously refuted.'[2]

While Edgar had probably heard about Lobengula's treasure, it does not appear that he ever went looking for it; he had got a job with a timber company, and would soon be off to explore forests for them to exploit. It took ten days for the family to travel up to Lobengula's old capital, Bulawayo. After a wobbly start – the family came down with the flu – a home was found in the suburbs, from where the girls were able to walk to school. Edgar was soon off doing forest work once again, and Geraldine found herself ensconced in the social life of Southern Rhodesia, which was quite a change from the busyness of running the *Kleinwonder* farm. Edgar was able to take his family into the Rhodesian bush as he had in Burma before Wendy was born, and so it was 'quite like old times.' Maybe the snake in the grass had finally gone, for their second house in Rhodesia was called 'The Happy House'.

As rumours of war gathered pace in mid-1939, the family prepared to move to a third home in Rhodesia, a thirty-two-acre farm. Before they moved, one day when Edgar was at

---

[1] Chilvers, Hedley, *The Seven Lost Trails of Africa: Being a Record of Sundry Expeditions, New and Old, in Search of Buried Treasure* (London: Cassell, 1930) [online] https://erroluys.com/biography3.html

[2] Holledge, James, 'Black King's Buried Loot', *The Sydney Morning Herald*, 4 August 1954 [online] https://trove.nla.gov.au/newspaper/article/29607652

'Now don't go raising any objections'

work, a man woke all the girls up walking up and down their stoep shouting that the end of the world was coming. He was almost right, for although it was not quite the end of the world, the world was never the same again after the Second World War – and this wime Edgar was determined to do his duty.

Worried as she was, Geraldine did not raise any objections.

24. 'Put old socks over your shoes'

The picture painted so far of Edgar is of a hard man, a man who could be emotionally cold, who could spend months or a year or more away from family, and not show any of the expected emotions upon being reunited. A man who enjoyed solitude in remote and even dangerous places, often with nobody but the peoples of the British Empire around him. By the year 1939, when he was forty-six years old, he had been without parents for over thirty years, spent most of twenty-five years alone in the jungles of Burma or travelling back and forth across the globe on ocean liners, or building a house in the vastness of Limpopo State. In sum, he had lived in India, Burma, Britain and South Africa, three more countries than most people will ever live in their lifetime, and once there, most of his time had been spent in places so far-flung that even today most people will never get there. Who do you know that has been to Mawlaik on the Upper Chindwin, or explored caves in the Mergui Archipelago, or spent days hunting endangered species in the Dawna Mountains – or even knows where these places are? Who do you know that has invested in property in the frontiers of a country still being mapped at least a decade before going to build their own house on it, even making their own bricks to do so? Who else do you know who has nearly had their head cleaved in half, almost died of malaria, learnt to speak four languages, and managed a laundry? This is all before we get to what can only be described as one heck of a war record.

Thus far, though, the life experiences just described, impressive as maybe they are, don't mitigate the testimony of his wife, who certainly suffered years of mental anguish and pain due to his character. Before Joy went off to boarding school and contracted pneumonia, she had a governess to teach her on the Kleinwonder farm. The relationship between Edgar and Geraldine had broken down to such an extent that he only spoke to his wife through the governess; the governess was so

'PUT OLD SOCKS OVER YOUR SHOES'

uncomfortable in the house that she sent a telegram to herself to provide the excuse to leave her employment – something Geraldine only found out years later after Edgar's death. So what about the children, little Joy and Wendy? Living in this tense environment must have had an impact upon their early years. What are their memories of their father?

Many of Joy's earliest recollections of her father are from before she was six years old. She remembered that there were 'often' animals and birds in the various homes in Burma, creatures that Edgar had found injured and nursed back to health. She remembered jungle tours where her father put her on his horse, and had a special safety structure built around the saddle so she couldn't fall out because she was only about eighteen months old. Also while out on tour, Edgar must have arranged for a special visitor at least once, for one Christmas, sitting on daddy's lap deep in the jungle, Father Christmas appeared!

Edgar had a 'great love of literature', and was 'always quoting' Dickens, Kipling and Tennyson, but especially Kipling. A particular favourite was also Longfellow's *The Song of Hiawatha*, with which he thoroughly entertained his little girl by reciting it with 'so much meaning, rhetoric, oratorical display and eloquence' that it 'came alive for me even when I was only a very small girl.' Henry Wadsworth Longfellow published his 'epic poem' *Hiawatha* in 1855. It comes in 22 chapters, and tells the story of a Native American warrior called Hiawatha, and his love for Minnehaha, a woman belonging to the Dakota tribe.

After leaving Burma and living through the difficult laundry years, Joy presumed Geraldine was looking after the newborn Wendy and cooking dinners, and 'so missed the fun my father and I were having.' This included reading A.A. Milne's poems together, Kipling's *The Jungle Book*, and taking early morning walks down country lanes to watch the sunrise and see all the birds and animals come to life. This latter was a 'magic time to be alone with my father'. Joy also learned some poems by heart and acted them, much to Edgar's amusement. In the cold months, they made ice cream together, putting the dishes containing their concoctions in the snow to freeze. Joy and Edgar ate these together: 'I don't think my mother liked them at all.'

Although writing that she was 'happily unaware of my parents' problems' in their home in England, she does recall being shocked at seeing her mother drop a full tray of cups and teapot on the floor and shouting, 'This is not my job, it's for the maid to take this to the kitchen' before turning tail and going back in her bedroom. It is with recollections such as this that glimpses of Edgar's wife are revealed, and how she was coping with the tense household environment at this time. Joy does, however, concede that 'It was not easy to live with Edgar as a husband', and that 'his wrath could be frightening.'

In South Africa, when Joy was aged between ten and thirteen, she remembers her father built a yacht for the lake and christened it *Tom Tiddler*. Edgar taught Joy to sail *Tom Tiddler*, but she remembers no sympathy when she made a mistake and the boom hit her in the head. She remembers a heron that was nursed back to health, who wandered around the house and came back to visit after it was able to leave. She also remembers Mac the bull mastiff who was going to be put down until Edgar said he would take him. This time the fierce dog was broken in successfully after being beaten with an iron fence pole. Although he continued to take down cattle, and even kill a visiting friend's dog when they arrived at *Kleinwonder*, Mac adored Edgar but nobody else, followed him everywhere, and was a well-behaved hunting companion.

Being a bit older by the time she lived at *Kleinwonder*, Joy was not so oblivious to the marital disharmony surrounding her, and she wondered why her father would not forgive and forget the whole sorry laundry business as the years went by. Edgar would tell his daughter to forgive her friends, like the one who lost her favourite book and didn't seem bothered, yet she

'PUT OLD SOCKS OVER YOUR SHOES'

couldn't understand why he couldn't get past his now very long-term baggage. Joy described an 'awful atmosphere' that would last for weeks sometimes, and nobody knew when the 'awful mood might return.' When it did, she recalled that 'Sometimes he would not speak to anyone', and certainly not to his wife for weeks.

Wendy put these terrible mood swings and change of character down to the head wound received in Burma during the Saya San Rebellion. She described 'brooding sulks', but where the rest of the family was scared of him, Wendy wrote that she 'felt a wave of sorrow for him rather than fear.'

Through it all though, for Joy, one of her lasting, happy memories is of being taught by Edgar to slide the length of a wooden floor in their family home. The secret, she was told, was to 'put old socks over your shoes.' What a dad thing to do.

Part II

The War (to the end of '44)

25. 'You must come back a colonel'

By the time Edgar finally enlisted, it was July 1940. Geraldine wrote that he 'was furious when he found how difficult it was to join up.' Part of the problem was that he was too old. To get around this inconvenience, Edgar lied about his age, hence his Army and SOE records have his date of birth as 1898 rather than 1893. He had kept himself extremely fit, which definitely helped, so at last he went off to start his training in Bulawayo. Training was most likely at Brady Barracks, which was renamed Mzilikazi Barracks in 2017 as part of the continuing process of decolonisation by Robert Mugabe's successor, President Emmerson Mnangagwa. Edgar found it hard, according to Geraldine, not because of his age or fitness levels, but because he now had to take orders. By October, however, Edgar was already promoted to Sergeant and was soon to be posted to East Africa.

Edgar was not the only more 'elderly' recruit to gain three stripes within months of enlisting. During training at Bulawayo, Edgar made firm friends with William Eustace Poles. This friendship forged in the hardships of initial enlistment proved to be of immense importance and endured throughout the war and beyond. Somehow, quite remarkably, they managed to spend practically the entire war together, even returning to Africa in 1946 on the same boat after winding up their affairs for Force 136.

Eustace Poles, according to his SOE personnel file, was born 19 June 1902 in Wentworth, Yorkshire. In his handwritten notes scribbled after the war, however, he refers to Edgar being a year senior to him, so perhaps he also lied about his age. In any event, in other post-war documents, he wrote that it was 'Due to considerable cunning I at last got into the army.' He was educated at Bedford School, an independent school founded in 1552, before leaving Britain for Southern Rhodesia at some point. He served in the colony's Mounted Police, which was a

'YOU MUST COME BACK A COLONEL'

'quasi military unit', so he managed to avoid a new recruit's course. It is Poles' papers that make it clear that both he and Edgar were on an instructor's course, which is why they finished as sergeants by October 1940.

Before Edgar left for East Africa, Geraldine accompanied Edgar to a farewell ball. The girls stayed over at a friend's house specially so their parents could go out, and Geraldine was very proud of her husband in his smart new uniform with his sergeant's stripes. At the same time, she felt all the fears and trepidation common to military wives as the day approached for Edgar to go to war. When that day came, Geraldine held it all in until after she had waved him goodbye. At the station she had 'laughingly said, "You must come back a colonel"', which is precisely what he went and did.

Being promoted to Lieutenant Colonel lay over three years away at this point, and of course there was every chance he would not achieve such seniority in such a short time from leaving Bulawayo as a sergeant. In fact, if Edgar hadn't ended up employed by the Special Operations Executive, it is unlikely he would have achieved this rank. It should also be added that he lobbied persistently to be posted precisely where he thought he would bring most value to the war effort, i.e. in the India-Burma theatre. His fortunate and powerful personality certainly played its part here too. In the modern British Army, even given the absence of the exigencies of total war, it normally takes an average of twelve years to make it to Major once commissioned as an officer; as an example, it took the founder of the Scouts, Lieutenant General Robert Baden-Powell, twenty-one years to make full colonel. He died in Kenya on 8 January 1941, just as Edgar arrived at the Royal Artillery Training Depot in that country. This was not the first time Edgar came close to the footsteps of the famous General; Baden-Powell had come to the relief of Bulawayo in 1896, when the Matabele and Shona fought the First Chimurenga, or War of Independence.

While Geraldine took the girls to Victoria Falls for Christmas 1940 because 'we couldn't face a Christmas all alone', Edgar sent a letter where he wrote 'I took three days leave allowed us for Christmas and New Year, a few days ago, and spent it camping in the veldt with another chap from here.' We can't know for sure, but the 'chap' was very possibly Poles, who was also an experienced hunter. Apparently they enjoyed 'very good game country' and shot a couple of buck for the pot.

The exact chronology of Edgar's service gets a bit tricky at this point, for on his Army Form B199A it has a section for campaigns, which indicates that Edgar fought in the Burma Rebellion of 1930–32 and in the Abyssinian Campaign of June 1940 to November 1941. There is no mention of serving in Abyssinia anywhere else in all the family documents, and no record of Edgar serving there is found in records at the National Archives.

In his personal documents, Poles does mention briefly that he 'went off with the 2/2 King's African Rifles (KAR) and got in at the tail end of the Abyssinian campaign.' That he joined 2/2 KAR is corroborated in the archives where Poles is recorded on the 'nominal roll of NCOs' from 25 January 1941.[1] The battalion only sailed from Kenya to Abyssinia on 24 May, arriving four days later. Poles was definitely back in Kenya by 5 July, as that is when he and Edgar started their officer training. Oddly, however, Poles wrote that he managed to get wounded 'during the messing about before the Battle of Gondar.' That battle took place 13–27 November 1941, just nineteen days after he and Edgar were commissioned Second Lieutenants, having passed out from Njoro Officer Cadet Training Unit (OCTU) on 25 October 1941.

Without active service on an officer's record, it is that much harder to pick up promotion, and both men were keen to

---

[1] National Archives, WO 169/2997, War Diary of 2/2 King's African Rifles, 1 January 1941 to 31 January 1941.

get in on the action. Poles was sufficiently worried that African regiments would not see any more action after Abyssinia that in an effort to get a decent posting he 'went all out' during OCTU, 'and by extreme cunning and no small amount of wangulation [sic] succeeded in passing out with the Sword of Honour'. Then, just to make sure, he lobbied for a posting to the Royal Artillery, who wanted subalterns up to twenty-five years old. Being over forty, he spent a whole morning in Nairobi trying to find somewhere to dye his hair brown and cover the grey. He needn't have worried quite so much – both he and Edgar subsequently passed gunnery school at Larkhill in Kenya and were posted to 54 Nyasaland Field Battery, 162 Regiment Royal Artillery on 31 December 1941.

With active service on his record, passing out in the top twenty of OCTU, and a decent regimental posting secured, Edgar was well on his path to 'coming back a colonel'.

26. 'I can't say I like the news from the Far East'

By the time Edgar and Eustace were celebrating their posting to the Artillery and welcoming in the year 1942, the Imperial Forces of Japan had made their next move in their bid to conquer their so-called 'Greater East Asia Co-Prosperity Sphere'. Pearl Harbor had been bombed, prompting Hitler to declare war on America on 11 December; at the same time, notwithstanding the international date line, Malaya and the Dutch East Indies were invaded. That long sliver of Burma where Edgar had enjoyed his posting to Mergui had also been invaded at its southernmost tip, with Japanese troops securing the aerodrome at Victoria Point (present day Kawthaung) by 15 December 1941. The Royal Navy's Z Force had been sunk off the coast of Malaya on 10 December, Rangoon had been bombed on Christmas Eve and Hong Kong fell on Christmas Day; the Philippines had been invaded and General MacArthur was preparing for a last stand on the last day of 1941.

In North Africa, General Auchinlek's Operation Crusader had just come to an end on 30 December after Rommel had inflicted heavy losses upon British armour; within three weeks Rommel would be back on the offensive in the desert. The U boats were the scourge of the Atlantic, and on 12 December Hitler ordered them to hit US shipping. In what the Germans called the 'Second Happy Time' due to being able to sink so much enemy tonnage with virtual impunity, news from everywhere was pretty depressing for the Allies. At least Moscow had held against the Nazi onslaught, even if only just.

By March 1942, when Edgar was posted to the island of Ceylon, the situation in the Far East had deteriorated more rapidly than any but the most pessimistic could ever have imagined. The impregnable fortress of Singapore had been proven easily pregnable, and its loss was a severe blow to British

'I CAN'T SAY I LIKE THE NEWS FROM THE FAR EAST'

prestige; then the apparently impenetrable jungle along the Burma-Siam border had proved entirely penetrable for a determined army. As Edgar boarded his boat bound for Ceylon, the Japanese occupied Rangoon. The defence of Ceylon and India had now become an issue of great urgency as the Japanese brought reinforcements to Burma to continue harrying British Empire forces north towards the Indo-Burmese border, and the Japanese Navy moved towards an almost defenceless Indian Ocean. Writing to Geraldine, Edgar said, 'I can't say I like the news from the Far East'. It seems a bit of an understatement. The British Empire had been comprehensively defeated on land, at sea, and in the air everywhere that they had engaged the Japanese thus far.

According to the War Diary of 21 East African Brigade, Edgar and Eustace embarked on 9 March in Mombasa and sailed at 0600 hrs on 10 March; fortuitously, 'Nothing of interest happened during the voyage.'[1] They reached Colombo on 21 March at 1230 hrs, but only docked at 1845 hrs because they had to wait for a pilot to take them in. They disembarked on 22 March. No tents had been arranged for the brigade so over 500 troops had to sleep out in the open, and sanitary provisions were almost non-existent. Being used to the outdoors, this probably didn't bother Edgar too much, but the war diarist was unamused.

Edgar and 21 East African Brigade Group were sent to Ceylon fully expecting the next Japanese attack to fall on the island. If Ceylon and its ports came under Japanese control, the fear was that shipping to both India and the North African front via the Suez Canal would be imperilled. With the Mediterranean under Axis control, the only way to secure Egypt against Rommel's Afrika Korps was to send troops and supplies via the Cape route. Ceylon wasn't even similar to the rest of Britain's Far Eastern colonies in that where there had been at

[1] National Archives, WO 169/6958, War Diary 21 East African Brigade, March 1942.

least some defences elsewhere, when Edgar and Eustace arrived, Ceylon had almost none. Nobody seems to have entertained the idea that the Japanese would have got anywhere near the island. This meant that Poles was able to write: 'We were the first troops in the island which as yet was unspoilt and uncontaminated by the effect of the heavy troop concentrations which would soon appear.' Even with their arrival, however, there still wasn't much: 'together with 2 batteries of 25 pounders from 303 Field Regiment, we were responsible for the defence of the northern third of the island. Seldom can a greater task have fallen on so few', Poles commented. It really was a case of straight off the boat to defend a now key Imperial possession where there were literally no positions to occupy and barely a plan in place to counter the impending attack of a hugely successful enemy.

In the military hierarchy, there was thus quite a sense of panic, and disagreement about how to deal with the continuing disaster unfolding across the Far East. General Archibald Wavell, who by this point had not particularly covered himself in glory as Commander in Chief Far East, argued for building up Northeast India as a 'bastion' of defence; the chiefs of staff disagreed.[2] In their view, Ceylon was the key to the defence of India. If the ports of Colombo and Trincomalee fell to the Japanese and they thereby won control of the Indian Ocean, any build-up of scarce resources in India would be isolated. Ceylon got priority. The British official historian of the War in the Far East, General Woodburn Kirby, wrote that the chiefs of staff were proved correct in the end.

By the end of March there was the equivalent of two divisions based in Ceylon. Edgar's 21 East African Brigade came under 34 Indian Division. There was also 16 British Brigade, plus 16 and 17 Australian Brigades committed to the defence. For air cover, there were four fighter squadrons, one bomber squadron, two Catalina (flying boat) squadrons and three Fleet

---

[2] S.W. Kirby, *The War Against Japan*, Vol. II (Uckfield: Military & Naval Press, 2004), p.107.

'I CAN'T SAY I LIKE THE NEWS FROM THE FAR EAST'

Air Arm squadrons. Wavell was worried; southern India was 'completely undefended'. Admiral Somerville 'could do nothing to prevent the invasion of south India or Ceylon.'[3] Based on these scant resources and arguments over how to respond to the rampaging Japanese, Kirby thus painted a very bleak picture for Ceylon at this point.

That picture then got still worse. With plans for the invasion of Madagascar in motion to wrest control of that island from Vichy French forces and to help ensure the safety of the shipping lanes, 22 East African Brigade were diverted there for Operation Ironclad. Then the Australian premier, John Curtin, ordered the two Australian brigades home because it looked like the Japanese were going to invade northern Australia. Darwin had been bombed on 19 February, with considerable loss of life and ships. At the same time, Gandhi decided to launch his Quit India campaign, tying down over 30,000 troops on internal security duties in India.[4] Nonetheless, it appears the chiefs of staff in London were sanguine: in a February communication, the defence of Ceylon was considered to be 'mainly a naval and air problem' and ground forces were therefore not so important.[5]

In the meantime, detached from all the worries of the grand strategists, Edgar and Eustace got on with doing what they did best, despite not much liking the news of the Far East war in which they now found themselves. They went hunting.

---

[3] *Ibid*, p.127.
[4] Richard Aldrich, *Intelligence and the War Against Japan* (Cambridge University Press, 2000), pp.159-60.
[5] National Archives, WO 106/4517, 28 February 1942.

27. 'No one else [...] worshipped the little red gods'

It was four days after the fall of Singapore, on 19 February, when the Secretary of State for the colonies, Walter Guinness (Baron Moyne) wrote to the Governor of Ceylon, Sir Andrew Caldecott, to inform him of the new status of his territory: it was now of the 'very highest importance' to the war:

> The government of Ceylon must not fail in the present crisis at any point, and that you must be prepared at any time to take up emergency powers.[1]

He could expect reinforcements of two squadrons of Fairey Fulmar naval aircraft and 52 heavy and 65 light anti-aircraft guns by 28 February. Wavell expected a Pearl Harbor-type attack on Ceylon, and in an appreciation of 8 April, the island was on alert to expect an all-out attack soon.[2] It came the next day, with many of those AA (anti-aircraft) guns and the Fulmars being put into action. In the period between the communication to the governor and the Japanese attack on 9 April, detailed plans for a scorched earth policy had been put in place, with explosives originally bound for Rangoon making their way to Ceylon instead at the beginning of March. Tea and rubber had been shipped off the island, for although it was felt that the Japanese did not need these commodities, 'we do!'[3]

The appreciation of 8 April was based on a Japanese attack on 5 April when the Japanese attacked Ceylon at 0800 hrs. This was thought to be a reconnaissance in force, and it

---

[6] National Archives, WO 106/4517, to Sir A Caldecott from Secretary of State for the Colonies, 19 February 1942.
[7] *Ibid*, Appreciation 8 April 1942.
[8] National Archives, CO 968/82/6, Scorched Earth Ceylon, February 1942.

'No one else [...] worshipped the little red gods'

caused a 'wave of alarm' according to Kirby.[1] The two heavy cruisers, the *Dorsetshire* and the *Cornwall*, were sunk. When the Japanese returned on 9 April, although the carrier *Hermes* and its escort, the destroyer *Vampire*, had left Trincomalee to avoid being hit in port, they were spotted and both sunk by Japanese aircraft. Additional losses on 9 April included the destroyer *Teredos*, the corvette *Hollyhock*, twenty-five merchant ships and fifty-nine aircraft. Despite these losses, Ashley Jackson writes 'But the Indian Ocean was still British and Eastern Fleet largely intact.'[2] Admiral Somerville had been ordered to keep his fleet 'in being', and he had managed this only by very careful manoeuvring of his assets based on intelligence from his naval reconnaissance aircraft – which included the Fairey Fulmars delivered a few weeks before.

Curiously, the Japanese didn't come back for more, 'But it could not, of course, be known at the time that the danger in the Indian Ocean was in fact over. To all appearances, it was greater than ever' wrote Kirby, but no invasion forces came because it was all a cover for the reinforcements landing in Burma from Singapore.[3] The Japanese, perhaps foolishly for them, went hunting elsewhere.

Meanwhile, Edgar and Eustace, according to the scribblings of Poles, were almost daily off in the Ceylonese jungle worshipping 'the little red gods':

> Edgar Peacock, my senior by a year, was an expert in heavy jungle as well as being a superb shot. Finding me a willing pupil it did not take long to initiate me in this type of country. He and I

---

[1] S.W. Kirby, *The War Against Japan*, Vol. II (Uckfield: Military & Naval Press, 2004), p.127.
[2] Jackson, Ashley, *War & Empire in Mauritius & the Indian Ocean* (Basingstoke: Palgrave, 2001), pp.35-9.
[3] S.W. Kirby, *The War Against Japan*, Vol. II (Uckfield: Military & Naval Press, 2004), p.131.

provided our company with venison: sambhur, chital, barking deer and wild pig. No one else in the battalion, nor any of our gunner comrades worshipped 'The Little Red Gods.'

Writing to his wife, Edgar made reference to hunting on Ceylon, and mentions Poles:

> One chap and only one, in our battery besides myself, is a proper jungle walla. He is Poles from S. Rhodesia, who has done a lot of shooting in his time.

It is curious that he writes as if Poles is someone new to him as they had already been through training together, but perhaps he had not mentioned him to his wife yet. In any event, he continued:

> We are much the same age and have palled up. The others naturally look on heavy forests as impenetrable and dangerous. There are plenty of spotted deer, pig, and some Sambur in these forests, and though they are shy and cunning, Poles and myself have been taking our toll of them. We have explored the jungle paths in our area and know where the deer and pig wander, so we have some quite good fun shooting at weekends and odd times.

Later, in what appears to be the same letter:

> I have the reputation of being quite mad because I wander all over these jungles with a rifle when sensible people are resting from the heat. But I know the ways through the jungle, and walking and shooting keeps me fit against the time when fitness will be essential in battle. We are living a rough life in these forests, often with only a blanket and a pack - rather fun I think, but everybody doesn't like my

'No one else [...] worshipped the little red gods'

notions of fun. I am off to try and kill a wild pig or something this evening, if I can. It is quite interesting jungle, but rather monotonous as there are no hills where we are.

This section's title which is Poles's reference to 'The Little Red Gods' is most likely unfamiliar to most, but for Eustace and Edgar, both very experienced hunters, this turn of phrase was something very familiar. Edgar loved Kipling, and in his poem 'The Feet of the Young Men', Kipling wrote about the Red Gods in each stanza, for example:

> Do you know the pile-built village where the sago-dealers trade
> Do you know the reek of fish and wet bamboo?
> Do you know the steaming stillness of the orchid-scented glade
> When the blazoned, bird-winged butterflies flap through?
> It is there that I am going with my camphor, net, and boxes,
> To a gentle, yellow pirate that I know
> To my little wailing lemurs, to my palms and flying-foxes,
> For the Red Gods call me out and I must go!

Kipling would have been familiar, but another contemporary (1880–1971) was Theophilus Nash Buckingham. Nash was an American hunter and conservationist, the author of at least nine books and many articles on hunting, in many of which he wrote about the Red Gods. It is the Red Gods who apparently call young men to nature:

> The calling of the red gods takes the hunter to the pure bosom of nature, whose every phase is replete with beauty, of good fellowship, of love for nature

and forgetfulness of the unspeakably disgusting vulgarities of the 'civilized' battle for life.[4]

Perhaps Edgar and Eustace needed the calling of the Red Gods more than ever as they got sucked further into the reality of the 'disgusting vulgarities' of the Second World War's battle for 'civilized' life.

Here's another poem which pays homage to the Red Gods:

Here's a little red song to the god of guts,
Who dwells in palaces, brothels, huts;
The little Red God with the craw of grit;
The god who never learned how to quit;
He is neither a fool with a frozen smile,
Or sad old toad in a cask of bile;
He can dance with a shoe-nail in his heel
And never a sign of his pain reveal;
He can hold a mob with an empty gun
And turn a tragedy into fun;
Kill a man in a flash, a breath,
Or snatch a friend from the claws of death;
Swallow the pill of assured defeat
And plan attack in his slow retreat;
Spin the wheel till the numbers dance
And bit his thumb at the god of Chance;
Drink straight water with whisky-soaks,
Or call for liquor with temperance folks;
Tearless stand at the graven stone,
Yet weep in the silence of night, alone;
Worship a sweet, white virgin's glove,
Or teach a courtesan how to love;
Dare the dullness of fireside bliss,

---

[4] 'Who are these red gods that call from nature?', *Farm Progress*, 18 April 2008 [online] https://www.farmprogress.com/farm-business/who-are-these-red-gods-that-call-from-nature-

'No one else [...] worshipped the little red gods'

Or stake his soul for a wanton's kiss;
Blind his soul to a woman's eyes
When she says she loves and he knows she lies;
Shovel dung in the city mart
To earn a crust for his chosen art;
Build where the builders all have failed,
And sail the seas that no man has sailed;
Run a tunnel or dam a stream,
Or damn the men who finance the dream;
Tell a pal what his work is worth,
Though he lose his last, best friend on earth;
Lend the critical monkey-elf
A razor -- hoping he'll kill himself;
Wear the garments he likes to wear,
Never dreaming that people stare;
Go to church if his conscience wills,
Or find his own -- in the far, blue hills.

He is kind and gentle, or harsh and gruff;
He is tender as love -- or he's rawhide tough;
A rough-necked rider in spurs and chaps,
Or well-groomed son of the town -- perhaps;
And this is the little Red God I sing,
Who cares not a wallop for anything
That walks or gallops, that crawls or struts,
No matter how clothed -- if it hasn't got guts.[5]

---

[5] 'The Little Red God', *Montclair University* [online] https://msuweb.montclair.edu/~furrg/int/lredgod.html

28. 'Take care of yourself darling, I love you very much'

Time is time, and house moves which included moving continents have seen to it that a rich archive of wartime letters have disappeared somewhere along the way. What's left are traces of the letters that Edgar sent to Geraldine between December 1940 when he departed after the ball, and February 1946 when he finally returned to Southern Rhodesia. Geraldine quoted some of them in her published biography of Edgar, and used a few more excerpts in her more intimate family memoir. Through these we get a few glimpses of Edgar, but of course they have been selected and curated by Geraldine. It seems Edgar was able to be warm and affectionate in his letters home, a marked contrast to how he seems to have been when actually at home. Geraldine wrote that he was 'writing regularly' and that his letters were 'full of interest and sympathy in all I was doing.'

Geraldine was doing a lot. No doubt similar to all the other women whose husbands were away at war, she suddenly had the entire responsibility for life at home. For Geraldine this meant running the farm, and managing the workers, and trying to make ends meet. She sold the dogs and the horses to reduce costs, and reduced the staff too. She concentrated on growing vegetables and flowers, and employed a few boys to ride bikes around the town with baskets of her produce to sell: 'The money began to come in, and things were doing quite well until we had a period of drought.' So then she started making bricks in the dryer months, and even built better quarters for her farm workers. Then she built a tennis court for Joy because she felt guilty that Joy was missing out on sports at school by having to come home with her younger sister. She also plumbed hot water into their bathroom and converted an open fire to an electric stove in the kitchen. Edgar wrote:

'TAKE CARE OF YOURSELF DARLING, I LOVE YOU VERY MUCH'

The more I think about it, the more I realise what a stout effort you are making. The care of the land and the boys, supplies to the Army under contract, and taking the kids to school, not to mention looking after them and a big house, and all the animals, is a pretty big thing for any woman. Now having impoverished ourselves in addition, makes it doubly difficult, and if anybody deserves a medal for war work you do. You are a Brick. Don't overdo things however, my dear, and get out and see people as much as you can, as a change from the daily routine.

Take care of yourself darling, I love you very much and appreciate more than you can imagine the splendid work you are doing and have done. This D____d war will end some time or other, and we shall celebrate it good and proper in some way.

At the same time, Edgar was impatient to get more involved in the war. In approximately early 1942, Edgar wrote that he was annoyed that he had not been sent to fight in the Far East: 'I could be useful in that war.' It would take another almost twenty months, but he was finally to get there. For the moment, though, he wrote, 'there seems every chance of my going forward into action in the near future with my present unit.' He had just been posted to 54 Nyasaland Field Battery, Royal Artillery, and was shortly to embark for Ceylon – where action was expected. As already seen above, the Japanese did not take the open goal and invade Ceylon, and the raids of 5 and 9 April were about the sum of it. The War Diary for 162 East African Field Regiment, Royal Artillery gives some idea of what Edgar was up to for the rest of April 1942: unsurprisingly, given the lack of preparedness on Ceylon, he was training and preparing for invasion.[1]

---

[1] National Archives, WO 172/1679, War Diary 162 (E.A) Field Regiment RA, April - November 1942.

JUNGLE WARRIOR

On 20 April a new regimental HQ was established to take command of 53 and 54 batteries, hence the overlapping War Diaries. Edgar, as a Second Lieutenant, was a section commander with A Troop. The new officer commanding, Major D.B. Anderson, arrived and held a conference with all the officers of the two batteries, which included Edgar's friend Eustace. The battery then got instructions to move to Kandy, located in central Ceylon. On 1 May, they were busy making new gun positions, and the next day they received the 25 Pounder Mark II, replacing their 18/25 Pounders which were now to be used for training the infantry in an anti-tank role. The war diarist mentions how, despite the new guns, they were short of gun stores, including telescopic sights and paralleloscopes which are both integral to effective gunnery.

On 3 May they were training with the communications equipment, and it was found that the W/T was only effective up to three miles due to climatic conditions; between three and eight miles the reception faded. On 7 May, 54 Battery was 'out on drill order and practised forward body movement.' This was preparatory to moving up to Mannar on 11 May. Mannar Island is in the northwest of Ceylon and points out across the Indian Ocean towards a chain of islands that extend towards India's Pamban Island in the southeast of Tamil Nadu. On Mannar, 54 Battery practised firing and anti-tank drills. By 15 May, the regiment was in a new camp at 'VAV' which is most likely Vavuniya, located almost equidistant from the northwest and northeast coasts. It rained hard, the camp was flooded, and vehicles had to be towed out of camp for more training which included 'leapfrogging', 'stepping up' and 'ranging by sound'. The rest of the month of May was spent building positions in the jungle and preparing for the next big defensive training scheme, named Exercise 'Hawk'.

By the end of May, the Japanese had taken all of Burma that they were going to occupy. The longest retreat in the British Army's history was more or less complete. The British

'TAKE CARE OF YOURSELF DARLING, I LOVE YOU VERY MUCH'

expectation was that the Japanese would keep going, follow the battered Burma Army, and invade India, but they stopped to consolidate their unexpected successes across Southeast Asia. The monsoon had started, which would have made crossing the mountainous Indo-Burmese border difficult, just as the rains were making life difficult for Edgar hundreds of miles southwest of Burma in Vavuniya. The excerpt from his letter above hints at his frustration at not being put to use where he had the skills and knowledge to make a difference, but a passage from another letter home makes his thoughts plain:

> You will have read in the papers of the air raids over Ceylon, and of course we are waiting to give the Japs a hot reception when and if they land here. Personally I do not see why we should wait for them to come. In my poor opinion we should have gone through to Burma before the rains came and hit them there. I know the overland routes and down the old Chindwin and Irrawaddy and I know what conditions in Burma will be during the rains from May to October. D-m these old fatheads who wouldn't let me join up till so late that I am only a Second Lieutenant instead of being far more senior with a stronger say in the conduct of this Eastern Campaign. It makes me furious to see the blunders that are due purely to ignorance of local conditions.

Edgar was not simply writing home about his frustration. He was a man of action, a man of determination, a man who spoke his mind, and he had already been telling anyone who would listen that he needed a posting to India with a view to getting into Burma.

29. 'Edgar was mysteriously whisked away'

June was pretty much the same for the men of 162 (East African) Field Regiment as May had been. The War Diary is compressed into a single sheet of paper, detailing briefly where Edgar and Eustace went and what they did there. Whereas in May they had practised deploying to the northwest looking out to India, in June they deployed to the northeast coast to a place called Mullaitivu, and worked centrally from Mankulam. Apart from these movements round the island, the time was spent making battle positions in the jungle and training with the infantry of 1/2 King's African Rifles (KAR). With the Japanese unobliging, Edgar's hopes of going into action were unrealized, and he was desperate to get to India where he could use 'his intimate knowledge of the forests of Upper Burma and his fluency in the language'. The Japanese had just occupied the Mawlaik area, where he had been District Forestry Officer for three years. His 'intimate knowledge' of this new front line just needed to come to the attention of the right person.

That Edgar felt that signing up was his duty is absolutely clear in the letters he sent to Geraldine. His wife had evidently written about the colonial gossip she had been part of, and he wasn't amused:

> Please, you must not tell me what people who have stayed behind say about my going out on service. It annoys me. I have done what I think is my duty, and there is no more to be said. Don't you think, also, that a woman whose husband has been decent enough to join up and do his best, should resent strongly any remarks like that from virtual strangers? This is hardly a suitable time, old girl, to dig at me with such things, and that remark, 'I wish I had somebody nice to buy a horse for me', was quite unnecessary and hurtful. After all there are

three horses at home for your use, and this is war time.

He continued, although it is unclear whether in the same letter:

> I do sincerely think you have done very well, most excellently well. Please darling, don't spoil it by this awful habit of digging at me and repeating what others say about me. Can't we live without argument even now? I would like you to see my line of duty as plainly as I do: but if you must listen to what others think about it, it is just too bad. I feel rather bad about all of this, not because I care a damn what the chaps who've stayed at home think, but I know how furiously and loyally many women would resist any such talk about their husbands on active service.

It must have been hard to reconcile doing his duty with being in command of a section of artillery, miles from Burma. Edgar told Geraldine that manoeuvres in Ceylon under battle conditions were pretty uncomfortable and that he was suffering from a boil and sciatica. Also from Ceylon, he wrote:

> The Big Noise of our show spoke to me the other day on manoeuvres. He knows my record and how I joined as a private etc. He frowned very fiercely and said, 'Ridiculous, ridiculous with your record to be a gunner subaltern. Well don't worry, I hope you'll wake up one morning and find yourself off where you want to go.'

Again, it is not known when this letter was written, but July in Ceylon was made somewhat more interesting by having Hurricanes simulate dive-bombing their artillery positions while explosions set by the Royal Engineers helped to make it a realistic 'Japanese' attack. There was more W/T training, and more manoeuvres. August followed much the same with the only unusual entry revealing that the reinforcements for the regiment were forty-eight Sudanese men who had once been in the employ of Mussolini. Training included Exercise 'Ox', and the batteries were redesignated so that Edgar's A Troop became C Troop. In September, Edgar's friend Eustace went off for four days on a cipher course, but otherwise more of the same anti-invasion training was the order of the day. In October, Exercises 'Dog', 'Cat' and 'Mouse' took up most of the month until 19 October.

Nearly six months of roaming over north Ceylon, digging and clearing gun positions in the jungle and practising moving up or retreating from wherever the Japanese could have invaded Ceylon was quite wearing:

> These are anxious times for all. We have to think a lot for the general good, and very little for ourselves and when it is all over, if we live, we shall be able to look anybody in the face, because we have done the right thing.
>
> The Jap has done well, because he thinks that it is much more important to die well than anything else: and is seldom taken prisoner. Many of us think the same: but I wish all of us did.

For months and months, Edgar had been shouting about 'why I should be of far more use in the Indian Army than here.' Some people 'quite saw the point', but the cogs turned slowly, until eventually, on 19 October 1942, Poles wrote that 'Edgar was mysteriously whisked away.'

30. '2/LT Peacock with all drivers'

The previous two chapters have relied on a specific source to help fill what would otherwise be a huge gap in the story of Edgar's war. Geraldine could only know what Edgar wanted to tell her, and only if that got past the censor. Getting an idea of what Edgar's eight months on the island of Ceylon was like therefore relies upon an official source, the War Diary. In one respect, this biography is very fortunate to have not one, but two War Diaries, to help us understand and bring extra colour to the general picture offered by the official historian of the war in the Far East and other historiography such as there is on this somewhat sparsely considered area of the Second World War.

As a source, unit War Diaries are hit and miss in terms of the amount of detail, and indeed what detail is provided; the detail is only what is considered important to the commanding officer. It is also very much impacted by time and conditions. As anyone who has kept a diary will know, having time and inclination to write will vary from day to day and week to week – and that's in peacetime. Mix in a bit of war and it becomes understandably harder, but it is also worth remembering that a War Diary is meant for the historical record and the author knows it will be read, unlike a private and personal diary. War Diaries being an official record means that they are mostly matter of fact, but they can sometimes be a place where the commanding officer felt able to vent frustrations, similar to a private diary.

Consequently, the two War Diaries for Edgar's unit, covering his time in Ceylon, are remarkably different, but also the same in that they share the facts of the unit's daily life, albeit what each diarist considered to be important. The 54th (Nyasaland) Field Battery diary documents the conditions and the frustrations much more than the newly created 162 (East African) Field Regiment diary does, for example, but put the two

JUNGLE WARRIOR

together and what we get is tremendous detail of what, where and when for Edgar's seven months on Ceylon.[1] Once Edgar joined SOE, being a top secret organisation, of course there is no official daily record, no War Diary exists, so details like this are missing:

> Colombo 21.3.42 Disembarked Colombo. Left 2/LT Poles with baggage party and 2/LT Peacock with all Drivers to await disembarkation of vehicles. Remainder by rail to Anaradhapura [sic]. Camped in station yard.
>
> Anuradhapura 23.3.42 Making camp and siting latrines. Men listless and unacclimatised.
>
> Anuradhapura 26.3.42 Askari [African troops] very listless and not very fit.
>
> Anuradhapura 27.3.42 Cholera inoculations following outbreak.
>
> Anuradhapura 28.3.42 More vehicles arrived from Colombo. 2/LT Poles with baggage party ex Colombo arrived. Only serious loss of equipment - 3 trail shoes and B.N.C.O's cutlery. Sudden epidemic of dysentry [sic]. 13 cases in two days. Suspect new food and conditions rather than sanitary conditions. Remaining vehicles arrived [and presumably 2/Lt Peacock!].

These abridged entries reveal not only that Edgar and Eustace remained in Colombo for a week after disembarkation, but also that it took a week to get the unit together in the face of an expected imminent invasion. If the invasion had come, the Japanese would have found British non-commissioned officers without their cutlery, and men *hors de combat* with dysentery and

---

[1] National Archives, WO 172/1680, 54 (Nyasaland) Field Battery, RA, War Diary, March - May 1942

143

'2/LT PEACOCK WITH ALL DRIVERS'

cholera. All of a sudden, that open goal for the Japanese to have taken Ceylon just got bigger, and yet:

> Anuradhapura 28.3.42 Training continued. Training curtailed owing to acute shortage of petrol.
>
> Anuradhapura 1.4.42 Training continued in Camp. Unable to train beyond owing petrol shortage.
>
> Anuradhapura 2.4.42 Training continued. 8 Men discharged hospital. Dysentry [sic] epidemic appears to be clearing.

By 3 April, 'Men showing more signs of getting used to the peculiarly unpleasant climate', and three more men were discharged from hospital, but on 6 April a lorry crashed and the Officer's Mess lorry overturned. Two men were injured and evacuated to hospital while another suffered a broken leg. Then on 9 April, Driver Ngulalo Kerio was badly burnt when his lorry caught fire; sadly, he died of wounds in hospital later the same day.

There is no mention made of the two Japanese attacks on Ceylon in early April in this War Diary either.

> Jungle Camp Mile 24 Mullaittivu-Mankulam Rd 11.4.42 Preparation of positions on both roads to the sea. Health and vitality of men improving. Dysenty [sic] cases but quick recovery. In previous week admissions to hospital 6 and discharge 11. Sgt Whiteside and 11 African Ranks attached from No 2 (Z) Field Ambulance for anti-malarial work. Sgt Whiteside not satisfied with camp site. Too low lying and malarious. Sent 2/LTs Poles and Peacock on detailed recce to find new site.

Both Edgar and Eustace were fit and well then, and their jungle knowledge was used to try and find a less malarial jungle camp just as it seemed the regiment's health was beginning to improve. Four days later, however, the dysentery came back and fourteen men were admitted to hospital. Ten days later, on 25 April: 'Epidemic not seriously affecting efficiency.' Three days later, five men were in hospital with malaria, but by 9 May the new jungle camp at milestone twenty-five was recorded as 'healthy and free of malaria.' All the while, positions were being hastily prepared and training going ahead as best it could for the expected invasion.

When set against this context of sickness, accidents, trying to prepare defences and to train, perhaps a greater sense of Edgar's urgency to get off Ceylon can be understood, but by May, Burma was almost entirely in Japanese hands.

31. 'A lecturer of considerable ability'

Edgar's unwavering confidence in eventually being posted to India is evident in a letter he penned as early as January 1942, shortly after arriving at artillery school at Larkhill in Kenya: 'I shall continue learning gunnery here until I receive orders to depart for India.' He went on to learn quite a bit about artillery in the ten months between writing this letter, and finally leaving 54 Nyasaland Field Battery in Ceylon. His first destination was Karachi, however, and not his old stomping grounds of the Upper Chindwin. Karachi was the home of the Intelligence School, about 2800 kilometres away from the Indo-Burmese border, in what is now Pakistan. The school had only been established in January 1941. Edgar wrote: 'I have to lecture on Forests and Forest warfare. I think you can guess some of the things I will say.' Before starting his lecturing, Edgar completed Intelligence Course No. 15. The report on his performance on this course has survived. Dated 27 November 1942, their assessment of Edgar was:

> A very capable, active, popular and efficient officer who has extensive experience of BURMA and a good knowledge of the languages used in that country. He is capable of shouldering great responsibility and is suitable for an active intelligence appointment in a specialist capacity in connection with BURMA. He would be very suitable as Div L.O. in a forward formation or for organising guerilla warfare.[1]

Back in Southern Rhodesia, however, Geraldine was in a bit of a predicament. While Edgar got on with writing lectures, his wife had gone to see the doctor about her sciatica. The doctor found 'a lump which had to be removed immediately, and would

---

[2] National Archives, HS 9/1158/1, personnel file for Lt. Col. Edgar Peacock.

take no excuses for delay.' Arrangements were made for their farm and for their daughter Wendy to be looked after (Joy was away at university), and Geraldine was admitted to hospital. Expecting to be in hospital a fortnight, Geraldine ultimately endured a four-month ordeal during which she nearly died. Even after leaving the hospital, Geraldine was very weak and required frequent hospital appointments to ensure her return to health. Edgar's anxieties were palpable: 'I am waiting anxiously to hear how your operation succeeded. I am so worried about you.'

While Geraldine fought her own battles on the home front, Edgar had been promoted to Captain to lend the authority of rank to his lectures. He admitted to Geraldine that he 'felt horribly shy at first in giving these lectures' but 'he had developed some power of oratory because there was never a stir or a sound even when he had had to go on steadily for two hours, and he was told they loved to listen to his jungle tales.' His superior officers at the school evidently agreed for in their report on Edgar, they wrote:

> He is a lecturer of considerable ability and skill who fires the imagination of young officers who all like him.[1]

When Geraldine had initially found out about her urgent operation, she must have been scared, and she wrote to Edgar, asking him to come home. He responded by writing 'What is the use of telling me to come back. It only depresses me.' When what was meant to be a fairly straightforward procedure went wrong due to blood poisoning, it must have been troubling for Edgar, and maybe he regretted those words:

> I am very troubled about the blood poisoning and your being in hospital for so long. I have sent a cable to the doctor, asking him to cable information

---
[1] National Archives, HS 9/1158/1, personnel file for Lt. Col. Edgar Peacock.

about you. I pray that the cable will give me good news.

Your letters and Joy's have been so cheery and hopeful, it has been difficult for me to realise how serious your illness has been. Only after hearing that you were still in hospital did I realise how serious it has been. You have been so brave about it all darling, and I do love you and admire your determination to surmount all the difficulties you have had to face.

The conditions we are working and living in are pretty awful. Continual rain and a fight against fever and sickness. It comforts me to hear that Joy has returned to Varsity, because that means you are recovering rapidly, or else she would not have left. Poor little Wendy must have had a thin time, all you darlings must have had a rotten time, however, I pray things are much better now. You have been so cheery and brave and considerate of me. You know I do appreciate that, even if I do not say so often, and that I do love you darling, and pray that you will make a quick recovery.

This letter probably dates from April or May 1943, when he was out on patrol on the Indo-Burmese border, now working for the Special Operations Executive.

Even as his report at the Intelligence School was being written in November 1942, there was correspondence in Army channels, now in Edgar's SOE file, which showed that an organisation known as GSI(K) wanted Edgar. GSI(K) was the deliberately nondescript cover name for SOE in the Far East, before it got designated with the more familiar name of Force 136 in March 1944. The 'GSI' part stood for 'General Staff Intelligence', but the K had no meaning attached to it, rather it was an identifier as there were other 'GSI's with a different letter designation. By April 1943, then, Edgar had got to where he always wanted to be, where he felt he would be of the most use in the war, and in a role that was perfect for his expertise. This expertise had first been recognized at the Intelligence School, and then by helping to retrain 7 Indian Division. Now in the jungles of the Upper Chindwin, in jungles that he said no British officer knew better than he did, he could start fighting his war.

32. 'Who knows all those jungles better than I do?'

Edgar's SOE file records him as having joined SOE on 4 March 1943. He had just spent the last two months training 7 Indian Division in what his wife called 'Mowgli Land'. With 7 Indian Division he had 'tried out old ideas and formulated new ones, and worked out jungle formations and battle techniques for large-scale guerilla warfare.' Edgar had enjoyed his time with 7 Indian Division, but being based in northwest India at Attock, 'it was no nearer Burma'. Geraldine wrote that he was 'most sorry to break his two month's association with that grand crowd of soldiers' to join SOE, but he said goodbye and good luck to his battalions and told them to continue practising bird calls and animal calls even though it sounded like a menagerie, as it was a better way of signalling than by blowing whistles.'

Later that year, 7 Indian Division deployed for the first time since it had been raised, and joined battle in the Arakan. The Arakan was the western coastal strip of Burma, separated from the central part of the country by the Mayu range of mountains. Perhaps training with Edgar contributed to the men's confidence in the jungle, for that 'grand crowd of soldiers' went on to fight the famous 'Battle of the Admin Box' in February 1944, a battle that has been seen as a turning point in the Burma campaign. Having been run out of Burma in 1942, and suffered morale-busting defeats in Arakan in 1943, the myth of the 'invincible Jap' who was apparently the master of jungle warfare was finally squashed. At the Admin Box, 7 Indian Division stayed in their positions despite being cut off, and then further held their nerve when their headquarters were overrun. Slim wrote that the 'fighting was everywhere hand-to-hand and desperate' to the extent that there was a request for an air drop of bayonets: 'The bayonets were dropped - and used.'[1] The

---
[2] Field Marshal Sir William Slim, *Defeat into Victory* (London: Pan, 1989), pp.240-41.

bloody and heroic actions of 7 Indian Division blunted the Japanese offensive known as *Ha-Go*, which was a feint in the Arakan to distract the Indian Army from the main invasion of India aimed at Imphal, Kohima and Dimapur further north.

At the same time that 7 Indian Division was fighting for its life in the jungles of Arakan, Edgar was in the jungle in northern Burma. By the time he was evacuated with appendicitis in May 1944, he had spent over a year on operations 'not far from many of the places [he and Geraldine] had been together in happier days.' He was near Mawlaik and the Chindwin River, leading an SOE group known as 'P Force'. The 'P' was taken from his name, 'Peacock', so his command was named after him (Peacock Force). It was not so unusual for officers' names to be used as the name of the operation they led, but Edgar appears to be the only case of this within SOE. For example, Morris Force was a Chindit column under the command of Brigadier 'Jumbo' Morris. What is unusual is that he had somehow managed to get his good friend Eustace Poles posted to join him.

Edgar left India for the Chindwin on 28 March 1943, but it is not obvious at what point Poles joined him. After Edgar had been 'mysteriously whisked away' from Ceylon, Poles wrote:

> We were agreed that I would join him in any enterprise that might emerge should he command sufficient influence. Shortly a signal came from India with orders for me to proceed to India forthwith where I was required to report to General Intelligence HQ New Delhi.'

It does seem quite extraordinary that Captain Peacock had somehow managed to 'command sufficient influence' that he could lift his choice of officer out of his regiment in distant Ceylon and have him taken on the strength of a 'cloak and dagger' organization nearly 1500 miles away. In early 1943, however, the Special Operations Executive was desperate to prove itself and justify its existence.

The decision to form SOE had been based on the idea that Britain needed some way of fighting back against the Nazis after the humiliating defeats of 1940 which had seen the British Army run out of continental Europe. On 19 July 1940, therefore, the papers were signed which had brought SOE into existence. Shrouded in secrecy and amidst security bordering on paranoia, SOE was ordered to train secret agents for infiltration into occupied Europe and to contact those who still wanted to fight the Wehrmacht with a view to raising guerrilla armies in the guts of the enemy. Expecting a war with Japan in the not too distant future, in August 1940, plans were put in motion to send an SOE mission to the Far East.

The man placed in charge of Operation Puma, more widely remembered now as the Oriental Mission, was Valentine St. John Killery. Killery had worked in Asia for years as a director of Imperial Chemical Industries (ICI) so he was considered an expert on the region, with the required networks to establish the Oriental Mission. Killery arrived in Singapore in May 1941, but his relations with the military and colonial authorities quickly soured. For their part, the military were suspicious of SOE as a secret organization of civilians who wanted to poach both scarce personnel and resources. As for the colonial leaders, they had strict instructions from the Foreign Office to do nothing which might provoke a war with Japan. Governors such as Shenton Thomas in Singapore and Consul General Josiah Crosby in Siam were also vehemently opposed to upsetting the colonial apple cart by recruiting Asians for special operations. Killery's plans for the Oriental Mission were therefore obstructed, and by the time war with Japan began, seven months to the day after Killery's arrival in Singapore, not a whole lot had been prepared in any of the countries within the Oriental Mission's remit.

JUNGLE WARRIOR

After the humiliation of 1942, the military looked for excuses to explain their poor performance. Instead of accepting that the Japanese triumphs were mostly due to being both outfought and outgunned, in the bitter recriminations which flew out from India where British Imperial forces licked their wounds, allegations of poor colonial leadership, exaggerated claims of anti-British fifth columns, and the incompetence of the Oriental Mission were asserted. Such internal fractures within the British establishment were probably inevitable considering that the Japanese had so savagely exposed the weaknesses of the Empire and entirely destroyed British prestige throughout the east. Indeed, nothing was to be the same again once the war was eventually won by August 1945, with the decolonization of India and Burma in 1947 and 1948 respectively, and the rise of nationalist challenges throughout the colonies of the European empires.

Accusations of a fifth column being responsible for defeat in Burma were particularly prevalent, but Edgar had worked for years with the same people who were all supposed to have been traitors, and was about to do so again. Of course there had been Burmese who had seen an opportunity to successfully oppose the British with the help of the Japanese; a decade before, Edgar had nearly had his head cleaved in half in a revolt against the colonial power, but Stanley Short, a missionary, believed that

> the epithet 'traitor', which was hurled by all and sundry both during and after the Burma campaign only applied to about 10 percent of the population.[1]

For some in the military, however, SOE had failed in 1942, and now wanted to continue working with a hostile indigenous population, syphoning now even scarcer resources from the

---
[1] Stanley Short, *On Burma's Easter Frontier* (London: Marshall, Morgan & Scott, 1945), p.137.

153

'Who knows all those jungles better than I do?'

Army. The Army's experience of SOE in the Middle East and Europe, as well as the campaigns in the Far East, meant that SOE's reputation was severely tarnished. SOE's detractors believed that the organization provided, quite simply, a poor or non-existent return for the investment of money, men and resources that it took.

33. 'Our small band of cut-throats'

In late 1942, just like the regular military, SOE was going through a very necessary period of restructuring and reorganization. The last Oriental Mission personnel had only made it out to India by September 1942. By then the Oriental Mission had been absorbed by the India Mission, and Killery had long since returned to London. The man in charge of the India Mission was Colin Mackenzie. Like Killery, Mackenzie had represented business interests in the Far East through his directorship of the firm J&P Coates. The Viceroy of India was also on the board of J&P, so Mackenzie and Lord Linlithgow had an established friendship which seems to have been of some significance to the survival of SOE in the late months of 1942.

Mackenzie had originally been placed in charge of an SOE mission which extended west from the Raj with responsibility for Afghanistan and Persia, in addition to India itself. With his absorption of the Oriental Mission, Mackenzie's geographical remit grew massively, taking on most of Southeast Asia and China. Consequently, SOE was reorganized into three groups. Burma was part of A Group, with Indo-China and Siam. Group B was responsible for Malaya, Sumatra and the Dutch East Indies; Group C was China only. Within each group, each target territory was known as a country section, so Edgar was part of Burma Country Section, which was abbreviated to BCS. Major Richard Forrester was in charge of BCS from July 1942 until April 1943. He had been employed by the Bombay Burmah Trading Corporation, so with his intimate knowledge of Burma, he had been promoted to head BCS and draw up plans for getting SOE back into action. On 26 August 1942, Forrester authored his 'Appreciation for SOE Operations in BURMA' in which he advocated for the deployment of Burma forestry officers to those regions of the country which they knew, and which would be unoccupied by enemy forces. He proposed

'OUR SMALL BAND OF CUT-THROATS'

eight parties be introduced into Burma to collect intelligence, number IV of which was:

Party of two officers based on IMPHAL for penetration to MAWLAIK 23° 35' N 94° 25' E area for operations against MAWLAIK - KALAW 23° 15' N 95° 20 E - YE-U 22° 45' N 95° 5' E districts.[1]

It was this area, proposed by Forrester in August 1942, to which Edgar (and Eustace) were finally headed in March 1943. Edgar had been held up in getting there because of the chaos of the general reorganization of Allied forces and the ensuing 'bun fight' between all the competing units to grab the Burma experts. A pencil-written addition to a typewritten document reveals that Edgar was held up by at least two months; an organization known as GSI(X) had managed to send Edgar to Eastern Army HQ despite the fact that GSI(K) had, to their knowledge at least, already claimed him. That said, in December 1942, when the note was written indicating Edgar had been pinched to work – as it turned out – with 7 Indian Division, SOE (known as GSI(K) at this point) was still in the throes of reorganization into country sections with only the 'nucleus of what later became Group 'A'' established. Forrester's successor as head of BCS, Ritchie Gardiner, wrote in his 1945 report that late 1942 and early 1943 was 'a period of intense activity, everyone rather groping in the dark and fighting against time to produce results under the mistaken impression that Allied forces would very shortly be returning to Burma.'[2]

By the time Poles arrived in India, 'Edgar had already collected the nucleus of an irregular force' which included Burmans and Karen 'oozies' (Mahouts), and it appears Edgar

---

[1] National Archives, HS 1/27, Major R.E. Forrester, 'Appreciation for SOE Operations in BURMA', August 1942.
[2] National Archives, HS 7/104, Ritchie Gardiner Report, Chapter Three, 'Reformation In India June-Dec 1942', 30 December 1945, p.1.

had already left for the front; Geraldine described how Eustace was arrested on the Manipur frontier 'because someone had given him the wrong fashion of identity card.' There are not many surviving documents in the SOE files which record much about the first patrols of Edgar and Eustace in the period between 28 March and October 1943, but this 'nucleus of an irregular force' was among the first SOE personnel to go back into Burma from India. In his private papers, Poles left two descriptions in different places which give a flavour of what he and Edgar were up to. This first excerpt is from some redrafted handwritten notes:

> We went to work teaching our growing force of volunteers, whom we led on armed reconnaissances, probing enemy strong points along the Chindwin River and from time to time ambushing Japanese fighting patrols in the Kabaw and Chindwin valleys, and in the high mountainous teak forests separating them.

This second extract is from a typewritten document. After describing Edgar as 'A great friend of mine', he wrote:

> I joined him in the Manipur Hills overlooking the Chindwin River. We two had great fun and games. Our role was practically an indipedent [sic] one and we at once set about raising our own private army. Those were great days. We took to the jungle with our small band of cut-throats and played 'man eating tiger' with the Jap posts on both sides of the Chindwin; murdering and grabbing prisoners and occasionally doing a reconnaissance across the river. We did a little to prepare the way for Wingate's first adventure.

The reference to Wingate and his first Chindit expedition, Operation Longcloth, is an interesting one for chronological reasons. The Chindits were the brainchild of General Orde

Wingate. His idea was that mobile columns of well-trained troops could exploit the jungle to attack the Japanese far behind the lines. They were to be supplied by air, and be used in support of an offensive by the Eastern Army. The Chindits were different to SOE in that they were designed to work as a Long Range Penetration Group (LRPG) similar to the fledgling SAS units that had been used to such effect in North Africa. Wingate's Chindits first crossed the Chindwin in February 1943, over a month before Edgar left for Manipur. Perhaps Poles meant that their 'small band of cut-throats' assisted with their return journey.

34. 'I am right in the front line as a guerrilla'

The monsoon hits the Indo-Burmese border where Edgar and Eustace were out on patrol from about early May, and continues until at least October. From June to August, the rain can be almost constant, before the warm weather comes from November to February. From February to May, the weather can be intensely hot across most of the country. While Edgar endured the monsoon, back in Southern Rhodesia, Geraldine wrote to Edgar asking him to come home, and included the opinions of others who evidently also thought he should return to Rhodesia. Edgar wrote back:

> I am not concerned with what our good friends at home think I ought to do. I am in no position to move back, and I would think shame to do so. I am afraid you do not understand my position, and of course, I cannot tell you much, but it is only the beginning, and there are many hardships ahead. Please do not help me to weaken by such talk. It has been beastly for you, the operation and everything, but you live among the amenities of civilisation, and this war has to be fought out. I couldn't return in any case. Please take things easily, darling, and do not over tax yourself.

A further couple of paragraphs reveal a bit of Edgar's perspective on these early P Force patrols:

> I can say so little, but I am right in the front line as a Guerrilla and you can imagine that it is difficult for me to give and receive mail except when I come back to base. My last patrol was a gruelling one in constant rain, with not a day's rest for sixteen days. We hit the enemy three times, and on each occasion killed some of them, without losing one of my men.

'I AM RIGHT IN THE FRONT LINE AS A GUERRILLA'

> We are resting at my base camp for a bit before going out again.
>
> We released a man who had been tortured for information, and who died during the action, but I am thankful to say that I shot four of the brutes responsible. I am in command of a pretty hard lot, and living conditions are (?) [sic] and uncomfortable, but I am quite fit. I am most anxious to receive another letter to say you are improving fast. This silence is awful, but I hope to hear before I go on patrol. If you can get a change to the coast, I hope you will arrange to do so.

Geraldine did make it to the coast for a month, but the hospital was too far away and she still required treatment. Edgar's wife and daughter got another scare when Geraldine suddenly went down with erysipelas, which they mistook for further blood poisoning. Erysipelas is a skin infection which is caused by streptococci, presenting mostly on the lower leg and face.

At some point in October, just as the weather got drier, Edgar was called back to Calcutta to attend a meeting about his work on the Chindwin. Plans were laid down and he was promoted to Major on 1 November 1943, less than a year after arriving in India as a Lieutenant. He was given some leave, and so he asked if he could go to Rhodesia to see Geraldine, but this request was turned down; only local leave or leave in India was permitted. Edgar therefore decided to take himself off to Kashmir for some rest and recuperation:

> My house boat has sitting, dining and bedrooms, pantry, kitchen etc. complete with cook and servants and fully furnished, very comfortable indeed and peaceful. I am concentrating on eating, sleeping and resting. I have had the boat house [sic] taken out of Srinager on to a lake where there are most beautiful views.

The valley of Kashmir is one of the most beautiful places I have ever seen, a succession of calm placid lakes lying between mountains which are now getting capped with early snows. It is cold and frosty in the flights and mornings, but clear and bright. You would rave over the beautiful views and not be happy until you had painted them. My overstrained muscles and brains have flopped and I spend most of my time resting and reading.

The war was taking its toll physically and mentally on all the Peacocks. For Edgar, the stresses and strains of operations in the no man's land between two armies, sitting in jungle camps in monsoon downpours, all the while thousands of miles away in the so-called safety of the 'Home Front' loved ones also nearly died was difficult to endure. Add to this the uncertainty of communications by letter, and the time between each eagerly anticipated delivery of news, and the river boat in Kashmir was a very well-needed spot of leave. Of course, it would not be long before Edgar was back on operations along the Chindwin, and he was right about the many hardships ahead: the Japanese were preparing to invade India.

35. 'A recapitulation'

On 5 November 1943, Edgar received a three-page 'recapitulation of our conversation on 4th November' from Colonel Mount Stephen Cumming.[1] Cumming had worked in the East for the firm Butterfield & Swire before the war, so shortly after he was commissioned into the Royal Artillery in 1939, he was scooped up by SOE for the Oriental Mission. He had arrived in Singapore in April 1941, almost eight months before the Japanese opened hostilities with the West on 7 December. After training in Singapore, Cumming had been assigned to Burma, from where he had trekked out to India by July 1942. In November 1943, when he met Edgar and subsequently wrote his 'recapitulation', he was the Liaison Officer for SOE's Group A of Far Eastern countries. A report about Cumming in his SOE file reveals that he and Edgar should have got along famously:

> A strong and sterling character that, due to his natural reticence, is sometimes under-rated by those who do not know him well. Has an almost infinite capacity for intelligent and hard work. Makes courageous decisions and does not suffer fools gladly. Observant and shrewd, with a sense of humour.[2]

It might also have helped that both Edgar and Colonel Cumming belonged to the Royal Artillery. With regiment and character aligned, it is not hard to imagine that the path was smoother for Edgar to be supported in his plans for the Chindwin and P Force. The intention for P Force was clearly set out for Edgar:

---

[1] National Archives, HS 1/3, Colonel M.S. Cumming to Major Peacock, A Recapitulation of Our Conversation, 4 November 1943.
[2] National Archives, HS 9/381/2, personnel file for Col. Mount Stephen Cumming.

(a) Organising a string of contacts in the rear of the enemy

(b) Undertaking open acts of sabotage against enemy outposts and communications

To carry this out, Edgar was required to 'recruit and train a self-contained force capable of defending itself and of movement without assistance from other formations'. The Burmese to be recruited were village elders and headmen who were to be trained so that Edgar could maintain an intelligence network; a second 'type' was described as 'the local strong man', who would be taught the craft of a guerrilla fighter.

Interestingly, Cumming mentions that Edgar should expect to receive men who had been trained for Operation Harlington, but who were now in need of employment elsewhere. The Harlington operation was a mission to the Karenni Hills to contact Captain Seagrim. Seagrim had, by accident or design, remained in Burma when the Japanese invaded. Part of the original Oriental Mission in Burma, Seagrim had recruited Karen personnel to act as a stay-behind group to attack the Japanese lines of communication in 1942. Operation Harlington was conceived as an early operation for SOE to get back into the eastern Karen Hills to ascertain the fate of Seagrim and start sending intelligence back to Calcutta in the short term. In the long term, it was to raise and train a guerrilla army far behind the front line.

To this end, in February 1943, four Karen officers were parachuted into Burma. They were deployed without a W/T set, which, although intentional at this early stage in SOE missions, proved to be a mistake. Once they had established if Seagrim was alive or not, and whether their Karen comrades were willing to fight the Japanese, they were to arrange a drop zone so that British officers with a W/T and supplies of weapons could be dropped into the hills. Unfortunately for SOE, a whole series of mistakes and bad luck precluded those British officers

'A RECAPITULATION'

from joining the original Karen parachutists until October, a huge eight months or so after the operation's launch. Head of Burma Country Section (BCS), Ritchie Gardiner, described it as 'quite the most depressing series of failures that we ever experienced' in his post-war report.[3] Over fifty failed sorties were flown in those eight months, and consequently Edgar was approached about leading an overland trip to find out what had happened. He never went, probably due to the experience of having sent a man overland for the same reasons to reach an SOE operation codenamed Dilwyn. It had taken over five months for Major Shan Lone, a Kachin officer, to reach his area of operations, and in the meantime Dilwyn II was successfully dropped.

The causes of the failures to insert the second group of operational personnel, for both operations, ranged from navigational error to battery acid being spilt on parachutes, to faulty bomb racks in the aged Hudson aircraft SOE had at its disposal. By the time Cumming wrote his instructions to Edgar, promising him Harlington personnel, Major Jimmy Nimmo, another original Oriental Mission man, had been parachuted into the Karen Hills. Nimmo was dropped on 13 October, with a W/T set, and he was in communication with Calcutta by 15 October. He went on to find Seagrim and the Karen party from the previous February, and to signal that it was safe to send in another British officer, Major Eric McCrindle. McCrindle touched down in December 1943. Harlington therefore finally got established nearly a year after the original party had been infiltrated.

The rest of the Harlington story, however, is not a happy one. In March 1944, the operation was successfully closed down by the Japanese after attacking both McCrindle and Nimmo's camps and killing them both. Seagrim managed to escape, but Japanese reprisals against Karen villagers convinced Seagrim to give himself up to prevent any more torture and murder. After a

[3] National Archives, HS 7/104, Gardiner Report, Chapter Four, p.9.

trial, Seagrim and seven Karen comrades were executed in September 1944 in Rangoon by firing squad.

This Harlington story is important to Edgar's war because the men Cumming promised were Karen, and Edgar went on to prove that Karen and Burman could work effectively together in the field during P Force operations. That this was possible was not necessarily known, for the nationalist Burmans in the Burma Independence Army (BIA), who had fought alongside the Japanese in the 1942 campaign, had carried out atrocities against the Karen living in both the Irrawaddy Delta area and in the Karen Hills. They had also been participants in the reprisals that led to Seagrim and his Karen friends giving themselves up. In February 1945, it was these Karen and Burmans, blooded together in P Force operations, who formed the nucleus of Operation Character, the name given to the revived Operation Harlington – which was to be led by Edgar.

36. 'It is now up to us to justify the confidence placed in us'

Before going on restorative leave on a Kashmiri houseboat, and having received his 'recapitulation' from Colonel Cumming, Edgar wrote to Flight Lieutenant John Swan on 7 November 1943.[1] Swan was in the P Force base on the Yu River, and Edgar needed to update him on the outcomes of his discussions in Calcutta. He started by writing:

> The Commander 4 Corps approves and is interested in our plans and has promised to assist as far as possible.

Before becoming the commander of 4 Corps in 1942, Lieutenant General Geoffrey Scoones had been Director of Military Operations and Intelligence in India, having served there as a general staff officer (GSO) since 1940. This background probably made him more receptive to what Edgar and SOE were offering him as commander of 4 Corps, as the narrative is usually that relations between SOE and the Army were somewhat strained at this time. Winning this support from a Corps commander, based on P Force patrol work during the first half of 1943, has to be seen as particularly significant. A clue as to why the support was forthcoming comes from a later paragraph of Edgar's communiqué to Swan:

> Men from the East bank are particularly required by us so we should leave space in our force for them. The limits of our recruiting will depend on our officer and N.C.O. strength. I suggest you recruit about 30 men from your neighbourhood as soon as possible. We can add 50 or more when we move to the river and when more officers arrive.

---

[4] National Archives, HS 1/3, Major Peacock to Fl/Lt. J.A. Swan, 'OPS. - Chindwin Area', 7 November 1943.

The east bank referred to is the east bank of the Chindwin River, where P Force was recruiting Burmans into SOE. As seen in the last chapter, some were to be trained and used as guerrilla fighters because of their intimate knowledge of the area, others were to be used as agents to glean intelligence from the villages where it was too dangerous for Caucasian personnel to go. Japanese reprisals against whole villages and the torture of individuals was a worry for SOE right through to the planning and execution of operations in 1945, but reprisals were just one of the many risks that needed to be taken in order to supply Scoones with the intelligence he and his boss at 14 Army, General Slim, desperately wanted in late 1943 and early 1944.

In addition to the expansion by eighty or so men referred to here, Edgar wrote that he expected SOE's Indian Field Broadcasting Units (IFBUs) to be deployed to the area in December, when Edgar returned with IFBU officers. Edgar hoped that the troops detailed with protecting these frontline propaganda and psychological warfare units would also be available to 'add 50 - 100 trained men to our defensive strength, assist in training our recruits and help with mule transport.' The IFBUs did get deployed to the Chindwin area, but not until late January and early February; there is nothing in the IFBU records or War Diary which confirms that they did indeed end up providing Edgar with the support he hoped for.[1] What we do know is that P Force was working closely with General Gracey's 20 Indian Division, specifically with 100 Brigade, as were number 202 and 203 IFBU.

Eleven days after writing to Swan, Edgar wrote to his second in command, Eustace, after having been to Meerut.[2] At Meerut, the decisions made in Calcutta were reviewed, presumably with the head of SOE in the Far East, Colin Mackenzie, and approved. Edgar wrote that 'It is now up to us

---

[1] National Archives, HS 1/333, IFBU War Diary, February to July 1944.
[2] National Archives, HS 1/3, Major Peacock to Captain Poles, 'CHINDWIN OPS', 18 November 1943.

to justify the confidence placed in us.' He then went on to explain the parameters within which P Force would have to operate in order to keep that confidence:

The Theatre and nature of our operations, our development policy, our personnel and kindred matters are dealt with by our own H.Q. which maintains such specialist groups as ourselves for work in co-operation with the Army.

The direction of our efforts lies in the Corps Commander who will advise us in co-operative measures and restrict or further our movements as the general situation demands, e.g. at the moment we are restricted in penetrative measures to 20 miles east of the Chindwin.

The co-ordination of our work with those of forward army and other units rests in the Div. and Bde. Comdrs. who issue from time to time orders calculated to prevent overlapping and clashes with friendly patrol, e.g. coloured identification ribbons for certain days of this week.

The measure of our success will not be read in unrelated actions, but in co-operative efforts timed to assist far greater army movements. The need for close and tactful liaison is obvious.

Within this frame there will be plenty of room for opportunist action whether in deep penetration sabotage, demolition on enemy L. of C. or plain killing; but none for unadvised actions which may upset the plans of Army Commanders. This is a very important side to our functions and must be kept always in mind. Army Commanders have again indicated their willingness to assist and support us as far as possible.

In effect we are a group of specialists with peculiar local knowledge, to be used for the harrying of enemy flanks and rear in accord with army movements.

This is especially important for setting out the precise relationship that SOE's P Force was to have with the Army, and crucial to how that relationship would develop in Burma in the coming two years. If P Force did not justify that confidence, then the future for SOE in India/Burma operations would be uncertain. It is also significant for suggesting that Edgar had a firm doctrinal understanding of how guerrilla operations must provide both tactical and strategic utility to regular forces. It is clear that even in 1943 not everybody understood how the irregular/regular relationship needed to work; it had been abundantly obvious amid the defeats of 1942 that few had understood it then too. Edgar would soon return, fresh from Kashmir, to the Chindwin, with his friend Eustace, to try and prove that confidence in P Force was well placed.

37. 'Such armed rabble are not merely useless, but may be a menace'

After Edgar returned to the Chindwin area some time in December, he continued to write 'periodic reports', presumably for both the Corps Commander and his SOE bosses. It appears that he must have also written them before going to his meeting in Calcutta and subsequent leave in Kashmir, for the one dated for the period 8 October to 25 December 1943 is titled 'EIGHTH PERIODIC REPORT ON SITUATION UPPER CHINDWIN'. Unfortunately, there is no trace of the first seven, which, it can be inferred, would have provided similar insight into the early patrol work of P Force.[1]

Edgar's personality comes bursting through the words in his report; he was obviously not afraid to type what he thought, and similar to Cumming, not one to suffer those he considered fools gladly. Where many career soldiers may have been less candid for the sake of their future employment prospects, Edgar had no such need to hold back; he knew that as soon as the war was won, he would be going back to his farm in Southern Rhodesia. From later events referred to in the surviving post-war correspondence with his friend Eustace and other Force 136 men found in the Poles papers, it is clear that his actions did not always win him friends in the 'right' places. Edgar, however, had a war to win and no army career to protect, and both he and Poles were direct in their criticisms where they thought criticism was due. The men and women of SOE have often been accused of being maverick characters, but this is arguably exactly what SOE needed for it to be able to acquit itself well in the Second World War.

Of immediate interest in this 'EIGHTH PERIODIC REPORT' is the clear explanation of the dispositions of 20 Indian Division, 100 Brigade, P Force and the Japanese. The

[3] The surviving 'Periodic Reports' can all be found in the National Archives, HS 1/3.

Japanese were creeping forward and had 'entrenched themselves at Kyukkyaw [sic].' Edgar writes that it was 'uncertain whether we shall commit ourselves to battle in order to take possession of KYAUK KYAW or merely stay near it to prevent further encroachment.' Kyauk Kyaw, most likely Kyauk Chaw in today's spelling, is midway between the Indo-Burmese border and the Chindwin River, and about 30km from Tamu – as the crow flies. It is located in the jungle-clad hills that make up the eastern side of the Kabaw Valley, which runs more or less north to south parallel to the border with India.

Since P Force was supposed to be acting in an intelligence and guerrilla role, this admission of possibly 'commit[ting] ourselves to battle' to reclaim Kyauk Kyaw could be seen as surprising. Was this Edgar pondering a difficult decision, namely to take a step away from his operational brief to perhaps exploit an opportunity, or was the use of 'ourselves' referring to the Allied side more generally, and that troops of 20 Indian Division were going to engage the Japanese at Kyauk Kyaw? The choice of language in original documents, although obviously not the intention of the authors, can lead historians into false assumptions if due diligence is not observed. It would be quite easy to take this as an example of Edgar being a maverick, unafraid to make 'courageous decisions', using the inference thus provided to conveniently fit a narrative – but that is not good history.

What does fit the narrative, and Edgar's character, is the next part of the report where he is absolutely scathing about a formation called the Kin Scouts. The Kin Scouts appear to be absent from histories of the Indo-Burma campaign, although they do make an appearance in a few documents in the SOE files. They were formed by the civil authorities, and Edgar wrote:

> The civil authorities have obtained permission to augment the number of their Kin Scouts all over the [Kabaw] valley. The procedure is simple: Burmans desirous of an easy life are called in,

'SUCH ARMED RABBLE ARE NOT MERELY USELESS, BUT MAY BE A MENACE'

> given a fortnight's so called training at the civil camp, a rifle, clothing and equipment and Rs. 32/8/- p.m., with orders to go back to their villages and to run away if anything stronger than a few B.T.A. [Burma Traitor Army, the popular name on the British side for the Burmans of the BIA] spies enter the area.[1] As there are no B.O's [British Officers] to care for them in forward areas these Kin Scouts can be relied upon implicitly - to run away or give themselves up to the Jap.
>
> The uses of the Kin Scouts can be defined thus:- Behind the Army for security and police measures they have definite purpose and use: in front of the Army such armed rabble are not merely useless, but may be a menace. They usurp the functions of the regular army without a tithe of its training or organisation. I can see no purpose in this indiscriminate movement beyond an effort to justify the existence of a large number of officials of the so-called Government of Burma.

Geraldine hinted at Edgar's lack of respect for the Government of Burma when she wrote, in *The Life of a Jungle Walla*, that Edgar had been to Simla, where the government was in exile. He had gone to see what he could find out from those who had been in Burma in 1942, 'but what he gathered only sickened him.' Whatever he may have thought about the civil authorities, the Kin Scouts were having direct consequences for P Force:

> The effect of the Kin Scout movement on my recruiting programme has been deplorable. I can offer no more than slightly better pecuniary terms, divorce from their villages and the promise of hard training and perhaps hard fighting. To give the

---

[1] 'Rs' is short for Rupees. The '8' is for the Annas (think pounds and pence or dollars and cents).

Burman his due, he is willing to come to us in fair numbers, but is naturally drawn by family ties and the tempting offers placed before him by the Civil Department.

I have protested to Corps and Div. and seen the Civil Authorities.

Not a man to be defeated in his duties, Edgar prepared to take two P Force patrols out before the New Year. He hoped to find 'by personal contact the type of recruit' he wanted. One patrol would be led by him and Flight Lieutenant Swan, while the other would be led by Captains Cope and Gibson. Thaungdut and Auktaung, on the west bank of the Chindwin, were their targets.

38. 'A pair of abbreviated bathing trunks'

In the weeks between arrival back at the Yu River camp and going out on patrol on 28 December, organization and training was the order of the day. Edgar was trying to procure officers and decent non-commissioned officers (NCOs) for P Force, but was facing the headache of competing requests for personnel, in addition to the frustrations caused by the Kin Scouts. Again, Edgar spoke 'truth to power' voicing his displeasure at what he considered to be 'a breach of military etiquette.'[1]

The officer at the centre of this 'breach of etiquette', through no fault of his own, was Captain Stanley White. Before the war, White had worked on Burma's rivers for four years with the Irrawaddy Flotilla Company.[2] His knowledge of the Chindwin was obviously in demand, and although he had been promised to SOE, and indeed has an SOE personnel file, the 'Corps Commander has retained Captain White at Imphal.' Edgar wrote that he could accept 'no responsibility for failure' when Army commanders decided to 'interfere with the movements of my officers without prior reference to me.' As far as Edgar was concerned he was owed 'an explanation with appropriate regrets', not least because, as Edgar saw it, his side had 'never failed them [the Army] in courtesy and cooperation.'

Not only fighting for personnel, Edgar was fighting for transport in these weeks too. Once again, he was quite unambiguous in his remarks:

> This is a sore point with us who have had the greatest difficulty in obtaining supplies and in making necessary army contacts, while members

---

[2] National Archives, HS 1/3, Major Peacock, 'EIGHTH PERIODIC REPORT ON SITUATION UPPER CHINDWIN 8TH OCTOBER to 25th DECEMBER, 1943', p.2.
[3] National Archives, HS 9/1583/4, Personnel file for Captain Stanley White.

of the Civil, Elephant Corps and 'Z' force and the army, fling dust at us in passing in their superfluity of Jeeps and 15 cwt. trucks.

He was not amused to have been left stranded on the road when his borrowed truck kept breaking down, and deplored the wasted time that should have been spent training his men. All he wanted was two jeeps and two trucks for supply and contact with the Army 'and not for mechanized patrols or anything of that sort.'

It was not all negative, however, for Edgar was very pleased with his Liaison Officer, Captain Kemball. Arnold Kemball had joined SOE in December 1942, and at this time was Liaison Officer between 4 Corps and SOE. Apparently he was 'A cheerful and popular officer who is conscientious and capable except for occasional lapses when he goes on the spree.'[1] He can't have gone off 'on a spree' while liaising for Edgar, or there would never have been the recommendation that he remained in his post as Liaison Officer. Meanwhile, in camp, the number of men in P Force was now up to forty. They were:

> all under intensive training. All, including officers, strip for P.T., and it is a pleasant sight to see Captain POLES leading the morning run in a pair of abbreviated bathing trunks! At least we don't lack enthusiasm.

Throughout the private papers, particularly in letters to Geraldine, Edgar mentions fitness. In the 1930s, even after he had left the Forestry Service, it might be recalled that Edgar had tried the popular Hay Diet to stay in shape. Now, back in the harsh environment of the Burmese forests and jungles once again, the fitness of his men would be a defining factor in the success of their patrols. Just as Wingate is famous for focusing on the fitness of his Chindits, so Edgar knew that the climate and conditions required extraordinary resilience. Edgar's own

---
[1] National Archives, HS 9/827/8, Personnel file for Major Arnold Kemball.

fitness, let alone the fitness of his men, would be severely tested in the next few months as they came under increasing pressure from the Japanese.

On 26 December, a first physical test began when the planned patrols left the Yu River base camp. Edgar submitted a patrol report for the period 29 December to 6 January, but it never made its way into an archival file for posterity. Instead, it is referred to in Edgar's 'NINTH PERIODIC REPORT' which covers the dates from these patrols leaving up to 23 January.[2] Both patrols appear to have made it to the banks of the Chindwin, meaning Edgar was able to report back on the conditions in the villages along the river. He also wrote further harsh words about the Kin Scouts and the Civil Affairs Service, but the remarkable news recorded here is that Edgar had had an audience with the divisional commander 'about this report' and that General Gracey had 'approved my views. He is taking necessary action.' Establishing a favourable relationship with Gracey was important, and some measure of how good this relationship became may be judged by the Eustace Poles papers where Eustace says that he and Edgar had two breakfasts with Gracey one day, and the second one was made by the general himself.

---

[2] National Archives, HS 1/3, Major Peacock, NINTH PERIODIC REPORT ON SITUATION UPPER CHINDWIN 26th DECEMBER, to 23rd JANUARY, 1944.'

39. 'Our part in the battle for KYAUK KYAW'

In his book *Defeat into Victory*, the Army Commander, General Slim, wrote a brief paragraph about the area that Edgar was patrolling in with his P Force:

> During and after the 1943 monsoon, in a series of patrol clashes and minor actions, we had steadily expanded the territory under our control in the Tamu area. The Kabaw Valley was re-entered; the Chindwin reached and crossed by patrols. Roads were being pushed forward as fast as our meagre resources in excavating machinery permitted and reconnaissances for the eventual offensive being carried out. All was going well here.[1]

Of course, Slim could not mention SOE when he wrote this in the 1950s, and naturally this is not a reference to the work of P Force alone, but it gives some sense of how important Slim felt patrolling and pushing forward from the Indo-Burmese border was. In the context of the impending Japanese assault, it was vital:

> I had not at my disposal the sources of information of the enemy's intentions that some more fortunate commanders in other theatres were able to invoke. We depended almost entirely on the intelligence gathered by our fighting patrols, and the superiority we had developed in this form of activity now paid a high dividend.[2]

Patrols by the Army, and P Force patrols like the two that had just been to the villages on the Chindwin in early 1944 provided the intelligence Slim needed to make his plans for the defence of

[3] Field Marshal Sir William Slim, *Defeat into Victory* (London: Pan, 1989), p.288.
[4] *Ibid*, p.289.

'OUR PART IN THE BATTLE FOR **KYAUK KYAW**'

India. Intelligence came in the form of 'Documents, diaries, marked maps, and even operation orders taken from Japanese killed in these patrol clashes'. Instead of seeing the Army and SOE as acting independently of each other, however, surviving documents submitted by Edgar reveal close cooperation.

Unlike his 'Patrol Report' for 29 December to 6 January, the report for 11–20 January – also referred to in Edgar's 'Ninth Periodic Report' – has survived.[1] It means that Edgar's comment in his Eighth Periodic Report about it being 'uncertain whether we shall commit ourselves to battle in order to take possession of KYAUK KYAW' can be clarified. With twelve Karen and Burmese other ranks (ORs), Major Peacock and Captain Poles were tasked:

> to approach Jap positions at YUWA as closely as possible, create a diversion and prevent Japs from sending reinforcements to KYAUKKYAW via YUWA

On 11 January, Edgar reported to the battalion commanders of the Northamptons and 3/8 Gurkhas and finalized plans for working with a section of the Madras Regiment and a section of Gurkhas. Moving forward the next day with Captain Noronha and his section of the Madras regiment, P Force contacted Captain Crece with his Gurkha platoon, and took one section away under the command of a havildar (sergeant). Having expressed his opinion of the Kin Scouts quite plainly, Edgar would have been aghast to read the 3/8 Gurkhas' War Diary entry for 12 January:

> MAJ PEACOCK'S party of 12 Kin Scouts [...] carrying out a nuisance raid on PAYAUK left pt2368 on 13.1.44[2]

---

[1] National Archives, HS 1/3, Major Peacock, 'PATROL REPORT 11th TO 20TH JANUARY, 1944'.
[2] National Archives, WO 172/5028, War Diary of 3/8 Gurkha Rifles, 12 January 1944.

JUNGLE WARRIOR

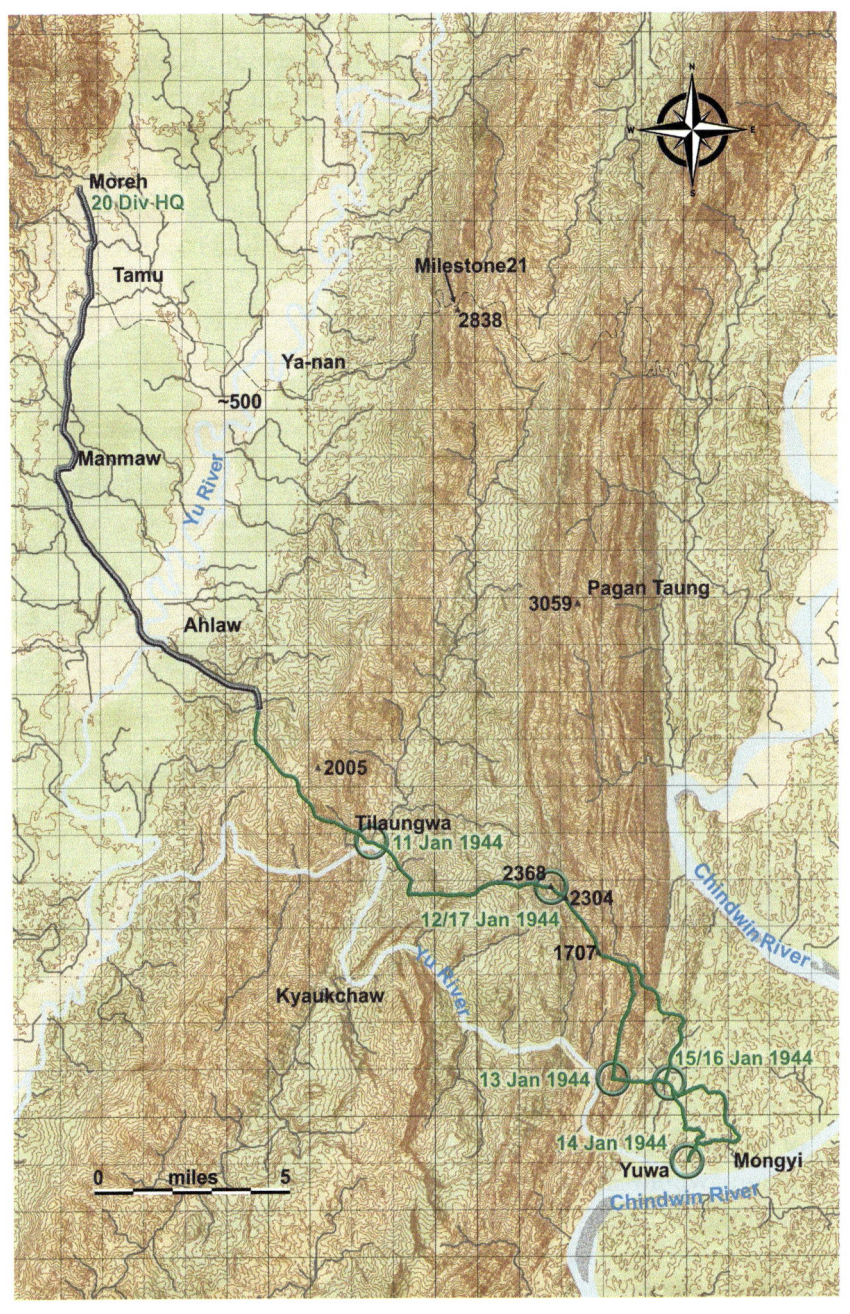

January patrol (overview)

'OUR PART IN THE BATTLE FOR **KYAUK KYAW**'

Nonetheless, on 13 January Edgar reported: 'I followed our old patrol route', dropping off the Gurkha section with orders to camp and patrol 'where the path leaves the main watershed'. Captain Noronha and his section were to be shown to their objective, but the Captain went down with fever, so he had to be left 'with map instructions and the hope that he might be fit enough the next day to make his point.' Edgar and Eustace continued to a point where they could see the lights in Yuwa, but they didn't observe any movements on the Yu River during the night.

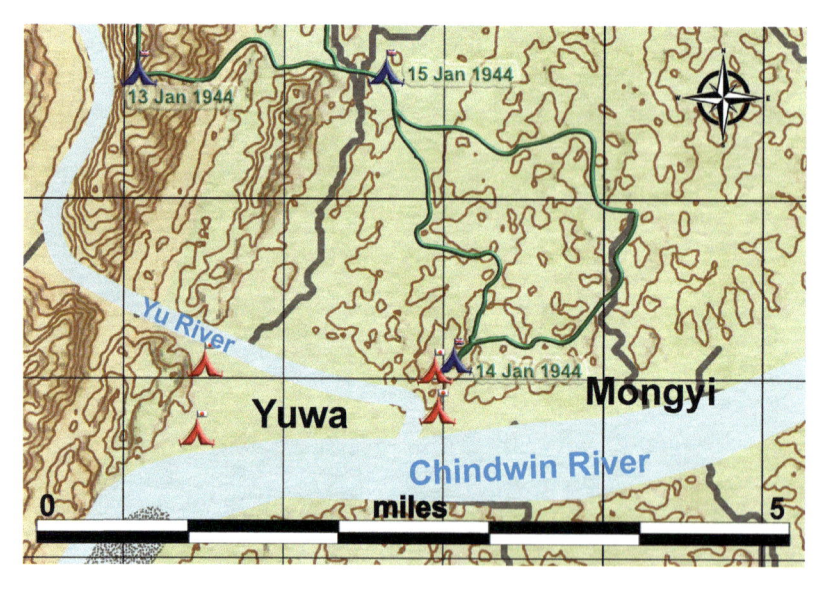

By 14 January, Edgar and his patrol were on a bluff overlooking the Yu River where it meets the Chindwin. Three villages including Yuwa were in sight, with Yuwa just 700 feet from their position. Two Japanese sentries came within 150 feet of where they were laid up, 'and could have been shot, but such action would have been premature.' Fires were observed burning all night on both banks of the Chindwin and at four other grid references. Having held his fire on 14 January, orders were to open up 'on any fair target' on 15 January, or await the bombing of Kyauk Kyaw and then shoot any target. In the

event, just before midday, Captain Noronha's section opened up, and villagers began running around in a panic. P Force joined in, shooting at all the Japanese posts observed in the time since their arrival, and anything else that presented itself. Edgar wrote:

> Since no attempt was made to return our fire from the post near us I sincerely hope that we blotted out its personnel; but of this I cannot be sure.

In true guerrilla style, after firing approximately 500 rounds, Edgar and his men moved off into the jungle north of their position to avoid being encircled, and took anti-ambush measures to reach a laying-up point for the night. The Japanese opened up with mortars, 'but [these] were directed at Captain NORONHA'S position.'

The 16 January was spent waiting in ambush all day for anticipated enemy follow-up patrols, but much to Edgar's 'great regret, nothing walked into our trap.' On the 17th, reunited with the Gurkha section, they watched the delayed bombing of Kyauk Kyaw, and on the 18th, the Northamptons attacked. Staying at Tilaungwa on 19 January, Edgar put his patrol at the disposal of the battalion commander:

> The men were very keen on taking part in the attack in any capacity, and I should have liked to set them on to locating snipers on the N. bank of the Yu. The battle plan, however, had been arranged and I suppose it was impossible to fit us in.

When no orders were received on 20 January and no hope was expected of joining in the fight for Kyauk Kyaw, P Force retired to their base camp. Edgar was happy that his 'Karen and Burmese ranks were very steady', and that both divisional and brigade commanders 'were pleased to express their appreciation to me personally.' Meanwhile, all had not gone well for the Northamptons. The trial in cooperation with the air force to secure the Japanese bunkers at Kyauk Kyaw 'was not too good', with some 'friendly fire' casualties.

'OUR PART IN THE BATTLE FOR KYAUK KYAW'

The details of the Japanese position in Kyauk Kyaw are to be found in the War Diary of 13/14 Frontier Force Rifles.[3] The Japanese had constructed eight bunkers with connecting trenches. There were observation posts carefully sited to protect the approaches and wire had been erected to bolster the defences. It was estimated that approximately 100 Japanese held the position. The attack had originally been due to take place on 12 January, but in an explanation of the first delay, some sense of the territory in which P Force was operating can be gained. Troops had been unable to receive adequate rations because the 'severity of the mountain tracks' meant that the supply mules were each limited to carrying 60lbs in weight. Then the heavens opened causing the 'hill tracts [to be] unsuitable for mules.'[4] When it stopped raining, the cloud precluded air support, meaning yet another postponement, and causing the Northamptonshires' War Diarist to record that the delay had caused much 'irritation and impatience'.[5] When at last the air attack went in, it cleared the foliage and the ground assault went ahead. Suffering significant casualties due to a clearer field of fire for the defenders, the position was finally in Allied hands by 25 January.

With the strong point of Kyauk Chaw now secured, the battalions involved could continue patrolling up to and beyond the Chindwin River, following the Operational Instruction issued by 20 Indian Division, an edited version of which appears in the War Diary of 3/8 Gurkha Rifles. The document could not be any clearer in what General Gracey wanted of his Division: 'The main intention is always to kill Japanese.' Furthermore, 'Every recce patrol, however small, can also kill or

---

[3] National Archives, WO 172/4985, War Diary of 14/13 Frontier Force Rifles, January 1944.

[4] National Archives, WO 172/5028, War Diary of 3/8 Gurkha Rifles, 9 January 1944.

[5] National Archives, WO 172/4908, War Diary of 1 Northamptons, January 1944.

capture Japanese. This is not so difficult as it sounds in the Jungle which, as we all know, helps to multiply even two men into 10 or more.' These confident words are certainly how Edgar viewed fighting the Japanese in the jungle, and from this it seems that the rest of the 14 Army was at last beginning to share Edgar's confidence.

A party of about sixty Japanese had managed to escape Kyauk Chaw, but they were subsequently ambushed on 23 January. This may have given substance to what Edgar reported as 'the usual rumours of Jap concentrations'; it is remarkable with so much going on, as made obvious by the various battalion War Diaries, that P Force sat waiting in so many unsprung ambushes. Looking ahead, however, Edgar wrote that there would 'be no retirement this rainy season from forward positions gained.' Back at Army headquarters in the meantime, General Slim was pondering over his choices for how to deal with the Japanese attack he was sure was brewing.

40. 'Some of us are going to suffer from disease and violence from the enemy'

Working in conjunction with the Army in such actions as the attack on the Japanese positions at Kyauk Kyaw and providing intelligence for the Army commander to piece together led Edgar to state in his Ninth Periodic Report that 'cordial relations with Army Commanders has been cemented by such little things as we have been able to do recently.' Also smoothing the way, however, were the SOE Liaison Officers placed at different levels within the military hierarchy. For any irregular or Special Operations unit to be effective, it has to act in concert with the aims and plans of the regular military, and it helps immensely if there is communication and trust between them. Major Noel Boyt seems to have done tremendously well in his capacity as Liaison Officer at achieving that trust.

Born on Boxing Day 1901, Boyt had worked for the firm Steel Brothers in Burma before the war as a forestry manager.[1] Boyt had joined the Army in Burma Reserve of Officers (ABRO) and then been recruited by SOE's Oriental Mission in 1942. During the first Burma campaign, Captain Boyt had been involved in one of the Oriental Mission's most successful actions. Along with fellow ABRO Captain Thompson and a company of Karen Rifles, Boyt had helped to stall the Japanese advance into central Burma, thereby contributing to the Army's escape across the Irrawaddy at Mandalay. He managed to escape to India by August or September 1942, and by May 1943 was working as a Liaison Officer. It is unclear whether he and Edgar knew each other, but Edgar was 'very glad' to hear that Major Boyt was coming to visit P Force at the end of January 1944.

Edgar intended to move P Force forward from its current base on the Yu River, and to continue to recruit Burmese for his patrols – as well as stay put for the rainy season of 1944. As P

---

[6] National Archives, HS 9/196/7, Personnel file for Major Noel Boyt.

Force grew and his patrol activity increased, Edgar thought it 'reasonable to suppose that some of us are going to suffer from disease and violence from the enemy' so he requested a Medical Officer (MO) join him.[1] The Medical Officer, Edgar wrote, would need to be someone who was 'strong and hearty without aspiration to fleshpots and great rank!' Major Boyt was to come and discuss such plans with Edgar as part of a tour of the Tamu area of the 4 Corps front.

Owing to bad weather conditions, Boyt was held up from arriving in Imphal by a day.[2] He met officers from P Force at Imphal on 29 January; Flight Lieutenant Swan, Captain Gibson and Captain Cope. Gibson drove Boyt to the P Force camp on the Yu River, but they missed Edgar by a few hours as he had gone out on patrol again. HQ ordered Boyt to await Edgar's return, so he remained at the Yu River base for the next week until Edgar returned on 7 February. On 8 February, Edgar and Boyt finally got down to business.

Boyt's report informs that Edgar planned on moving his base to the Chindwin in the vicinity of Yuwa, which was why he was awaiting the outcome of the battle for Kyauk Kyaw. With the Japanese removed from Kyauk Kyaw there would be no threat to the rear of P Force when they moved base. It might also explain a bit about why they were so keen to get involved in the assault earlier in January. Had they got more involved and taken casualties, the need for a Medical Officer would have been starker, but as it was, Boyt agreed that Edgar needed a Medical Officer as well as an Assistant Medical Officer for patrol work. Boyt also wrote:

---

[1] National Archives, HS 1/3, Major Peacock, NINTH PERIODIC REPORT ON SITUATION UPPER CHINDWIN 26th DECEMBER, to 23rd JANUARY, 1944', p.2.
[2] National Archives, HS 1/3, Major Boyt, 'MAJOR BOYT'S REPORT ON HIS VISIT TO TAMU AREA', 12 February 1944.

It would appear that Peacock, with his knowledge of the area and jungle knowledge, has been almost directing the battles!

While this is, perhaps, a puzzling perception of the battle for Kyauk Kyaw given Edgar's own reports on the matter, it is another source which continues to add gravitas in respect to Edgar's work with P Force.

The strength of P Force by early February was now ninety-nine ORs (other ranks) and four officers, with the expectation of growth to 250 ORs and eight officers 'within a few weeks.' Boyt was 'much surprised at the progress' made at the Yu camp. In his opinion the 'local 'junglies' are turning out into good smart soldiers'. There was of course some weeding out, but Edgar was injecting his customary drive and pace into his project, shown by Edgar's own request that he be able to advise recruits that 'they are subject to be returned without explanation as in Commando Units. We have neither the time nor the machinery for following the routine of regular units.' Keen to get P Force up to 1000 men, it is possible to see why Edgar wanted to be allowed this expediency.

Interestingly, Boyt also wrote about 'a little friction' between Edgar and Eustace. It appears that Poles was signing off orders and signals as second in command. That was not the only friction with officers, however, for the four officers now named in P Force were Peacock, Poles, Gibson and Penty: 'The trouble regarding Fl/Lt. Swan and Capt. Cope is reported on separately.' Unfortunately, it seems that separate report did not survive either, along with a few other attachments to Boyt's Report. In his Ninth Periodic Report, a reference to problems with Captain Cope indicated that Edgar had nearly returned him, because 'Young officers should learn not to talk too much'. It appeared that the matter was settled, though, as Edgar wrote he was now 'working well' and would hopefully 'be of much value to this force.' In reference to Swan, the comment was that he was 'much happier; but there are incompatibilities'.

Of course, it is daft to expect everyone to get on, or be the right person for the unit, but the brief insight into these relationships adds that granular detail to what was already a demanding job in a harsh environment, with a commanding officer who said himself that he was 'naturally intolerant of anything which softens the standards we have set.' As February slipped into March 1944, those standards were soon to be appreciated as the men of P Force fought for their survival, cut off from India.

41. 'The lower Yu is much too peaceful'

When Edgar and Eustace came in from their patrol of 30 January to 7 February with their twenty-two Karen and Burmese men, they had again been thwarted in their expectation of springing an ambush.[1] The men had been put on 'hard rations' (in other words no cooking) and they had lain in wait from 2–4 February, watching day and night for any Japanese movement along the Yu River and the road on the river's right bank. In the end, Edgar crossed the river to recce the road and found that it had not been used at all; there were just the naked footprints of two pedestrians. Although there had been no contact with the enemy, P Force was able to report that this was not a route being used by the Japanese; sometimes it is just as useful to know that something does not exist, no matter how much it had been expected.

The next part of the report, dated 5 February, reveals that Edgar was ordered to report to the Brigadier at Kyauk Kyaw, where on 6 February Edgar was able to inspect the Japanese bunkers. Kyauk Kyaw had obviously been taken by 32 Brigade by then, so Edgar felt able to push ahead with plans to move his base forward, and to give his thoughts about 'the possibilities of roads being made along and across the main watershed between the KABAW and CHINDWIN valleys.' His overall assessment was that the gap between 80 and 32 Brigades (both 20 Indian Division), some sixteen miles, could be significantly improved with 'a little jungle clearing and spade work' along game trails that P Force had used. In his estimation, a whole day could be saved, which in terms of tactical needs could make the vital difference. Edgar was obviously niggled, though; in his estimation 'The lower Yu is much too peaceful and quiet and unused to be true.' This comment indicates that Edgar was suspicious of Japanese intentions, but was this in the

[3] National Archives, HS 1/3, Major Peacock, 'PATROL REPORT - 30th JAN. to 7th. FEB. 1944.'

context of the local battle for Kyauk Kyaw, or the amassing Japanese divisions poised to 'March on Delhi'? The patrol report does, under the heading of 'Objects', set out his mission as being 'In concert with second phase of battle to cut the river and road near the mouth of the Dalein C[haung]', so the inference is that he was still ignorant of any planned invasion of India.

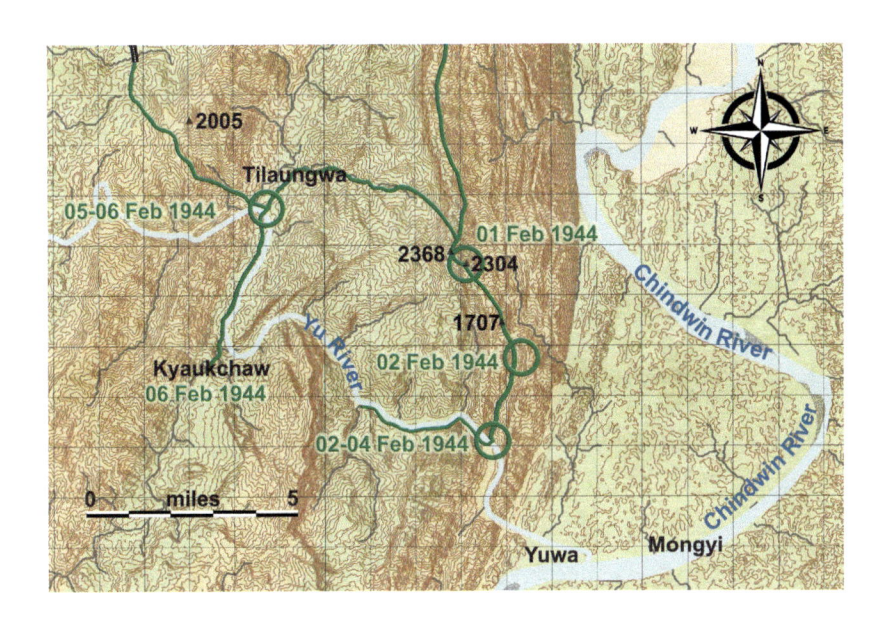

In any event, Edgar returned to base and found Major Noel Boyt waiting for him, and plans were made which did not account for any Japanese advance. The documents setting out these plans and objectives for this next stage in the development of P Force operations have survived, but there appear to be no more patrol or periodic reports. Edgar received his 'DIRECTIVE FOR O.C. G.S.I.(K) OPERATIONAL TRAINING BASE, CHINDWIN AREA' before 20 February and he was certainly working on its content when the Japanese made their move.[1]

---

[1] National Archives, HS 1/3, 'DIRECTIVE FOR O.C. G.S.I.(K) OPERATIONAL TRAINING BASE, CHINDWIN AREA.'

'THE LOWER YU IS MUCH TOO PEACEFUL'

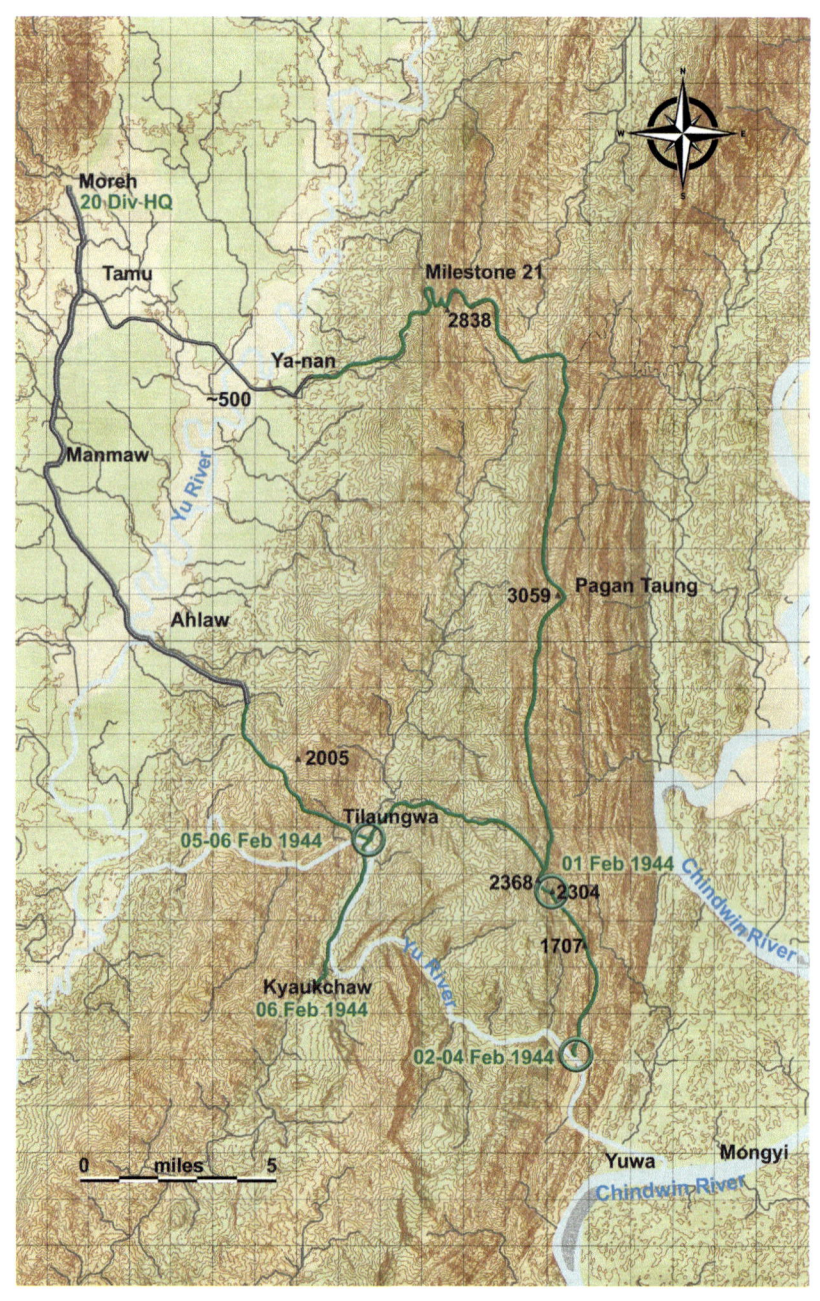

February patrol (overview)

When Edgar and Eustace had established their Yu River base, it had been well forward of 20 Indian Division and therefore isolated. By early February, this was no longer the case as regular units had advanced into the hills between the Kabaw and Chindwin valleys, pushing the Japanese out of villages such as Kyauk Kyaw. A new operational base, further forward, was to be set up where Edgar would:

> train a cadre of officers and N.C.O's with a view to their becoming capable of acting as Instructors in the handling of irregular forces of the various BURMESE races behind the enemy lines in conjunction with, but not necessarily with the support of, regular formations.

It is important to note the specificity of working 'in conjunction' with the Army as SOE is often seen as an organization mired in security and secrecy pursuing its own goals rather than supporting the broader war effort. It is this close relationship with the Army that ultimately led to such massive operational successes in Burma in 1945. The directive continued:

> (b) In the second stage to use this cadre to train up to 50 fresh officers and N.C.O's, who have military experience and S.O.E. training, but no knowledge of Burma, to handle irregular forces

These men would be used in 'short range S.O.E. work' including infiltrating behind the Japanese to attack lines of communication, supply dumps and other targets as 'agreed on with the G.O.C. 4 CORPS'. Edgar was given a ceiling of 150 recruits, although men to be used as agents were not to be included in this number. All patrols had to be authorized by the Corps commander, and all intelligence reported. The training was to focus on:

> (a) The handling of Burmese irregulars and their reaction to control

(b) All aspects of living under jungle conditions

(c) All aspects of jungle warfare with particular stress on setting up hidden bases

(d) The use of weapons in the jungle and the adaptation of explosives and mechanisms to jungle warfare and their co-ordination with native forms of ambushes and booby traps.

42. 'If this is the case our position is serious.'

At the same time as Edgar was out patrolling the Chindwin and Boyt awaited his arrival back in the Yu River camp, further southwest the Japanese offensive in the Arakan began. The Japanese 28 Army's attack was codenamed *Ha Go*; its intention was to draw forces away from the Chindwin front where P Force was probing forward in cooperation with 20 Indian Division. The opening moves of *Ha Go* created a serious situation for 7 Indian Division, the division which Edgar had helped train for two months back in early 1943, but British commanders held their nerve and did not respond as the Japanese expected, neither retreating locally nor redeploying troops regionally. By now, General Slim knew that the main offensive was coming for Imphal and Kohima, with the ultimate objective of capturing the railhead at Dimapur. The opening moves of the Japanese invasion of India were underway.

As it became clear that the soldiers of British 15 Corps would hold against the Japanese 28 Army in the Arakan towards the end of February, the Japanese 15 Army made its final preparations for advancing over the border into Manipur towards Imphal in the first week of March. Edgar and Eustace were out on patrol when forces drawn from 15 and 33 Divisions, with tank support, entered the Kabaw Valley. According to Poles:

> The enemy advance up the Kabaw Valley in 1944 drove XIV Army into the Chin Hills. We, ourselves consigned to a special mission were far in advance of Divisional forward troops. Owing to a signals breakdown we remained unaware of the Army's retreat and discovered our predicament only on emerging onto the Yu River when we found the Kabaw Valley in Japanese hands with their AFVs [armoured fighting vehicles] astride the only road

'IF THIS IS THE CASE OUR POSITION IS SERIOUS.'

at Tamu beyond which like summer lightning there were continuous flashes of gunfire. The Japanese were between us and the forward elements of 19 Division [19 Indian Division didn't get deployed to Imphal until July 1944, Poles must have meant 20 Indian Division].

The Japanese advance had been launched a week earlier than the 15 March date predicted by the intelligence boffins. Despite this, Edgar and Eustace had been ordered to proceed on patrol, setting out on 13 March. Eustace kept a diary where he set out these orders:

To proceed to R.P.2368 on Kabaw - Chindwin watershed and establish defensive position. Patrol area PAKAN TAUNG - KABULWANG (exclusive) YU WA - NGAPUN (inclusive) to PAKAN TAUNG. To Discover [sic] enemy movements this area. Keep contact with enemy and report. Communications W/T to DIV H/Q.

These instructions are confirmed in the War Diary of 32 Brigade in an entry for 12 March:

Maj. Peacock, GSI(K) with party was leaving on 13 Mar to patrol base in area THANBAYA SL0562 where he would watch area NGANPUN - YUWA - Pt2368 - KADUGYAUNG.[1]

They were going out in strength; 56 Karen and Burman other ranks, plus seven officers and NCOs including Edgar, Eustace and Captain Gibson. It was evidently supposed to be a long patrol too, as they marched off 'carrying 14 days rations - demolition stores, 2' mortar and Bombs H.E. 18. Illuminating grenades 96. 2/40lt batteries & wireless set.' Their packs therefore weighed around 60lbs, or 27.2kg. That first day, 13 March, was 'very hot' which made for slow progress with

[1] National Archives, WO 172/4406, War Diary of 32 Brigade, 12 March 1944.

frequent stops. One of their party 'collapsed [with] heat stroke' but his load was redistributed and on they went, making camp 'after climbing cliff face at N.W. shoulder of PAKAN TAUNG.' The next day they continued along the ridge they had been following, suffering in the heat because there was 'little shade'.

On 15 March they arrived at an old Gurkha post where they settled in and manned the defences. Patrols went out to see what was happening on the 'neighbouring heights', but also to get water which was by now 'becoming very scarce'. The W/T was set up but they were unable to contact Divisional HQ. Signalman Bate believed the mistake was Division's and that they were using the wrong frequency, so it was decided that he would go back with Jemadar Tun Sein and six other ranks (ORs) to try and resolve the problem on 16 March. Meanwhile, Eustace and Gibson had been out on patrol, setting booby traps and finding evidence of recent Japanese activity. On 16 March, Edgar and Eustace patrolled together and found the tracks and debris of a 'large Jap detachment' which was estimated at about five days old. By their estimation, the Japanese troops were new to Burma as they didn't know how to cut the bamboo; they were also 'very careless' because amongst the debris were ration tins, cheroots, and a shoulder title giving away rank and unit number. Of course, this intelligence couldn't be passed back to Division at this point, but a booby trap of four grenades was set across this track.

The entry for 17 March is quite long, but starts with the return of Jemadar Tun Sein by 3 pm. Tun Sein had gone back with Signalman Bate. He reported that he had left Bate at a Gurkha post and that there was no sign of the Japanese along the ridge. Earlier that same day, the three British officers had each taken patrols out in different directions. At 0830, Eustace heard two explosions which sounded as if they came from their camp and the ridge taken by Edgar. There was also some firing which sounded like a Sten gun; unperturbed, Eustace 'rigged a booby trap behind me and continued my patrol.' Having crossed

'IF THIS IS THE CASE OUR POSITION IS SERIOUS.'

a saddle and climbed to the Tambaya track, Eustace found 'considerable recent enemy patrol movements' but 'no enemy seen'. After setting another booby trap, this time on the saddle, his patrol made for camp but 'sounds like sporadic rifle fire' were coming from the direction in which they were heading. It turned out to be a forest fire and the 'rifle' shots were the burning bamboos. Edgar and Gibson returned with just Gibson reporting signs of the enemy on the path from Payaung Chaung. Booby traps were left and details shared to avoid any accidents. In the evening, after Tun Sein's return, there was heavy firing in the southern part of the Kabaw Valley, lots of lights going up above Kyauk Kyaw and a 'bright glow over YU WA village.' Lights on the Chindwin indicated motor boats in use crossing the river. Havildar Kolu Ban, in charge of the W/T, said that the set was working fine, but there was still no contact with Division.

On 18 March, booby traps set off in the fire were replaced. It was here that the type of grenade trap that was to be used so effectively in 1945 was perfected. Eustace details at least four traps, using three or four No.36 grenades linked by Cordtex, hidden in bamboo clumps or among fallen bamboo. Cordtex is a detonating wire that is used extensively in mining today. According to the Oxford Dictionary, the earliest known use of the word 'Cordtex' dates from 1935. By 1945, the men of P Force were using Cordtex to link nearly forty grenades over a 250-yard distance, with devastating results. For now though, still out of comms with Division, Eustace went back to make contact. The battalion holding the Sittaung Road had withdrawn about 24 hours before; at Milestone (MS) 17, 'Camp abandoned'; at 'M.S 15 (Bde H/Q) Camp abandoned. Heavy gun fire from KABAW valley in direction of TAMU.' Men in his patrol were exhausted, but he led them three miles into the jungle to sleep. Eustace correctly surmised that 'our forces have withdrawn not only from the Chindwin but also the North & South KABAW'. He wasn't quite sure if it was the expected Japanese attack yet, so he wrote 'If this is the case our position is serious.'

43. 'Big flap and panic'

General Slim had decided that his best course of action, when the Japanese attack came, was for his three divisions of 4 Corps to concentrate on Imphal. Spread out as they were was seen as 'an invitation to their destruction in detail.'[1] A fighting retreat, maintaining contact with the enemy to draw the Japanese to the battlefield chosen by Slim, was the plan which had been decided as the only realistic option to achieve a decisive success. This, then, was why Eustace found all the positions abandoned: 20 Indian Division had received its orders to retire, and had not been able to pass them on to Edgar and P Force because of the problems with the W/T. Eustace returned to camp on 20 March with his exhausted men, arriving about the same time as Edgar. If the Army was in a 'big flap and panic' as it struggled to cope with the unfolding Japanese onslaught, P Force was soon to have their own more immediate personal one.[2] Not only were they cut off behind the enemy offensive, but Havildar Kolu Ban now reported that 'Capt Gibson [had] blown himself up whilst inspecting [a] booby trap'. Edgar immediately went out to bring him in while Eustace 'set about boiling towelling, cutting up clothing for bandaging and generally preparing for Capt. Gibson's reception.' Edgar had pushed for a Medical Officer to be attached to P Force, and they needed one now.

Gibson arrived at about 3 pm after the 'fearful task' of ascending to the ridge carrying him on a makeshift stretcher. Eustace goes on to describe 'about 20 grenade splinter wounds from left shoulder to left heel.' They washed and dressed Gibson's wounds 'as well as possible' and administered morphine. Meanwhile, Edgar was 'in a state of collapse from heat-stroke', and all the men were 'in a highly nervous state' because while they had attended to Gibson, news of the military

---
[2] Field Marshal Sir William Slim, *Defeat into Victory* (London: Pan, 1989), p.290.
[3] Major Eustace Poles, Private Papers.

43. 'BIG FLAP AND PANIC'

situation that Eustace had discovered earlier was shared – contrary to orders – by one of his men.

A conference was held and decisions made. Any non-essential stores were to be left behind; this included the W/T batteries, mortar bombs and demolition stores. A sturdy bamboo litter was made for the casualty and under cover of darkness, P Force moved out. Progress in the dark with a litter, on steep jungly hillsides was 'almost impossible', however, so the decision was made to lie up for the night.

The 21 March 1944 is described in Eustace's diary as 'A terrible day.' It's worth quoting the diary in full:

> The section advance guard - 4 men with dahs [a Burmese short sword or machete] cutting a way for John's litter. Next the litter carried by 6 men and in rear the rest of the force, supplying relief at the litter and guarding our rear.
>
> Edgar in a very bad way - Heat exhaustion extreme. In spite of this he keeps ahead with the advance guard and is continually checking up [on] the men and generally organising. A wonderful example of the will driving a sick body.
>
> Made a strong gruel from remains of our very depleted rations and I think this did Maj Peacock [&?] John some good.
>
> Camped near water below the PAGAN TAUNG - Progress for day about 1 M.I.H [Miles in the Hour, now more commonly MPH].

It's interesting how here Eustace has swapped the formalities so that it is no longer 'Edgar', but 'Major Peacock', and how Captain Gibson has now become 'John'. It somehow seems to both show respect for Edgar at this particular time, and to make the casualty more familiar and cared about. Although the predicament Edgar and his P Force command found themselves in does not sound very fortunate, Edgar's leadership was living up to the second part of his Anglo-Saxon name: powerful. Eustace was certainly impressed.

The 22 March was somewhat better than the previous day:

> Marched to Gurkha post near M.S 21 sending a patrol forward onto the SITTAUNG road - no sign of Jap movement up this road yet.
>
> Camped at abandoned Gurkha post.
>
> Heavy gun fire from direction of MOREH but could only see reflection of gun flashes in the sky to the west, An intermediate range of hills lying between our position and the KABAW valley. Maj Peacock feeling a little better today. Heavy showers.

Eustace was not wrong about the heavy gunfire from the direction of Moreh. Slim recorded that 'After dark on the 22nd March the Japanese attacked our Moreh positions, but were repulsed and lost more tanks.'[1] Moreh is two miles north of Tamu, sitting astride the Indo-Burmese border. Units of 20 Indian Division had been ordered there on 16 or 17 March, the days in which P Force were out on at least three separate patrols and confronted by the jungle fire which had sounded like small arms in action. On 20 March, while P Force tended to the wounded Captain Gibson, 'one of the few tank versus tank actions of the campaign took place' in which the Third Dragoon Guards were triumphant, but in Slim's words, by 22 March, 20 Indian Division was 'now heavily pressed'. Slim had by now negotiated and ordered what the Japanese had wanted a reverse of in February when they launched *Ha Go*; 5 and 7 Indian Division were flown in from Arakan to reinforce the Imphal front. Poles scribbled in his diary that there was a 'big flap and

---
[1] Field Marshal Sir William Slim, *Defeat into Victory* (London: Pan, 1989), p.304.

43. 'BIG FLAP AND PANIC'

panic'; Slim wrote that he 'had badly underestimated the Japanese capacity for large-scale, long-range infiltration'.

The general situation for Allied forces in the opening fortnight of Operation *U Go*, the main Japanese thrust against India, was exceedingly tense. On a more personal level, for Edgar, the predicament in which P Force found itself was particularly tricky. There was still a long and difficult way to go if Edgar and his men were to reach safety. Even without the wounded Gibson, the challenge was huge; hard decisions had to be made on 23 March.

44. 'Edgar and I held a conference'

Since beginning their attempt to get back through the lines, P Force had not yet run into any Japanese. This was because the two main Japanese thrusts were north and south of where Edgar had his patrols out. To the north, the Japanese had crossed the Chindwin between Tonhe and Thaungdut; to Edgar's south they had crossed close to Edgar's old home of Mawlaik in the Yazagyo area. Part of this southern advance continued up the Kabaw Valley to converge with units of the northern crossing at Tamu and Moreh. At Moreh, 20 Indian Division had amassed supplies for its own offensive, but much to Gracey's disappointment, the Japanese attacked first and his Corps commander, Scoones, ordered the division back to Moreh. At Moreh, Gracey wanted to stand and fight, but Slim's 'underestimation' meant that 20 Indian Division had to 'lend' some units to meet a larger Japanese thrust to the north heading for Sangshak. Sangshak is northeast of Imphal, while Moreh is to the southeast. It would mean destroying the stores at Moreh, and leaving the road leading on to the Imphal plain from Tamu via Palel more vulnerable. These were the discussions between senior British commanders as Edgar's P Force reached MS 21 on the road from Sittaung to Tamu.

On 23 March, P Force continued on the Sittaung road, 'and pushed ahead with all speed to reach the Yu River.' The men were beginning to struggle with exhaustion and sore feet as they went into camp in a position 'deserted some days ago'. Lots of heavy gunfire was heard during the night from the direction of Moreh and west of Moreh. A recce patrol was sent forward to Tamu, which returned at 2030 hrs. They reported that the Japanese were sleeping in the headman's house, and that friendly forces had retreated two or three days previously:

> Men very jumpy and frightened and quite worn out. Spoke to them. They expressed their loyalty to

'EDGAR AND I HELD A CONFERENCE'

follow us wherever we might go but said that they were too fatigued to carry John Gibson further.

Clearly something had to be done, and some hard decisions were made. Eustace wrote:

> 'Edgar and I held a conference & decided moving John further quite impossible.'

We can only imagine how John must have felt when he was told, but Eustace wrote that once it was explained, Gibson 'accepted it with great bravery.' Leaving him on a bed in a hut in their own old camp on the Yu River with food and water for four days: 'He promised that he would do nothing to endanger his life in that time.' It then began to rain, heavily.

On 24 March, shortly after moving off, Eustace fell over and the neck of his water bottle cracked a rib. He was in a lot of pain, but he could walk slowly. He had also knocked himself out, so in addition he felt faint and sick. Later, crossing the Moreh-Mintha Road, there were 'no signs of large Jap movements.' Probably near Kuntaung (spelled Kundaung in the diary) there were signs of Japanese forces and notes in Japanese characters stuck to trees, which meant they 'took to the Jungle again.' That afternoon it rained and became 'bitterly cold', and they ran into a Japanese patrol. Avoiding a firefight, they gave the enemy the slip, Eustace writing that 'under the circumstances we dare not engage the Jap patrol.' It is worth a pause at this point to remember how Eustace spoke about P Force after the war in his notes, as compared to these diary entries. Admittedly he was referring to 1943, rather than 1944, but gone were these 'halcyon' times:

> Those were great days. We took to the jungle with our small band of cut-throats and played 'man eating tiger' with the Jap posts on both sides of the Chindwin.

By now, in 1944, they were scavenging food from an abandoned Gurkha post for their evening meal. This was despite having found hidden dumps of grain where the villagers were already protecting their food supply from the depredations of the Japanese. That night rain fell and Eustace had 'severe pains' from his fall, but he was 'hopeful' because he could 'still walk though only slowly.'

On 25 March, a dozen of P Force, Burmans from villages on the Chindwin, came forward to say that they would like to 'take the chance' of returning to their villages. They were worn out, and probably more than a little worried about their families. To strengthen their case, they pointed out that they were slowing the rest of the men down. Initially writing 'Edgar', Eustace amended to 'Major Peacock' in this next example of Edgar's sound leadership; all the men were given the opportunity to go home if they wanted to. Nobody else did. In what Eustace described as 'an example of great loyalty as every man believed our army to be in full retreat before the Japanese', the rest of P Force 'expressed their intention to follow us'. The twelve handed in their rifles, saluted, 'and several were crying openly' as they took their leave.

Pressing on, the remaining fifty men of P Force laboured up the 'boulder strewn' Kundaung Chaung with blistered feet and exhausted bodies. Eustace was in a lot of pain, and the chaung was sunless and 'bitterly cold.' The sound of battle up on the ridge above was a morale booster, however, as it meant that friendly forces were within a few miles – and that they hadn't retreated as far as Palel or Imphal. This was confirmed when Saw Na Mu and Maung returned two hours after setting out to recce the ridge. A Gurkha battalion was in position above them. An hour later at 1830 hrs, P Force was welcomed into the Gurkha battalion's HQ where they were 'looked after with utmost kindness.'

P Force had made it through, but Captain John Gibson was still alone in a jungle camp, pondering his fate. He was two days into his four days of rations.

45. 'Give me madness every time'

Weary as they were, there was just one thing on Edgar's mind: Captain Gibson had to be rescued. The next day, 26 March, the men were left resting with 3/1 Gurkhas while Edgar and Eustace got in a jeep. They were bound for 20 Indian Division's HQ. It was here that they had the two breakfasts, one of which was made by General Gracey himself. Eustace wrote that we '[c]annot satisfy our hunger.' They had already had a snack with the Gurkhas and breakfast with 80 Brigade before arriving at divisional HQ. Bodily replenishment aside, they were there for permission to take some fresh men and effect a hugely ambitious casualty recovery. Brigadier Mackenzie, in charge of 32 Brigade, agreed to provide Edgar with a patrol of Gurkhas, while Edgar refused to allow Eustace to go too. Both decisions were correct; instead, Eustace went to 'see Edgar on his way' and only after wishing them good luck did he go to the surgeon who confirmed that his lower rib was fractured.

The account of these twelve days in March comes almost exclusively from the diary of Captain Poles. Without it, the more intimate details of what Edgar and his P Force were up to during these days would have been almost entirely lost to history. As has already been made clear, Edgar's original letters home have all been lost in the upheaval of life and the realities of decolonization after the war, but fortunately Edgar's voice has not been completely lost due to Geraldine's determination to document her husband's war. Writing to his wife soon after the rescue of Captain Gibson, Edgar wrote:

> During the last two weeks I have suffered the most awful mental and physical torment and feel queer at finding myself alive and well still. Eustace, John myself and over 50 of my men were sent forward on a task just before the Japs put in the big push against us. We were told we would be warned if the

troops had to retire but the wireless went wrong and we heard nothing till too late. The sound of gunfire seemed to have gone backwards and I sent Eustace back to a certain post to find out what was happening. He came back with the news that all our troops had gone back and that we were cut off with the Japs between. The same day I got a touch of the sun and felt pretty sick but didn't much bother about the news because I felt pretty sure I could get back through the Jap lines. A little later, however, John walked into a booby trap and was blown up. He was very seriously wounded and quite unable to walk.

I do not like to think of the days that followed. We made a bamboo stretcher and carried him for 3 days over hills and through jungle till the men were exhausted and our food nearly finished then our scouts found the Japs and that night it rained heavily as if our sufferings were not already sufficient. Heaven only knew how far our troops were, and the noise of bombing and gunfire made it appear as if they had gone right away. To try and go on carrying John would have meant inevitable disaster and to leave him was, likewise, impossible. If we could only know where our troops were and the Jap strength we might try. The only thing to do was to leave him hidden temporarily with all the food and water necessary and try to break through quickly, find out the battle position and then come back for him. This we did marching into the jungle at night.

The fates did not relent and Eustace fell down a steep place and cracked a rib and could only move with great pain, and it rained again. All that day we walked, slipping between Jap patrols and making for where I hoped to find our troops. I dared not fight for fear of being committed and thus risking the chance to get through and bringing help for John. The next day, thank the Lord, we found our own troops, but to the last minute we did not know whether they were Japs or not. I immediately went to the Commander, got transport and pushed off to the front nearest John's position. Here I got a band of fresh men, waited till nightfall, and then back through the Jap lines without being seen. I was horribly scared that John had been found and killed and it was an intense relief to find him alive. I got him into the stretcher and we made our way back before dawn safely. It was the most awful good luck not hitting a Jap force or post going and coming back and, of course, there was the usual bombing and shelling going on to make things more lively. However we rushed John to a field ambulance and out of the fighting area. His wounds are bad but he will recover alright. When this was over I lay down and slept - then back to base where my men were resting - then eat and sleep; sleep and eat. The retirement was only so far but enough to give me days of intense anxiety with a wounded officer on our hands. The battle is still going on confusedly and as soon as we are rested and re-equipped I suppose we'll be out on another show.

Returning to the Poles diary, in his diary entry for 27 March 1944, Eustace wrote:

0700 hrs Edgar [strike through in the original] Maj Peacock with Saw Na Mu, Moluku and the Gurkha patrol return with John Gibson. Maj Peacock & his party of 20 Gurkhas went straight down the main MOREH - TAMU road, through the Jap lines.

Met no enemy patrols but saw verey lights [a flare] fired from New TAMU as they went past.

A very gallant feat on Edgar's Maj Peacock's part - worn out with fatigue and responsibility and greatly distressed as to John Gibson's fate. But for his courage & determination it would not have been possible to bring John out. The Gurkha patrol was frightened and on edge & panicked badly on two occasions. Our two Karens behaved in an exemplary manner.

We both believed that the chances of finding J. Gibson alive were very slight and it was a very welcome surprise to find that his condition had in fact improved since we had seen him three days previously. The surgeon pronounced him in good shape & he is being evacuated through 14 C.C.S.

Maj Peacock and I conveyed our thanks to Brig. Mackenzie and returned to SIBONG. That night there was a good deal of gun fire from MOREH in the SOUTH and KONGKANG in the NORTH.

The rescue made it into the War Diary for 3/8 Gurkha Rifles, where they were a bit more positive about their part in the Gibson episode:

1730 hrs Patrol of 20 men from C Coy, under comd [command] Hav. [Havildar (Sergeant)] DHANSANKAR PUN left MOREH with Maj PEACOCK on an errand of mercy to bring back a wounded British officer of Maj PEACOCK's party from YA-NAN (8688) where he had been left with food + water after being wounded on 23rd March. Patrol moved almost directly by road throughout night 26/27 March, picked up the wounded officer about 2300 hrs and carried him back to MOREH, arriving back in Bn [Battalion] lines at 0700 hrs; in view of the fact that the enemy was known to have been in the area of the wounded man in some strength this was a very creditable performance and reflects very highly upon the patrol commander, Hav. DHANSANKAR PUN.[1]

Writing to Geraldine of the rescue after Edgar had died in the 1950s, Eustace wrote:

> We got through all but Gibson and it was then that Edgar went back from Moreh through Tamu to the Yu down the main road, blatantly passing through the Japanese Army to effect an epic rescue. God knows how he did it. I don't to this day. Our men had reached the limit of their endurance and I was a casualty only just managing to crawl home, so Edgar borrowed a Platoon of Gurkhas and did the job alone.

General Gracey, providing the foreword to Geraldine's *The Life of a Jungle Walla*, wrote:

> When he came to me [and I cooked him breakfast] and insisted that I must help him to go and get Capt. Gibson back, I thought he was mad, but if loyalty without thought of self is madness, give me madness every time. His stark courage and obstinate persistence got him there and back, when very few would have started.

Given the circumstances, and that it was with the full knowledge of senior officers on the spot, Edgar was recommended for the immediate award of the Military Cross (MC), which was accepted. The recommendation reads:

---

[1] National Archives, WO 172/5028, War Diary of 3/8 Gurkha Rifles, 26 March 1944.

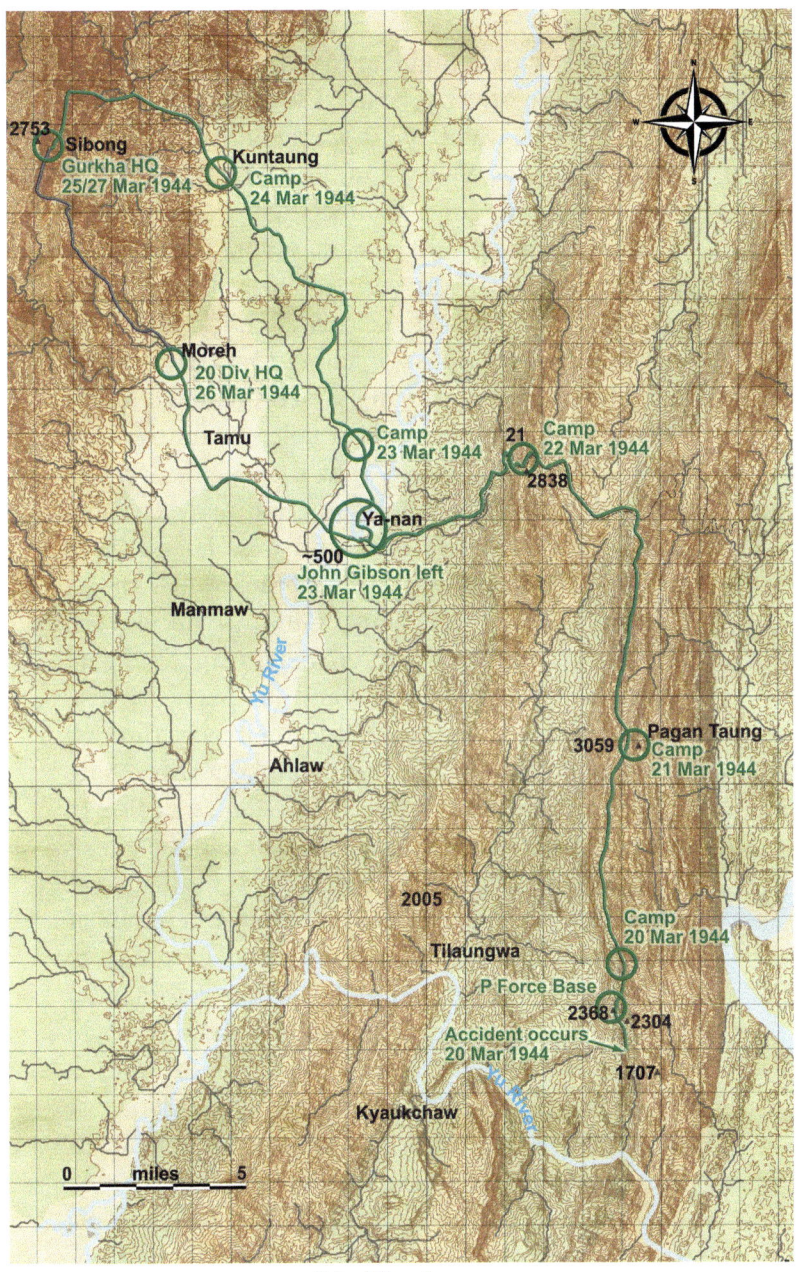

John Gibson's rescue

'GIVE ME MADNESS EVERY TIME'

Major E. H. Peacock was in command of a Special Force of Burmans and Karens which shortly before the Japanese advance started was sent on March 13th 1944 to watch the approaches from Yu Wa into the Kabaw Valley. On 23rd March 1944, the day before this long distance patrol was due to withdraw, one of his officers, Capt. J. Gibson, a very heavy man, was very seriously injured by a grenade, and had to be carried back over very difficult country by slow stages. On arrival at his old camp site at the Yu River crossing, Major Peacock, whose wireless had failed to function for several days, discovered that the enemy were in possession of Tamu and Hesin and between them and Moreh and was uncertain how far our own troops had withdrawn. It was imperative to get assistance quickly for Capt. Gibson who was left hidden at the Yu River crossing with food and water, while Maj. Peacock and his party, by now considerably exhausted, made their way through the jungle via the northern flank of Moreh to Sibong where he contacted our forces again. In spite of his considerable exhaustion and the effects of heatstroke from which he was suffering, Maj. Peacock's sole concern was the safety and rescue of Capt. Gibson. He wasted no time in going to Moreh and after consultation with the commander of the Moreh garrison, left Moreh the next night with an escort of Gurkhas and two Karens to fetch in Capt. Gibson. At this time [some Japanese forces] including tanks and guns were in Nakala, Tamu and Hesin areas, but no exact information was available. Without thought for his personal safety, he took this party successfully under cover of darkness, straight through Tamu and Hesin villages to the Yu River crossing and safely brought back

Capt. Gibson, who was still alive, the same night. It was entirely due to Maj. Peacock's dogged determination, drive, unselfishness and great courage that Capt. Gibson's life was saved.

Captain Gibson went on to recover from his wounds and join two further operations in Burma before himself being awarded the MC for his work with Force 136 in Malaya during 1945.

On 28 March, the day after returning with Captain Gibson, Edgar and Eustace and the rest of P Force were driven to Imphal where they reported to their Liaison Officer, Major Goddard. It might seem that Edgar and Eustace were now out of the proverbial frying pan, but they were just as certainly about to go into the proverbial fire – the Battle of Imphal.

46. 'All ranks are rum drinkers'

The twin battles of Imphal and Kohima were where the Japanese Army suffered their greatest defeat of the entire Second World War. Their 15 Army, comprising approximately 115,000 men, had assembled along the Chindwin River with the intent to 'March on Delhi'. Imphal was the capital of Manipur state, and the 14 Army's main hub at the end of a long line of communications stretching back through Kohima to the Dimapur railhead 115 miles away. Facing the Japanese around Imphal were the British 17, 20 and 23 Indian Divisions plus two brigades, approximately 70,000 troops.

The Japanese started their offensive at the southern end of the Kabaw Valley on 7 March, eight days earlier than British intelligence had predicted. Although the Allies knew the Japanese were coming, in the opening days of the offensive 17 Indian Division was almost cut off from Imphal. The threat was serious, and if successful it would have altered the course of the next three months of intense combat. It took the deployment of 4 Corps' reserves to stabilize the situation, but when another major Japanese thrust to the north of Edgar came on 15 March, it meant that troops from 20 Indian Division defending Moreh and Tamu had to be diverted. The arrival of Edgar and P Force in Moreh ten days later was therefore a welcome addition to the defence of the road to Imphal from Tamu, especially as Moreh had to be abandoned to the enemy at the end of March owing to the now obvious danger posed by the thrust to the northeast of Imphal at Sangshak. Two of 20 Indian Division's brigades, 80 and 100, retired into prepared defences while 32 Brigade went into reserve.

Surmising that P Force was a welcome addition is actually of more significance than it might seem. From archival records, there is a gap in the chronology of P Force from March to June in the SOE files. Although P Force was officially attached to 20 Indian Division, in the chaos of the Japanese offensive, from the end of February the 20 Indian Division HQ files for this period show they did not know where Edgar was (not least because their W/T set was not working).[1] The next definite location of P Force from the SOE files places Edgar and his men in a transit camp called 'Tweed' from June 1944, while reference to 'Peacock's Det.' in 20 Indian Division's records continues blank. Archival records of the individual Burmans and Karen in P Force have different dates for them leaving P Force between March and June, which suggested the dissolution of P Force after the rescue of Captain Gibson. Some of the dates are explained by the revelation that some Burmans chose to go back to their villages in March as the Japanese attack developed.[2] What is brand new, however, and bridges the locational gap of those remaining in P Force between the end of March and the beginning of June, is a short sentence scribbled by Poles after the war:

> Eventually we won through and accompanied our retreating forces to Palel where we occupied a defensive 'Box' position during the decisive Battle of Imphal.

He says no more about it there, for the next sentence is about being withdrawn from the battle to Camp Tweed, but now it is known that P Force was in a 'box' at Palel. Palel was further up the road from Moreh towards Imphal. This road was one of three main roads into Imphal, entering the town from the southeast. The road from Bishenpur came in from the southwest, while the road from Kohima came in to the north of Imphal. The Japanese attacked Imphal from all three roads so,

---

[1] National Archives, WO 172/4318, War Diary HQ 20 Indian Division, January to June 1944.
[2] For the original records of indigenous personnel, see National Archives HS 1/29 - HS 1/43. These have all been curated and added to Richard Duckett, 'The Men of SOE Burma' [online] https://soeinburma.com/the-men-of-soe-burma/

'ALL RANKS ARE RUM DRINKERS'

essentially, Edgar's SOE unit helped to block one of these three major routes. This is exciting because until now, presumably no historians have identified that SOE fought at this turning-point battle; if they have, it has never made its way into any account of the fighting at Imphal.

It is frustrating, of course, that the Poles diary has numerous pages torn out, but some of the remaining pages cover from 20–29 April. These now have context because the location of P Force at Palel is known. These pages reveal that Edgar and his men were in the sector of the front held by 100 Brigade. Fortuitously, chits that never got torn out and delivered offer significant insights, such as asking for rations or informing brigade HQ of where booby traps and ambush demolitions had been placed. On 26 April, for example, Poles wrote out the following:

Peacock's Det.

26 Apr '44

O.C.

75 [indecipherable]

Will you kindly supply anti mosquito cream for my force. Strength 108.

As we are employed on advanced ambushes it is essential we do not use a powerful smelling kind of cream.

[signature]

2 i/c Capt RA

For O/C

'Peacock's Det.' of 108 men somewhere near Palel was now nearly a company-sized force then, and they were on the offensive, rather than merely sitting in a defensive box waiting to be attacked. The last thing they needed was to be sat in an ambush that the Japanese could smell a mile off, or to be left to the mercy of the malarial mosquitoes that the Imphal area is renowned for. The breakdown of the 108 men is revealed on another page; seventy-nine belonged to Peacock's Detachment, with twenty men from 4/10 Gurkha Rifles, and nine men from 3/1 Gurkha Rifles. On that same chit asking about rations, Poles wrote:

> All ranks are rum drinkers. We have many pipe smokers and would be glad of a little tobacco if & when a supply is available.

Details of the defences for their box are also revealed. In the dead ground beyond the wire, nine anti-tank mines had been rigged up, along with verey lights. They would only be armed when 'warning is received of an impending enemy attack.' Ambush positions were prepared, with thirty-one grenades linked by Cordtex over a distance of 180 yards in one example; a second had twenty-five grenades over 120 yards, and a third had the same number of grenades over 100 yards. These Cordtex traps could only be detonated when the ambush position was occupied and someone used the pull switch, therefore they could not be accidentally set off and be a danger to friendly forces. This Cordtex ambush technique, perfected by P Force while on advanced patrols across the Kabaw Valley during 1943 and early 1944 was thus also used at the Battle of Imphal; and later on in 1945 it was used to devastating effect in Operation Character.

The scraps left by Poles are corroborated and a little more information about SOE and Edgar's role in the Battle of Imphal can be gathered from combing the War Diaries of the units indicated by Poles. There are at least six references to 'Peacock's Force' in the diary of 4/10 Gurkhas. These indicate a proactive role, from providing intelligence from patrols such as the one on 20 April which found '40 Japs in a Nullah about one mile east of YAPO', to being in an ambush position on 8 May to cover 4/10's HQ Battalion as it came back into Palel.[3]

---

[3] National Archives, WO 172/5034, War Diary of 4/10 Gurkhas, April and May 1944.

'ALL RANKS ARE RUM DRINKERS'

In the grand scheme of things, SOE's contribution to the great Battle of Imphal may seem small, but the fact that SOE was present at all has only now been appreciated. The 'March on Delhi' claimed sixty percent of the 115,000 Japanese troops who started the offensive.[4] It was an epic defeat, made possible by many, many small actions, and it was all these 'little' contributions which made the whole such a stunning victory for Slim's army. After the success of Imphal and Kohima, 14 Army was able to drive all the way to Rangoon, reclaiming the country from Japan, never suffering another defeat and thereby putting some of the ghosts of 1942 to bed – and Edgar played a part in that.

---

[4] Lyman, Robert, *A War of Empires: Japan, India, Burma & Britain 1941-1945* (Oxford: Osprey, 2021), Appendix 4, p.509.

47. 'Now darling don't panic'

To P Force, it seemed that it was the Japanese invasion of Manipur which put paid to Edgar's plans to spend the rainy season out in front of 20 Indian Division in a new camp, near Manmaw on the west bank of the Chindwin River. In fact, unbeknown to Edgar and Eustace, their superiors in SOE had written to Lieutenant General Scoones – which the General received on 20 March – indicating that there were new plans to be considered.[1] On the day that Captain Gibson had had his accident, Scoones received the chit that told him 'It is now almost certain' that SOE wanted Peacock, 'his second in command and a number of his Karen N.C.O's for another task early next winter.' It was suggested that Scoones would have to give them up by the end of July or early August. As things turned out, Edgar was evacuated from Palel in May; he needed an appendectomy. Poles was therefore left in charge, while Edgar went and had emergency surgery.

Since Edgar had justified the confidence placed in him, and General Gracey spoke 'most highly of this Force', it was not proposed that P Force necessarily be terminated. It was suggested that a new pair of commanding officers be found to replace Edgar and Eustace so that the intelligence network and patrolling could continue. The eventuality was that no new officers were found to take on a renewed P Force and it fell to the IFBUs to help spearhead the 14 Army's advance into Burma and provide intelligence for the Army commanders.

Shortly after Edgar was flown out, and with the Battle of Imphal obviously now finally going against the Japanese, most of the Burmans and Karen of P Force were extracted from Palel. Their destination was Camp Tweed, a brand new transit camp, where

---

[5] National Archives, HS 1/3, to Lt.Gen. G.A.P. Scoones. Undated and unsigned.

P Force was to recuperate after an eventful five months in the field. Things did not quite work out as planned, though:

> Burma Country Section [...] in July 1944 obtained a camp S.E. of Calcutta in rather inaccessible hill country - [...] since at that time they were expecting a large accession to their ranks in the shape of Major Peacock and his Burmese levies [the term levy is used a lot to describe the men recruited by SOE in Burma], known as 'P Force', some 80 strong, who had been employed as irregular recce troops with XIV Army in Burma. [...] This venture was, however, doomed to disaster as shortly after all plans had been made for opening up the camps (known collectively as Camp Tweed) the area was condemned on medical grounds. This was a great blow and presented an immediate and urgent problem[1]

Part of the justification for notifying the army of their intention to reclaim Edgar and his core of officers and NCOs was that P Force was not 'carrying out a true G.S.I.(K) role.' There is some truth in this. SOE was never meant to be a clandestine organization which operated across the front line as P Force had been doing: in India and Burma, V Force, Z Force, the Chin Levies and the North Kachin Levies were available for such close-range irregular roles. SOE was supposed to operate deep behind enemy lines, where other units were unable to. This is exactly what was in mind for the 'task early next winter'; after some R&R, P Force was going to have a period of training before being deployed deep into Burma. The long-awaited aircraft needed to support such long-range operations had just arrived in February 1944, so SOE's India Mission could finally spread its wings – once personnel had been parachute trained.

---

[1] National Archives, HS 1/115, 'History of SOE Training in India', Part 1, section B Historical, 40 -41.

Writing to Geraldine, Edgar said that, with his MC, he had 'quite a splash of colour' on his uniform now. It included 'something else in pale blue and white', but Edgar was unable to say much more about it other than 'it would make your hair curl if you knew what I had been doing.' At fifty-one years of age, Edgar had been jumping out of aircraft, and had qualified for his parachute wings. Geraldine only found out late in 1945 that her husband had jumped into Burma. She wrote: 'He knew I would be cross with him for parachuting, and so I was. It was a wonder he was still alive to tell the tale.'

Having recovered from his appendicitis and been parachute trained, as Christmas approached, Edgar was on leave in Kashmir again. He wrote to Geraldine to tell her about his recuperation in the colder climate, and that he had been out to a dinner and dance on his way back to Calcutta. With the prospect of another Christmas without her husband, and no presents arriving for her and the children due to 'restrictions' on what he could post, and with lots of news of meeting lady friends and going out dancing into the early hours, Geraldine had another dose of the green-eyed monster. She asked if Edgar had been alone on the houseboat in Kashmir. Edgar replied reassuringly:

> Of course I was alone on the houseboat, silly! Did you expect me to have a girl friend with me? Of course I am behaving myself, darling. There is so much one would like to write about one's doings, but it is impossible of course to do so. We have to consider security the whole time. I am in a jungle camp again, and not liking it too well, as it rains and rains. It was so lovely in Kashmir, and at least I had nearly a month of good food and climate and feel better for it.

In a later letter, probably penned early in 1945, Edgar had to write reassuringly once again:

Without going into details, which of course I can't, I want to tell you that I may in the future be in places where I cannot get at a post office of any kind to write and receive letters. If and when that is the case, you will receive a weekly letter from an official source to tell you that I am all right. You must not get worried about me if and when you receive such letters. As soon as I am able to send letters myself I shall do so.

Now darling don't panic, I am pretty well able to take care of myself, and nothing for you to worry about. This war has to be finished, and it is people like old Eustace and myself and many another, who have to see it through. You would not like me to do otherwise.

Geraldine was evidently pleased with the correspondence she was receiving, for she wrote that Edgar always sent 'such wonderful letters', and perhaps with some benefit of hindsight she continued 'it was hard to imagine all the horrors he was living through.' On top of worrying about her husband, her own health and keeping the farm going, Geraldine heard from England that her mother's health was deteriorating. On hearing this news, Edgar wrote:

I am sorry to hear about your Mother, but darling, when one is so old like that, I suppose it is natural. These are the tragedies of life, and there is so much suffering in the world today that one wonders whether it is worth being born.

48. 'Riddled with malaria'

In March 1944, while the Japanese pushed into Manipur State and Edgar was effecting his rescue of Captain Gibson, SOE got rid of the rather mundane moniker of 'GSI(K)' and was rebranded 'Force 136'. With the rebrand, and nearly three years of training, reorganization and operational experience behind them, and not least the delivery of Dakota and Liberator aircraft, Force 136 was finally ready to fulfil its true role. The work of P Force may not have been a 'true GSI(K) role', but not only had Edgar fulfilled the part of his Intelligence School report of 1942 which read that he 'would be very suitable as Div I.O. [Divisional Intelligence Officer] in a forward formation'; he had also justified 'the confidence placed in' him. Both Edgar and Eustace had won friends in high – and the right – places, a General who had even cooked them breakfast; and a Military Cross had been won after going through the Japanese lines three times in twelve hours. This was all points earned for the credit side of Force 136's ledger, a ledger which had spent a long time in deficit. Edgar and Eustace and P Force had won a not inconsiderable amount of trust in the utility of SOE, and once Slim was shown in December 1944 that Force 136 could be of use to his plans, 1945 was set to become SOE's finest hour of the entire war. This finest hour was to be in Burma, however, thousands of miles away from the war in Europe.

Hitler unleashed his last huge assault on Western Europe through the Ardennes on 16 December 1944. It was the same day that the British 2 Division crossed the Chindwin. After the mauling of Japanese forces at Imphal and Kohima, Slim decided on hot pursuit in an operation codenamed Capital. The initial aim of Operation Capital was to chase the remnants of the Japanese 15 Army back into Burma, and bring the rest of Burma Area Army to battle on the Shwebo Plain, in front of the mighty Irrawaddy River. Not playing Slim's ball, the Japanese crossed the river to regroup on the far bank, which necessitated a change of plan. Operation Capital was about to become Operation Extended Capital. With resources still not flowing to the Southeast Asia Command (SEAC) theatre from a war so close to finishing in Europe, Slim decided to go for Rangoon overland. It was going to be a finely run race, for where the Japanese had butchered themselves in Manipur at the end of over-extended lines of communication, now the situation would be reversed and it was Slim who would suffer logistical failure if the monsoon arrived before Rangoon had been liberated. The efficacy of air supply had been proved, but the distances and altitudes needed to clear the 'hills' separating Burma from India and to supply his divisions would – according to all contemporary thought – be impossible once the rains arrived. Slim needed whatever help might give him an extra advantage to beat the rains and take Rangoon, so using Force 136 was really a no-brainer as long as it meant that SOE operated within their own means.

Edgar had formed a highly trained company-sized formation of 'junglie' Burmans and Karen; four officers, seventeen NCOs, and 104 Riflemen. Most of these men came out of the Battle of Imphal in June and went, temporarily, to Camp Tweed. Edgar wrote:

> On withdrawal from IMPHAL we were sent in June 1944 to a place called TWEED Camp in BENGAL, where the condition for rehabilitation and training during the rains could not have been worse anywhere in any part of INDIA. Riddled with malaria; with crude encampments close to villages in which splenetic infection in children was over 80%; over 100 miles from the nearest large town and supply depot, and subject to constant heavy rain, training was quite impossible and rehabilitation a miserable farce.

Given that Mountbatten, after his arrival as theatre commander in 1943, had made malaria one of his key priorities, and that considerable 'scientific vigour' had been put into combating malaria, the Camp Tweed failure is inexcusable really. Mountbatten reported that in 1943, 120 men were a malaria casualty for every single combat casualty. This ratio of 120/1 was reduced to 20/1 by 1944 and 10/1 in 1945. If even Edgar the 'jungle man' and his experienced 'junglie' men could not train in Camp Tweed, it must have been bad. Edgar continued:

> Under protest this dreadful camp was inspected by medical authorities and forthwith condemned. We were then hurriedly removed and, no provision having been made elsewhere, the Force was sent to M.E.25, a disused artillery camp about 40 miles from COLOMBO, amongst coconut and rubber plantations. Most of the men fell sick of a virulent fever which the M.O. regarded as originating in TWEED Camp, and the whole Force had to be hospitalised for 6 weeks. On their journey to M.E.25 these fever-stricken little men were put through a parachuting course at CHAKLALA where their conduct earned them the highest praise from their R.A.F. instructors. They passed this course with credit and this short period is outstanding in its record of kindness to our men and efficiency of organisation.

Military Establishment 25 (ME25), also known as Eastern Warfare School, Ceylon (EWS(C)), opened in June 1943 and had become the main training school for paramilitary courses. Initially, ME25 was located in Koddiyar Bay near Trincomalee. In July 1944, the base was shifted to Horana, outside Colombo. Later that year, Horana became the destination for SOE teams known as Jedburghs who had volunteered for more SOE work after completing their missions in Europe. Edgar and his men were reorganized into Special Groups of about twenty men, and they were going to be joined by the Jedburghs. Having trained together in Ceylon, they would soon be emplaning to jump into the Karen Hills on an operation codenamed Character. Their mission was to protect the flank of Slim's XIV Army as Operation Extended Capital raced for Rangoon to beat the monsoon rains. Far behind the lines, Edgar and his men would now be fulfilling a 'true' SOE role: Force 136 was finally going to war in earnest.

Part III

Operation Character And Beyond (February 1945 to March 1955)

49. 'Of training in jungle warfare the less said the better'

Before the Japanese invaded Manipur in March 1944, Edgar 'was advised of a plan for entering KARENNI ahead of our contemplated invasion of BURMA.'[1] Of course, India Mission had been planning to get back into Karenni since August 1942, when the then head of Burma Section had written his appreciation of SOE activities in the wake of the retreat from Burma. In mid-1943, Edgar records that he was asked to plan an overland trip to the Karen Hills, during the period between the first Operation Harlington personnel being flown in and the repeated failures to get a British officer in after them. In the end, Majors Nimmo and McCrindle were successfully dropped to try and find Major Seagrim, which they did. Subsequently, for a brief period of about eight or nine weeks, India Mission had three officers working W/T sets, sending intelligence to Calcutta from the Karen Hills. That the Karen were willing to fight was the good news, but then all three W/T sets went off air. The Harlington network had been shut down by the Japanese. From Edgar's report, it seems that the idea of forming 'Special Groups' dates from this time, and Poles states categorically that the plan for the Karen Hills was Edgar's.[2]

The opening of Horana as a base for SOE training in July 1944 was fortuitous timing, for by this point, the idea of Special Groups had gained traction. Consisting of 100 men, P Force would finally form three Special Groups, but India Mission had recruited Kachins and Chins, and secured men from the Burma Sappers and Miners as well as the Burma Rifles, meaning that thirteen Special Groups – about 260 men in total – were all moved into Horana during the last three

---

[1] National Archives, HS 7/106, report of Lt. Col. Peacock, 3 November 1945.
[2] Major Eustace Poles, Private Papers.

'OF TRAINING IN JUNGLE WARFARE THE LESS SAID THE BETTER'

months of 1944.[1] These Far Eastern personnel were added to by the arrival of the Jedburgh men from Europe. The overall plan was for Special Groups to assist the reconquest of Burma from the immediate Chindwin area to 900 miles further south in central and southern Burma, as well as in the Arakan.

To train the Special Groups, the training staff needed to expand to cope with the influx. The number of officers increased from ten to fifteen, and NCOs increased from five to sixteen. A request to London for experienced instructors secured a new commandant for ME25 (Military Establishment 25, Ceylon) from November 1944; Lieutenant Colonel Musgrave was a Burma veteran from 1942 who was flown out from Europe. He was brought to Ceylon from his job as commandant of STS 65 (Special Training School 65, Peterborough). The post of Chief Training Officer was filled by Major Oliver Brown, and he was joined by the very experienced Captains Bellamy and Thompson from mid-November; both had served under Musgrave training SOE teams at STS 65. More locally, 'two first class officers' were obtained from the Burma Rifles; Majors Scott and Macpherson had both been Chindits, and they were 'of invaluable assistance' in readying the Special Groups for jungle warfare and for Burma. It was envisaged that ME25 would become the new STS 65, and that operations would go ahead in the Far East very much like the successful operations recently completed in Europe, 'although in vastly different circumstances'. All the hard-won lessons of Europe, along with the new technology which had not yet made its way to the Far East, were part of the value that this injection of European personnel brought with them:

> The paramilitary schools soon contained quite a proportion of what might be called 'professional' S.O.E. instructors which made for the continuance of a high esprit de corps and increasing technical efficiency. All had, however, to undergo a period of

[3] National Archives, HS 7/115, SOE Training in India, 1942 - 1945.

adaptation to Far Eastern conditions and the normal practice was for each officer himself to 'walk' a course and undergo the Basic Jungle Training before taking on a course of his own.[1]

Consequently, Edgar was able to write that, although ME25 was 'unsuitable for training in jungle warfare', they were treated very well by the staff at ME25. Edgar continued:

> At this establishment the training in weapons was good, in demolitions excellent, and the attention given to the men and organisation generally was good. Of training in jungle warfare the less said the better, but was not discreditable in instructors fresh from European theatres of war.[2]

While Edgar was training in Ceylon, back in Southern Rhodesia, Geraldine was preparing for another Christmas without him. She had written to tell Edgar of Wendy's success at riding, recently winning a trophy for jumping at a gymkhana. Edgar replied that Geraldine should give her a kiss and a 'friendly clout on the head' for her achievement. He also sent money for them to buy Christmas presents from him, whilst being thrilled to receive 'Christmas plum pudding, cake and sweets' from Geraldine. He planned to share them with his officers.

Geraldine began to worry about the future at this time, wondering if the farm would be enough for Edgar when he got back. In a letter to Edgar, she suggested selling the farm, and that Edgar take a job she had seen advertised as game warden in the Kruger National Park. Evidently Edgar was not best pleased:

> Darling, you are the absolute limit to talk about selling up our house and land, and for me to get a job somewhere else, but all this lies in the future

[1] National Archives, HS 7/115, SOE Training in India, 1942 - 1945.
[2] National Archives, HS 7/106, report of Lt. Col. Peacock, 3 November 1945.

'OF TRAINING IN JUNGLE WARFARE THE LESS SAID THE BETTER'

and we shall have to discuss things together and then decide what to do.

In one of the last letters Geraldine was to receive for four months, Edgar wrote:

The war seems to be taking a turn for the better on all fronts, and with any luck it may finish by the end of this year, who knows. I have my part to play still and it will be a combatants [sic] part, and not in the back areas. I know you will understand how I feel about it, not trying to obtain staff jobs and promotion etc. I would rather leave that sort of thing to other people.

And so it was that Edgar left Ceylon with his three P Force Special Groups for Calcutta, arriving there on 16 February 1945. Within a week he would be playing his part as a combatant, as so candidly explained to his wife.

50. 'Bedlam reigned'

The voyage from Trincomalee to Calcutta was made aboard the cruiser HMS *Newcastle*. Immediately after landing, Edgar and his men travelled to Jessore, home of 357 and 358 Special Duty (SD) Squadrons. Equipped with Liberator and Dakota aircraft, these two RAF squadrons were responsible for most of the clandestine flights within Southeast Asia Command, dropping both personnel and stores. Before the formation of 357 Squadron in February 1944, SOE had been served by 1576 SD Flight which had consisted of just six Lockheed Hudsons. These six aircraft were based at the RAF's Air Landing School in Chaklala, near Rawalpindi in today's Pakistan. In the middle of 1943, with SOE desperate to get British officers and a W/T set into the Karen Hills to make contact with Captain Seagrim, four were unserviceable by May, and in June the Flight was down to just one aircraft. It was clear that the old Hudsons needed replacing by an aircraft with greater capabilities. In September 1943, therefore, an appeal for Liberators was sent to London.[1]

Without Liberators, it was argued that the SOE's 'work will come to a dead stop.' On 1 February 1944, India Mission finally got its Liberators, and 1576 Flight became 357 Special Duties (SD) Squadron based at Jessore in present day Bangladesh. The transformation in operational ability was immediate. In the eight months between June 1943 and the delivery of the Liberators in February 1944, just twenty-three sorties had been attempted. In March 1944 alone, twenty-four sorties were attempted, leading to the description of March as an 'epoch making month for SD operations' by the head of SOE's Burma Section.[2] By the time Edgar arrived at Jessore from Ceylon, 358 Squadron had been formed (November 1944),

---

[1] National Archives, HS 1/201, George Taylor to Air Ministry, 'Liberators for SOE India', 11 September 1943.
[2] National Archives, HS 1/201, Squadron Leader Coleman, 'Brief History of Clandestine Air Operations'.

and Dakota aircraft had been delivered along with crews specifically trained for flying conditions in Southeast Asia.

With Special Groups and aircrew trained by early 1945, and aircraft allocated to squadrons assigned explicitly for SOE operations such as Operation Character, it might have seemed that everything was in place and all systems were 'Go'! The Army Commander, General Slim, was onside, having been convinced − at least in part − by the work of P Force and the value which General Gracey had placed on Edgar's work during 1943 and 1944. At least four things, however, were to make the launching of the major mission of Edgar's war tense and difficult.

Firstly, at a strategic level, Edgar's Special Groups of Operation Character were not going behind the lines without Force 136 support elsewhere. Since 1942, there had been discussions with Burmese Nationalists, and gradually a network of agents had been built up with a view to gaining the support of the Burma National Army (BNA). The Burma National Army, under the leadership of Aung San, had originally invaded Burma with the Japanese Army to win their independence from the British Empire. At that time, it had been called the Burma Independence Army, and it had been responsible for atrocities against the Karen people in the Irrawaddy Delta and in the Karen Hills. Perceived as a fifth column, many British officials and officers didn't want anything to do with what they called the 'Burma Traitor Army'. Nonetheless, Burmese Nationalist accounts make it clear that the middle-ranking officers of the BNA had been restive for some time, wanting to turn upon their new Japanese masters from as early as 1943.[3] That they hadn't was down to the top tier of Nationalists, holding them back until they thought the time was right. As a consequence of all this secret work since 1942, Edgar's mission in the Karen Hills was

---

[3] U Maung Maung, *Burmese Nationalist Movements 1940 - 1948* (Edinburgh: Kiscadale, 1989).

supposed to be supported by more Force 136 teams in an operation codenamed Nation.

The Nation teams were also to consist of Jedburghs who had volunteered for more SOE operations after their exploits in Europe and the Mediterranean. It was believed that since they had worked with resistance groups such as the Maquis in France, they had the skills and experience to handle the Burmese Nationalists. Teams of Jeds were poised to fly out of India at the same time as Edgar to operate south of Meiktila. Slim hoped that between these two operations, Force 136 might be able to give him the extra edge needed to defeat a still fanatical enemy before the rains came. On 13 February, however, Brigadier Prescott of the Civil Affairs Service (Burma) wrote to General Leese at the relatively new Allied Land Forces Southeast Asia (ALFSEA) arguing that under no circumstances should the Burmese Nationalists be armed.[4] In his opinion, they were 'pro-Burman only', they had 'backed the wrong horse' by siding with the Japanese, and that arming both the Burmans and the Karen would only produce a civil war similar to that which Greece was then experiencing. Leese was convinced, and the nine Nation teams were thrust into turmoil. It took the intervention of Mountbatten as supreme commander to reverse the decision of Leese and get the Nation Jeds back on task in support of Slim's Operation Extended Capital.[5]

Secondly, in Jessore, Edgar and the 'original' Special Groups of P Force were getting tetchy with the newcomers. Despite being poised for their parachute infiltration of the Karen Hills, there was considerable resentment. In Edgar's words:

---

[4] National Archives, WO 203/58, Brigadier Prescott to Advanced HQ ALFSEA, 'Assistance to Allied Land Forces in Burma by Pro-Allied Burmese Elements', 13 February 1945.
[5] National Archives, WO 203/4332, Mountbatten to Leese, 27 February 1945.

'Bedlam reigned'

> Each group was to take a Jed team (recently arrived from Europe) consisting of two Officers and a Wireless Operator, with whom we had not previously associated, and whose duties were defined as (a) for obtaining intelligence, and (b) for training Levies. Since these Officers had never been in BURMA, knew nothing of the language and were dependent entirely on the veterans of the Special Groups, the situation became confused. It was further learned that the Commander of Group 3 was to take with him an Officer with whom he was strongly antipathetic and another who was to come under his command in the first phase of the Operation, but was later to take command of him and assume the title of Area Commander.
>
> Bedlam reigned![6]

Evidently, there were a few arguments about command, for at least three accounts exist of this particular pre-operational tension. Sergeant Glyn Loosmore, a Jed fresh from France, wrote about meeting Edgar in Ceylon:

> He was an expert on Burmese flora and fauna and spoke Burmese fluently. He had at one time commanded his own small army – P Force – and he was displeased with the treatment accorded to his men, and dismayed to find that HQ planned to send him back to Burma as one of three Commanders of equal status.[7]

Major Trofimov, also a Jed fresh from France, confided to his diary:

---

[6] National Archives, HS 7/106, report of Lt. Col. Peacock, 3 November 1945.
[7] Glyn Loosmore, *The Jeds: A Postscript*, Section H, 'Preparing for Burma: 2 The Practice', p.1.

Briefing at Calcutta Burma Country Section [BCS], the actual brief was OK but the squabbling between the three officers of Peacock Force over who was to be in overall command was disgraceful, so I left them to it and was shortly joined by (Ronnie) Critchley who obviously felt the same.[8]

The pilot of 357 Squadron who flew Edgar and his men in, Terence O'Brien, wrote that

Peacock had not been happy about becoming part of a trinity, having already commanded his own guerrilla force, and at the planning meetings in Calcutta he tended to carry on as if he still held the stage - 'a real prima donna', Gardiner [head of BCS] said wearily.[9]

Thirdly, the briefing for the mission: as if issues with support and command were not enough, many of the officers who ended up leading parts of Operation Character and wrote post-operational reports recorded that their briefing for the mission in Calcutta left a lot to be desired. Edgar wrote:

The briefing officer had not been in BURMA and knew very little about the conditions obtaining in KARENNI.

Major Denning, later commander of Walrus area Red, wrote:

I hardly know where to begin. Several hours of verbose nothingness left us with the impression that those responsible had not the courage to admit they had no knowledge of our area or tasks, and that they were too lazy to make the effort.[10]

---

[8] Aubrey Trofimov, *A Most Irregular War: SOE Burma, Major Trofimov's Diary, 1944-45* (Devon Press, 2023), p.48.
[9] Terence O'Brien, The Moonlight War (London: Collins, 1987), p.200.
[10] National Archives, HS 7/106, report of Major Dening, Walrus Red, p.1.

'BEDLAM REIGNED'

Obviously still unhappy writing his reports some nine months later, even after the success of the operation, Edgar wrote:

> I further made it plain that all elements [by which he meant the Jeds] would be strictly under command of the Special Group Commanders and would take orders irrespective of the briefing conditions.
>
> We then returned to JESSORE in an atmosphere clouded by disagreements and doubts.

Those doubts were largely linked to the fourth issue, drop zones. It was clear to Edgar that his intended drop zone was unsuitable, and that a new plan needed to be made there and then, at the briefing. So he made one, having apparently been asked to do so. Edgar recommended that they all drop at Major Turrall's location for a show of strength to help persuade the Karen to join the fight, and because the landing area looked safe for parachutists. Gardiner insisted that the original drop zones be used, an 'insistence [which] nearly wrecked the Operation' according to Edgar.

51. 'I never could understand the hurry'

Returning to Jessore with these issues still on his mind, Edgar bore the pressures and responsibilities of command with his usual stoicism and determination to succeed. As Edgar's grandson has said, the descriptions of Edgar's behaviour at the briefing – as illustrated by the earlier quotes– 'doesn't put him in a good light'. While the family records and this biography thus far make it clear that Edgar was 'not an easy character', there can be some sympathy with the speculative view that Edgar probably didn't want 'to put his life into the hands of men who he thought were less able to protect it than he was'. He was, quite rightly, absolutely sure of his knowledge of the Burmese people and their environment; when Edgar had asked 'who knows all those jungles better than I do?' back in 1942, it was not an idle rhetorical question. Apart from the people still living in them, in other words the indigenous populations, probably not many others did. So what had Edgar done about it? He had gone out and recruited indigenous 'junglie' Burmese into P Force, forming and training his Special Groups from men who were experts in their homeland. Being joined for operations by newcomers with no experience of the East, and then briefed for that operation by people who even the newcomers didn't have much confidence in – mixed with a healthy dose of the normal pre-operational trepidation – couldn't have been easy. Edgar was probably asking the same question as his grandson eighty years later: why were the Jeds forced on them?

The answers to this are mostly found scattered within the surviving SOE files. As Force 136 wound down in late 1945, it wasn't just operational officers who wrote reports. Unfortunately, war is a recurring, if not ceaseless, part of human activity, so reflections on all aspects were collected presumably with a view to perusal and future application in another war. In the report from the training section of Force 136, the scarcity of British operational personnel is made clear from the outset. Until the

'I NEVER COULD UNDERSTAND THE HURRY'

Jedburghs came out from Europe, Burma, Malaya and Siam Country Sections had just forty operational officers between them. It was not only officers, but also W/T operators who were desperately needed. The Jedburghs were able to arrive just as operations in the Far East were greatly expanded:

> the grafting of these reinforcements onto the Country Sections' existing plan and the marriage of European operational techniques with the local knowledge and experience of the Country Section Officers and native levies can be said to have been a conspicuous success, both in training and in the field. It is for comment that although in most cases the new arrivals from Europe had, owing to the speed of events, to be put into the field with the bare minimum of acclimatisation and of jungle and medical training, the general performance was remarkable.[1]

It was the 'grafting' at the beginning which was the irritant, made more pronounced by the lack of confidence due to a lack of knowledge of what the Jedburghs were bringing to the operation. What they brought was operational experience of training and organizing and fighting with resistance forces in Europe, along with expertise in using all the latest technology that only made it to the Far East with them. Chief in all these were the S-Phone and the Rebecca-Eureka system. The S-Phone allowed men on the ground to talk to the pilots of supply aircraft, while the Rebecca-Eureka system consisted of specialized radar which allowed drop zones to be homed in on, providing much needed accuracy when operating above a sea of green or in thick cloud. What a difference it might have made had it been available between February and October 1943 when so many sorties to contact the Harlington team failed.

---

[1] National Archives, HS 7/115, SOE Training in India, 1942 - 1945

The speed of events referred to is something that Edgar bemoaned in his report, writing that he 'never could understand the hurry', which no doubt added a little more freneticism to the whole situation. The lack of training apparently due to the pace needed to get operations launched is encountered again and again. Sergeant Harry Verlander, who arrived at ME25 as late as 3 March 1945, wrote in his memoir that:

> Training was practically non-existent, it being assumed we were all more or less experienced, having already been involved with the real thing, albeit in another theatre of war. There was to be some jungle training given, the nearest over 50 miles away. Even this was not thought to be very much like that which would be encountered.[2]

When Harry was approximately halfway through his five-week journey from Liverpool to the Far East, Edgar and the Special Groups were at Jessore preparing to go. The intimate details of this tiny moment in Edgar's war, the few days before his big drop, would have been lost to history were it not for the remarkable work of Terry O'Brien.[3] Even if he did have the ulterior motive of attempting to meet the women serving in the First Aid Nursing Yeomanry (FANY), by his own admission he was 'constantly devising reasons to query minor details of operations' at Force 136 headquarters. Along with his contemporaneous scribblings in four exercise books filled while in command of a flight of Dakotas of 357 Special Duty Squadron, the detail and insight provided in his subsequent book *The Moonlight War* is unique. He also informs us that the Operational Record Books 'for 357 Squadron are not complete; some operations, such as my original attempt to land Colonel Peacock, have escaped record'. Useful to know.

---

[2] Harry Verlander, *My War in SOE* (Bromley: Independent Books, 2010), p.170.
[3] Terence O'Brien, *The Moonlight War* (London: Collins, 1987).

52. 'They told me seven o'clock'

Those were the first words that Edgar said to Squadron Leader Terence O'Brien.[1] Edgar's choice of words was taken as a 'critical comment' while the Squadron Leader had his hand firmly shaken beside the Dakota he would soon be piloting for Edgar. The time was five past seven.

Edgar's men were lined up ready to emplane, while Major Turrall's men were a 'chattering throng' towards which Edgar 'glanced in disapproval'. It was mid-February, apparently, and O'Brien wrote that the men were going to do a practice parachute jump. We know that P Force only arrived in Jessore on 16 February, and that the 17th was spent in Calcutta at the briefing. Since the date of launch was 20 February, were they really risking a practice jump on 18 or 19 February? It seems unlikely. Perhaps, therefore, it is simply an error, or maybe a vehicle to continue painting a picture of Edgar with a bit of 'poetic' licence:

> Ten minutes later I banked the aircraft steeply to watch him make his descent on the practice DZ [Drop Zone], the first of a stick of five. He tugged the shroud lines, landed with flexed knees exactly as in drill, then immediately stood upright and thumped the parachute release. The colonel was not a man to go rolling about on the ground to ease a fall.

That O'Brien was able to see Edgar land in such detail, 'thumping' his parachute release, perhaps seems a bit fanciful, but it helps drive his narrative for the majority of this particular chapter. The details are not always correct, as he has Edgar

---

[1] This section draws heavily on Terence O'Brien, *The Moonlight War*, Chapter 13, pp. 199-212.

down as having been in command of 'a large guerrilla group operating behind the lines on the Arakan front', a place where Edgar never served, and the 'importance of that front' certainly didn't 'diminish' towards the end of 1944. Every source the historian encounters will have its faults, but what is important here is the impression that Edgar left on O'Brien, even forty years later when he wrote his book.

Just as Edgar had not liked the reconnaissance photos of his proposed drop zone, O'Brien didn't either. Having been on the ground with the Chindits, he was familiar with the terrain from a perspective other than his pilot's chair. O'Brien was sufficiently worried to decide to go and speak to Edgar:

> Force 136 had three basha huts for their people out to the west of the airfield. At the far end of the huts was a single amherstia tree, and at this season it was covered with an immense number of vermilion flowers, the petals tipped by gold - it reminded me of a Christmas tree, all its tiny candles alight. Colonel Peacock was sitting outside in a chair by the tree, oiling his revolver. He nodded a silent greeting and went on pushing the cleaning rod down the barrel of the .38 as he waited for what I had to say. With his head lowered I could see through his black hair a long pallid scar across the skull where a dah had nearly ended his life in a Burmese uprising in 1915 [sic: it was the Saya San Rebellion 1930-32].

The exchange which followed, as described by O'Brien, is uncomfortable. After sharing his thoughts about the drop zone, Edgar's 'manner changed at once' as he got animated about 'those fools in Calcutta'. The sense of the continued stress of the fight at the briefing is palpable in O'Brien's account. Edgar obviously hoped that O'Brien might become an ally and prevail upon 'the idiots in Calcutta' to change his drop zone, but O'Brien said that he and the RAF 'could not interfere in such

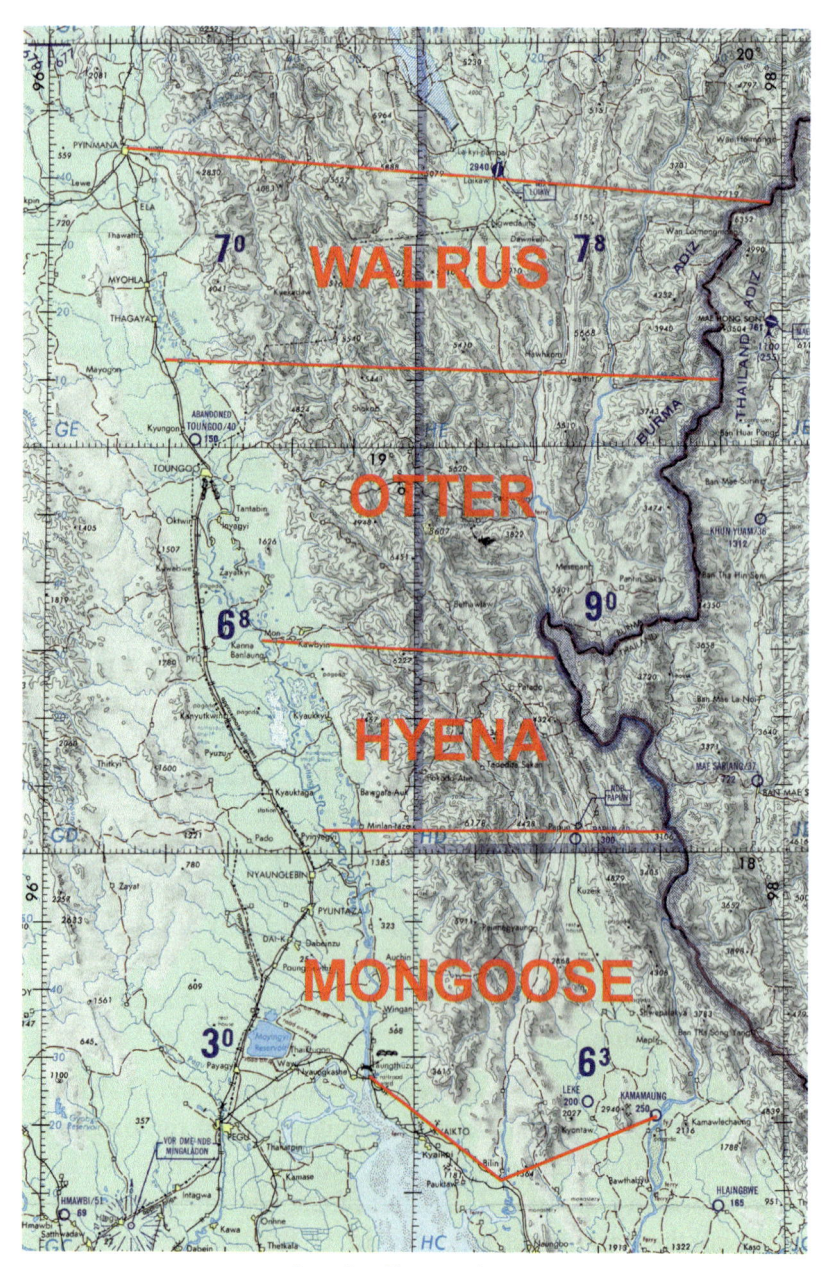

Operation Character Areas

matters', at which point Edgar 'became curtly uninterested in further conversation'. Conversation must have continued, however, for O'Brien mentioned he had been with the Chindits and 'his [Edgar's] manner abruptly changed again. He looked up in approval. 'You're a jungle wallah, then?"

The outcome of this encounter seems to have been that O'Brien formed a specific contingency plan to deal with the situation if indeed the proposed landing ground was unsuitable. He had already chosen to fly Edgar in himself, so that if there were any disagreements about jumping, he was the one to deal with Edgar.

So it was that on 20 February, O'Brien was able to observe Peacock organizing his men ready for boarding their Dakotas for the big drop into the Karen Hills. The aircraft took off just after dusk and after a five-hour flight, the drop zone was beneath them. O'Brien writes 'It was a shocker.' The photographs did not reveal all its difficulties from the pilot's point of view, nor how steep the clearing was from a parachutist's perspective. Not only that, fires were extinguished and figures were seen 'scattering' as the aircraft made its first pass. After searching for an alternative in the hinterland and drawing a blank, O'Brien decided to abort the drop. The navigator went to get Edgar, and O'Brien 'prepared for battle', expecting Edgar to protest:

> O'Brien: 'I can't let you go. Two reasons: the site is too dangerous, and I'm pretty sure there are Japs camped on it.'
>
> Edgar: 'It's your decision, but I think you're right. Those fires looked fishy to me.'

In his own post-operational report, Edgar wrote of the failed infiltration:

> I was jumping No. 1 and had the doubtful privilege of standing at 'action station' at the open door for

half an hour while the pilot flew to and from the so-called DZ, considering whether it was fair to make us jump. I had a very fine view of this wretched DZ and the lights on it, and, when the pilot refused to let us jump, I did not insist.

With that, the other aircraft were told to abort, and Edgar and his team settled down for the return trip to Jessore. Meanwhile, Turrall's drop had been a success, and Edgar felt vindicated in his criticisms of the Force 136 staff in Calcutta. P Force was consequently scheduled to land at Pyagawpu, Turrall's landing area, on the night of 23 February. They might have told Edgar seven o'clock, but they had also told him 20 February, changed the command structure of the operation, foisted the Jedburghs upon him, given him a terrible choice of drop zone, and provided an inadequate briefing of local conditions. What else could possibly go wrong?

53. 'Unswerving loyalty' Part One

In fact, Major Rupert Guy Turrall and his 'Hyena' Special Group had not had such a straightforward jump on 20 February as Edgar's and O'Brien's accounts would imply. Turrall's post-operational report contains excerpts from his W/T comms with Calcutta, which makes it clear that stores were lost in the forest up to two miles from the drop zone, and that the last of his missing men were only recovered on 24 February.[1] Turrall's second message was rather off-putting considering that Edgar's 'Otter' drop had failed: 'Jap aware our presence and on spot within 12 hours.' It turned out that it was just one Japanese soldier who was manning the local police station. Nonetheless, as O'Brien wrote, the head of BCS, Ritchie Gardiner had 'immediately' signalled Turrall to accept the others on his drop zone, as Turrall's report shows:

> 21 Feb HQ CALCUTTA
>
> PEACOCKS sortie failed last night account weather and unsatisfactory DZ ... can you arrange reception and if so what is earliest date ...

Interesting to note that weather was blamed by BCS, at least in part, for the abortive sortie. Captain Ansell wrote that blaming the weather was 'a bit of face-saving, as the weather could hardly have been better'.[2] In any event, Turrall replied:

> Will receive PEACOCK ... at our DZ PYAGAWPU. Desirable expedite arrival as THUGYI now expects early Jap interference ... Imperative 200 rifles complete with ammo to coincide with arrival PEACOCK.[3]

---

[1] National Archives, HS 7/106, report of Major Turrall, 'Hyena' group.
[2] Captain Ansell quoted in Geraldine Peacock, *The Life of a Jungle Walla* (Ilfracombe: Arthur Stockwell, 1958) p.75.
[3] National Archives, HS 7/106, report of Major Turrall, 'Hyena' group.

'UNSWERVING LOYALTY' PART ONE

There is quite certainly a typo in the next message from Calcutta:

> propose drop PEACOCK Party and 200 rifles Friday 3rd. Two Dakotas personnel and stores followed by two Libs arms and ammo. TOT 1st aircraft 2100 hrs. 2nd aircraft 30 mins later ... We can drop Poles Party but prefer ...

The 23 February 1945 was a Friday, and there was never any consideration of dropping on 3 March, which in any case was a Saturday. Presumably this was only a mistake in Turrall's write-up, rather than causing more unwanted confusion at the time of launching Operation Character.

Also of note in this message is the possibility of dropping Eustace's 'Ferret' Special Group too. O'Brien wrote that it being the full moon period, all aircraft had other sorties scheduled, himself taking a Secret Intelligence Service (SIS) mission, so Eustace's Ferret group could only follow when aircraft became available. As far as Eustace was concerned, however, he was never going to go the same night as Edgar because the Pyagawpu site was too far from Ferret's area of operations. Edgar was supposed to move out from the Hyena area and find a closer drop zone to 'save 'FERRET' group a long and exhausting march'. Eustace was therefore awaiting a signal from Edgar that would take a few days at least as Edgar would have to travel north from the Hyena area.[4]

There doesn't appear to be any comment about the landing of the Otter group in Turrall's report, so in contrast to Hyena, it must have gone without too much of a hitch. Edgar 'found Major TURRALL safe but with only 4 recruits.' Based on this lack of recruits, Edgar signalled for Ferret to also drop to

---

[4] Major Poles, like most of the officers in charge of various parts of Operation Character, wrote a post-operational report in 1945. It is an appendix to Edgar's report, but it resides in the National Archives HS 1/11, not HS 7/106 where most of the reports are situated.

the Hyena drop zone for a show of strength. This drop did not go so well, and actually caused some friction into the years after the war. Eustace managed to break another rib; Captain Duncan Guthrie, one of the Jeds from France, broke his ankle; Rifleman Maung Lu Dan also broke an ankle; Rifleman Maung Sa Kyai was unable to walk because of a sprained ankle; Edgar wrote that, in addition, 'there were a dozen lesser casualties owing to faulty droppings and descents on trees'.

Guthrie's explanation for his injury was that he left the aircraft after the red light came on. One of the Karen had hesitated and needed 'winkling out', in other words a good shove out the door by Guthrie, but he overcommitted and also ended up exiting the aircraft. Seeing that he was going to land on what he thought were trees, and having been told he would probably lose his reproductive capabilities if he landed on one without crossing his legs, he landed awkwardly on a more benign little bush rather than a tree, and therefore much closer to the ground than he expected.[5] In addition, the air was apparently thinner, making descent faster that night, and both Edgar and O'Brien observed that the men were weighed down with a substantial amount of kit.

It was Guthrie's injury which continued to cause rancour in the post-war years. He was not evacuated or seen to by a doctor until several months later, with the result that his break mal-fused. He had a limp for the rest of his life. Documents kept in the Imperial War Museum reveal how he believed he could have avoided a lifelong disability if he had been tended to in good time, and his obvious anger about it.[6] He was not the only one who believed he could have been spared long-term damage; Dr Bupesh Dewanjea was originally going to be parachuted in immediately that February to tend to the injured men. He did not deploy until nearly a month later based on signals from the field which said he was not urgently needed. Keen to see the two

---

[5] O'Brien, *The Moonlight War*, p.209.
[6] Imperial War Museum (IWM), 12840, Papers of Captain D.D. Guthrie.

men with broken ankles after he arrived, he was apparently told he 'should not bother unnecessarily about them.' They were being kept hidden and fed by Karen villagers in an area 'thick with enemy search parties.'[7]

Nonetheless, and notwithstanding the casualties, there were now over sixty men at Pyagawpu, with at least ten tons of weapons and other stores. This appears to have been the clincher. The local Karen headmen called a meeting and they voted to join the Character teams, having now been persuaded that the British had returned for good. Edgar wrote that once the Karen had taken this vote to fight, they 'never swerved from their decision.' Edgar felt vindicated once again, for he had said back in Calcutta that a show of strength was needed to persuade the Karen to fight after suffering all the brutality of the Harlington reprisals in the hunt for McCrindle, Nimmo and Seagrim just a year before. Without Karen support, Operation Character would never have been able to achieve what it did. As Edgar wrote, the credit for the success of Character 'lies in the people of the Karen Hills whose record of unswerving loyalty is second to none in the Empire, and whose loyalty alone justified an Operation so far ahead of our invading Army.'

Successful completion of the mission lay many months ahead in late February 1945, and nothing was by any means guaranteed at this stage. Both Otter and Ferret were some distance from their designated area of operations, there were significant casualties from the parachute infiltration, and the Japanese were apparently already closing in.

---

[7] Richard Duckett, 'A Doctor on Special Operations', SOE in Burma [online] https://soeinburma.com/2017/10/14/a-doctor-on-special-operations/

JUNGLE WARRIOR

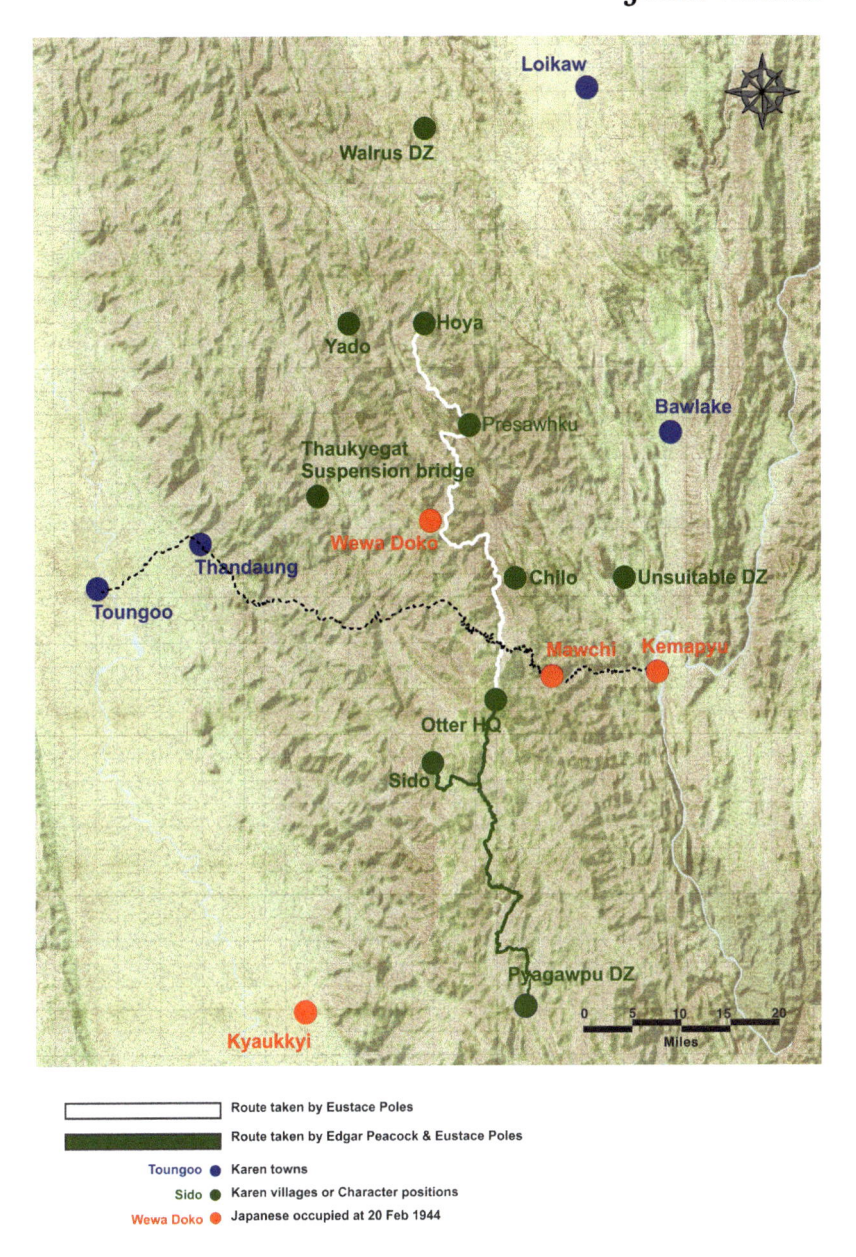

Map legend:
- Route taken by Eustace Poles
- Route taken by Edgar Peacock & Eustace Poles
- Toungoo ● Karen towns
- Sido ● Karen villages or Character positions
- Wewa Doko ● Japanese occupied at 20 Feb 1944

Locations shown on map: Loikaw, Walrus DZ, Hoya, Yado, Presawhku, Bawlake, Thaukyegat Suspension bridge, Wewa Doko, Thandaung, Toungoo, Chilo, Unsuitable DZ, Mawchi, Kemapyu, Otter HQ, Sido, Pyagawpu DZ, Kyaukkyi

54. 'Ideal for my purposes'

Against substantial odds, and not without considerable friction, the first three teams of Operation Character were in the field. They had narrowly managed to convince the Karen to join the fight by a landing in strength at Pyagawpu, and enough weapons had also been dropped to start arming and training the volunteers who now began to arrive in large numbers. Among those who rallied to the Character teams were many old soldiers who had served in the Burmese colonial units such as the Burma Rifles and the Burma Frontier Force. By 1942 when the Japanese invaded, rapid wartime expansion meant that there were approximately 20,000 men from Burma's various ethnic groups fighting for the British Empire. Of the 20,000 or so in the various colonial units, just 6140 made the retreat to India.[1] Many of the men were told to go back to their villages, hide their weapons, and be ready to rejoin the fighting when the British returned. Even allowing for casualties in the first Burma campaign, men taken as forced labour by the Japanese, and those murdered in Japanese atrocities, there were still a substantial number of trained men in the Karen Hills, including many who had worked with Seagrim in the intervening years. These men would form an important core of recruits for the Character teams, helping not only to train but also to administer the 12,000 men who would fight in the coming months as part of what they called 'Spider Group'.

Edgar wrote that he stayed at Pyagawpu for a week before moving off to his Otter area. In his report he says that 'control of the Operation at this time devolved largely upon myself' and he set about getting the teams organized. He was able to do this because although the signals from Turrall had indicated that the Japanese were aware of their presence and were expected to descend on them, it turned out that the Japanese consisted of exactly one, and all his Karen policemen

---

[1] National Archives, WO 106/2677, 13 June 1942.

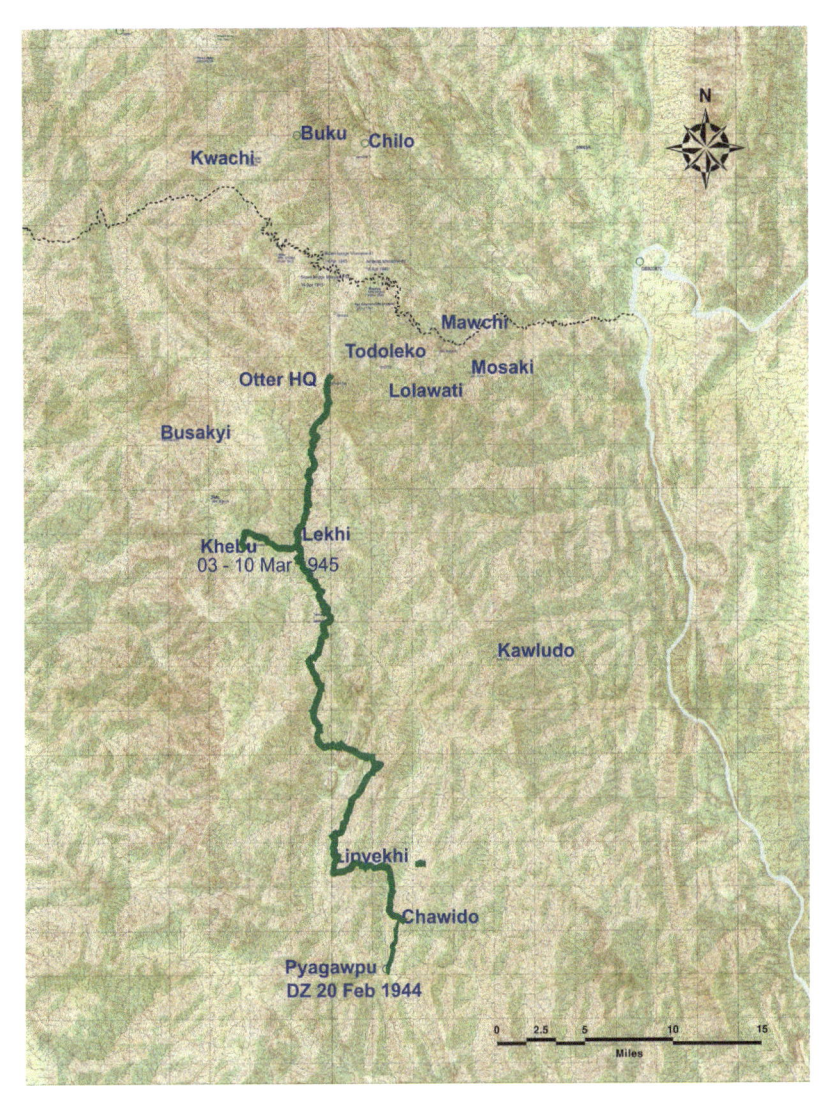

Operation Character initial march

had abandoned him immediately to join the parachutists. Apparently, unsure of what to do, he dawdled for a few days before going to report the landings, and suffering the inevitable loss of face at having had his men desert him. By the end of that week, Edgar reckoned over 500 Karen had been armed; and the Japanese now really were beginning to close in. By the time Edgar left, followed a few days later by Eustace, Turrall wrote that they were 'being actively hunted.'

According to Eustace, Edgar and his Otter team plus fifty newly recruited levies moved out from the Hyena area on 28 February, leaving Eustace to catch up when he had recovered enough to march. Apart from his broken rib, Eustace recorded that he had 'injury to pleura. The pleura is the membrane between the lungs and the chest wall, a vital part of the respiratory tract.' It was not until 6 March that Eustace felt able to lead his Ferret team off. They were some 80 miles from their area of operations, and two men had broken ankles. As they prepared to leave, a third casualty was created when Sergeant Moore severely burnt his hand on a flare which he was using to destroy stores they couldn't carry away. Sergeant Moore promptly passed out, so there were three men to carry on stretchers. At least Rifleman Maung Sa Kyai's sprain was better. That day, they made just two miles, the terrain being so difficult.

Three Japanese columns were reported to be converging on Pyagawpu from the directions of Papun, Kyaukkyi, and Toungoo. Fearing they might be surrounded, and anxious to give Hyena group 'freedom of action', a tough decision had to be made; it was obvious that carrying three casualties on stretchers was endangering the whole Special Group. The headman of Chawido village agreed to hide Guthrie, Lu Dan and Sergeant Moore, and for them to be looked after. Turrall was 'to rescue them as soon as an opportunity should occur.' Guthrie later published *Jungle Diary* in which he wrote: 'We hid there, depending on the simple kindness of those Karens, for three months.'[2] He and Lu Dan were finally flown out in a Lysander on Tuesday, 22 May 1945.

Unencumbered by non-ambulatory comrades, Eustace was able to catch up with Edgar by 7 March at a village called Khebu. They stayed here until 10 March, recruiting, picking up intelligence, and taking supply drops. By 17 March, Otter and Ferret had reached Sosiso on the Nattaung ridge. At 7500 feet with pine trees for cover, and clearings to take supply drops, Edgar decided to make his base here. Sosiso, he wrote, 'was ideal for my purposes.' It presented first-rate defensive positions, overlooked the Mawchi Road and indeed the mining town of Mawchi around eight kilometres distant. The place was still remote enough that it 'was seldom used by anyone'. In fact, it proved so ideal for his purposes that it became Edgar's headquarters for the next seven months or so.

The town of Mawchi was linked to 'civilisation' by a road which ran more or less due west for 67 miles to Toungoo. Situated on the banks of the Sittang River approximately 172 miles north of Rangoon (Yangon), Toungoo was a Burmese capital in the sixteenth century. The main road and railway from Rangoon pass through Toungoo on their way to Mandalay, 233 miles further north. At the same time as Otter and Edgar were digging their defences on Sosiso and making their mountain home, the final encounters were being fought in the Battle for Mandalay. It was a little over 400 miles from Mandalay to 14 Army's objective of Rangoon, and if the Character teams were going to be of any use in helping them get there, time was of the essence. The Japanese were heading for Toungoo to regroup and block the Allied advance. Character's job was to prevent 15 Division of the Japanese 15 Army from retreating from Loikaw through Mawchi to Toungoo. A fourth Special Group, codenamed Walrus and led by Lieutenant Colonel John Cromarty Tulloch, was hurriedly parachuted in on 24 March. The Japanese would now need to travel through three Character

---

[2] Duncan Guthrie, *Jungle Diary* (London: Macmillan, 1946), p.

Special Group areas: Walrus, Eustace's Ferret, and Edgar's Otter.

Similar to form thus far, however, Edgar and Eustace were shortly to be caused immense frustration and anger by those 'fools' in Calcutta. Eustace and his Ferret team left Sosiso on 18 March; 'all were determined to reach our operational area without further delay.' Eustace estimated that they were still a good 70 miles away from where they needed to be, with 'broken, mountainous country' to navigate. At this point, Ferret had no idea that another Special Group had been briefed in Calcutta under the same codename of Ferret. To the confusion of Lieutenant Colonel Tulloch, the Ferret name had then suddenly been changed to Walrus.[3]

On 23 March, the day before Walrus arrived, Eustace and his Ferret team, after marching for five days on one day's rations, clothed in 'sweat soaked rags' and with their boots 'held together by bamboo twine', finally arrived in their area of operations. 'Morale was extremely high' despite their exertions. That same afternoon, 'we received a signal from Calcutta which ordered us to turn back at once and attach ourselves to OTTER.' It seems the Gods of War were unable to entertain a Peacock/Poles separation.

---

[3] National Archives, HS 7/106, report of Lt. Col. John Cromarty-Tulloch.

Left: Edgar Peacock newly promoted to Sergeant in October 1940, aged 47
Right: Major Eustace 'Pixie' Poles, in 1945

Bottom left: Major Bill Nimmo, brother of Major James Nimmo who died trying to contact Hugh Seagrim in 1943.

Bottom centre: Captain Frank Ansell, Ferret Group, Operation Character.

Bottom right: Sergeant. Len Pearson MM. Recommended for DCM.

255

PHOTOS 2

Operation Character country

The Karenni mountains looking east. The mountain path from Mount Sosiso to Otter HQ can be seen running roughly northwards at bottom left.

A parade of the three sections of Operation Character in the days following their drop into Pyagawpu. The commencement of Operation Character.

The drop zone of Pyagawpu was the only one of the three initially selected deemed safe to use. Even so, it was 35 miles (as the crow flies) south of the Mawchi Road operational area. The men had to move there, unseen, through enemy occupied mountains and villages.

PHOTOS 2

Elephants were pressed into service to help Peacock's Otter Group move north from Khebu.

Officer's mess beneath tented parachutes at Khebu. Note the cut bamboo furniture.

A view from Mawchi towards Nattaung

Young and old, every Karen who could bear arms joined the Special Forces of Operation Character

PHOTOS 2

Lieutenant Colonel 'Pop' Tulloch, commander of Walrus Group. A notorious soldier of fortune!

Sergeant Carey and Major Young at Otter Head Quarters on Sosiso 1945.

HQ Mess at Sosiso. Stove made out of containers.
L-R Lt Col Peacock, Maj Young, Sgt Carey, Capt Buchanan, Maj Saw Butler, Sgt Carver, Capt Hemphill, Sgt Charlesworth, Capt Macleod, Capt Bawe, Sgt Cottingham

Major Saw Butler DSO MC. A highly regarded member of 'P Force' and a crucial member of Otter Group, Operation Character.

PHOTOS 2

Right: An enemy truck blown up. Captain Vivian poses with 'P Force' Levies

Blown up and hurled off the road down the khud [sic] side. The fate of hundreds of Jap transport vehicles. Saw Moluku poses.

Note the Scottish 'Jock' soldier with Lieutenant Colonel Peacock and members of 'P Force' Otter Group beside a wrecked enemy truck.

Collecting a supply drop at Khebu.

Photos 2

The Bridge by Mile 81 - Mawchi Road - blown up by Otter Group in April 1945.

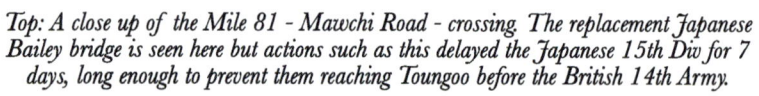

Top: A close up of the Mile 81 - Mawchi Road - crossing. The replacement Japanese Bailey bridge is seen here but actions such as this delayed the Japanese 15th Div for 7 days, long enough to prevent them reaching Toungoo before the British 14th Army.

JUNGLE WARRIOR

The bridge at milestone 81 - Mawchi Road - was blown as enemy vehicles were crossing!

Skeletons of enemy soldiers lay thickly beside the destroyed vehicles

Photos 2

Edgar Peacock's Otter Group in a captured enemy truck on the Mawchi Road

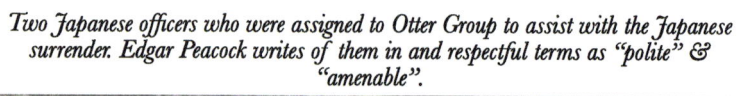

Two Japanese officers who were assigned to Otter Group to assist with the Japanese surrender. Edgar Peacock writes of them in and respectful terms as "polite" & "amenable".

JUNGLE WARRIOR

A dump of enemy small arms and ammunition surrendered to 'P Force'. Captain Vivian poses.

Japanese tanks surrendered to 'P Force' at Kemapyu L to R - Captain Vivian, Lieutenant Colonel Peacock & Captain Taschereau

PHOTOS 2

Officers and V.C.Os of Peacock's Group

Otter Karen Levies at Mawchi, late 1945. Lieutenant Colonel Peacock 3rd from left

Lieutenant Colonel Peacock and some Gurkha V.C.Os

V.C.Os, members of Otter Group

Photos 2

Lieutenant Colonel Edgar Peacock DSO MC & Bar, the creator of 'P Force' and the man who conceived, planned and initially led the Karenni Operations.

Major Eustace 'Pixie' Poles, commander of Ferret Group at the liberation ceremony in Thandaung in 1945.

JUNGLE WARRIOR

Written by Maj. Eustace Poles at the end of the war:

"The survivors of all three groups of 'P Force' at the end of hostilities and nine months behind enemy lines. Written off by army command - supply drops discontinued and never relieved by army formations.

These men were responsible for protecting the left flank of XIV Army; killing thousands of the enemy and destroying hundreds of his vehicles.

Burmans & Karens, all volunteers, 99.0% originally junglies recruited and trained in the Kabaw Valley.

A band of comrades whose loyalty is unsurpassed."

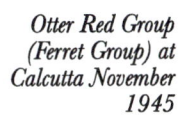

Otter Red Group
(Ferret Group) at
Calcutta November
1945

55. 'We awaited instructions for offensive operations'

In the Force 136 training report for the war, it is written:

> It was in a sense unfortunate that the Force 136 role in Burma, originally envisaged as that of offensive guerilla action against the enemy L's of C. [Lines of Communication], particularly railways and road transport, was at the last moment radically altered to that of reconnaissance and intelligence only, until offensive operations were ordered by the Army.[1]

This is part of the reason for the confusion and anger in Calcutta on 17 February, particularly over command arrangements. What Edgar had expected, indeed been briefed and prepared for since early 1944, was to take his P Force deep behind the lines to create havoc, not skulk about in an intelligence role. Indeed, the original Charter which established SOE was explicit about its role being, primarily, 'irregular offensive operations' leaving intelligence to MI5 and MI6. The whole *raison d'être* for SOE's formation in the summer of 1940 was to take the fight back to the Axis powers in any way Britain could after the disasters on the continent that year. It was slightly different for the Far East, at first. Whereas in Europe the war with the Axis powers was well under way, in the Far East, the original SOE mission arrived in Singapore before war with Japan started. The Foreign Office did not want to do anything which might provoke Japan, recognizing that Britain was already fighting for survival in Europe. With this in mind, the man in charge of the Oriental Mission, Valentine St. John Killery, had drawn up a Charter for the Far East which had specified intelligence as a priority while SOE built up its organization in *expectation* of a war with Japan. In the event of war, two things were added to the Far East Charter – post-occupational left-

[1] National Archives, HS 7/115, SOE Training in India, 1942 - 1945.

behind groups and paramilitary training for guerrilla operations. Having been at war with Japan for over three years by February 1945, what explains the 'last moment' alteration to an intelligence role that caused such consternation?

The simple answer is General William Slim; the more complicated answer is politics.[1] On 30 December 1944, the officer in charge of A Group of Force 136 (responsible for Burma, Malaya, Siam), Lieutenant Colonel Mount Stephen Cumming, had an audience with Slim at the latter's 14 Army HQ. Cumming had requested the meeting because he had been told that Slim 'was dissatisfied with Force 136'. Slim did not believe that Force 136 was achieving very much, and as far as he was concerned, the American Office of Strategic Services (OSS) were doing a far superior job. Slim had already made the recommendation that Force 136 be pulled from operating in Burma and that 'responsibility for activities behind the lines in that country be handed over to Det. 101 of OSS.' Cumming went to see Slim to save Force 136 from being relegated from the Burma campaign. He was successful in this, coming away with the agreement that Force 136 operations would now come under the control of the Army, and that the primary task of Force 136 was to provide Slim with intelligence.

Despite another meeting on 4 January in which Royal Navy Captain Garnons-Williams of Priorities Division (P Division) made it clear to officers at ALFSEA that amalgamating SOE with OSS, or getting rid of SOE in Burma altogether, 'betrayed an ignorance of the functions of the clandestine services', the intrigue within British circles continued through the month of January. By 25 January, ALFSEA were still

---

[2] For documents related to these arguments in the discussion which follows, see National Archives, CAB 101/198; HS 1/298, 'Account of meeting held at Barrackpore', 4 January 1945; HS 7/104 Gardiner report, Chapter 6; WO 203/58, ALFSEA to Commander NCAC and A Group Force 136, 25 January 1945; WO 203/53, HQ 14 Corps to AHQ ALFSEA, 29 January 1945.

insisting that any plan to arm any of the Burmese people had to be approved by them and the Chief Civil Affairs Officer. Nearly a month after the agreement between Cumming and Slim, it seems ludicrous that ALFSEA had not been informed of Slim's intentions, nor that hundreds of Force 136 personnel were poised to go on operations during the February moon. ALFSEA had evidently even sent out a questionnaire asking 15 Indian Corps HQ in Arakan their opinions on the various secret groups operating on their front. The reply from British 15 Corps on 29 January advocated either dropping Force 136 altogether, or combining it with Z Force with a primary role of intelligence gathering.

By 31 January, the head of Force 136, Colin Mackenzie, wrote to Mountbatten that 'The principle of arming Kachins, Karens, Arakanese, etc has already been conceded', but P Division was only informed by ALFSEA that approval for arming the Karen in specific areas for Operation Character had been approved on 5 February. Arguments about arming the Nationalist Burma Defence Army and the more left-wing Anti-Fascist Organisation (AFO) rattled on – despite Mackenzie setting out for Mountbatten precise politically sound reasons for proceeding with SOE's BDA/AFO plans. In the end, as mentioned already, it took the forceful intervention of Mountbatten on 27 February to finally secure the deployment of Nation teams which were an important source of coordinated support for Operation Character.

Just how much of this complicated, high-level, political wrangling Edgar and Eustace and the Force 136 Special Groups knew about is unclear since it doesn't feature in any of the officers' reports, but Squadron Leader O'Brien knew about it. He wrote:

> The nature of the operation changed presently, and a single commander was no longer practical. The XIV Army finally decided that Force 136 could be useful, not in guerrilla activities but in

gathering intelligence, so Character was expanded to cover three separate areas in the Karen Hills, each an independent command.

The three officers in charge of Otter, Ferret, and Hyena were, therefore, awaiting the order from General Slim to go on the offensive. In the meantime, they were to send back as much intelligence as they could, as well as recruiting and training and arming the Karen volunteers. Edgar sent messages to Gurkhas who had remained in Burma since 1942, and others who worked in the Mawchi Mines. These 'old soldiers' and his Special Group men were used to train and organize the recruits 'into Sections, Platoons and Companies and [to] establish a series of Platoon Areas and Point Sections that defended the DZ in considerable depth all along the Ridge.' Furthermore, by 23 March, a month after exiting his Dakota, Edgar:

> had recruited and partly trained 350 Levies and issued rifles to 350 Static Levies without a single shot fired at a Jap; meanwhile the Army had taken MANDALAY and we awaited instructions for offensive operations.

Mandalay was Burma's second city after Rangoon. It is 390 miles due north of Rangoon on the main highway; symbolically, Mandalay was also the old capital of the Burmese kings.

56. 'Our equanimity was somewhat shaken'

Edgar may have had strict instructions not to start shooting, but the Japanese were under no such orders. Edgar's patrols had been spotted by the Japanese on 13 March near Busakyi, and the garrison at Mawchi had heard rumours of parachutists. It was in the Japanese interest to find and attack the men of Operation Character as swiftly as possible, before they established themselves, before they recruited many locals, and before supplies were dropped. It is probably testimony to the difficulties posed by the terrain that it took a fortnight for the Japanese to mount a company-sized attack on Edgar's position on Sosiso. By then, 700 levies had been recruited and partially trained, and the DZ on Sosiso had taken its first drop. A Japanese company consisted of about 180 men, organized into three platoons of around fifty-four men, plus headquarters staff and the commander, who was usually a captain. With 350 mobile levies plus the men of his Special Group on Sosiso, Edgar's first enemy contact of Operation Character had a 2/1 advantage, but most of his new recruits had never fired a rifle before.

It was just as well, then, that the Japanese 'behaved in a very brave but foolish manner', in Edgar's opinion. They approached defensive positions sited above 'very steep open spurs' which provided 'very good practice for our Levies'. The attack was driven off, but not without the loss of one dead and four wounded levies. Captain Macleod was also 'badly wounded'. Captain (later Major) John Macleod had been commissioned in 1943, and pretty soon found himself in SOE as an instructor at a training school.[1] Posted to ME25 in Ceylon from mid-1944, Macleod had dropped into Burma with Edgar on 23 February. In this attack, he had taken a bullet through the shoulder, but despite being described as 'seriously wounded' in

[1] National Archives, HS 9/968/2, Personnel file for Major John Macleod. Note spelling of surname is different to National Archives catalogue (McLeod) as advised by Macleod's grandson.

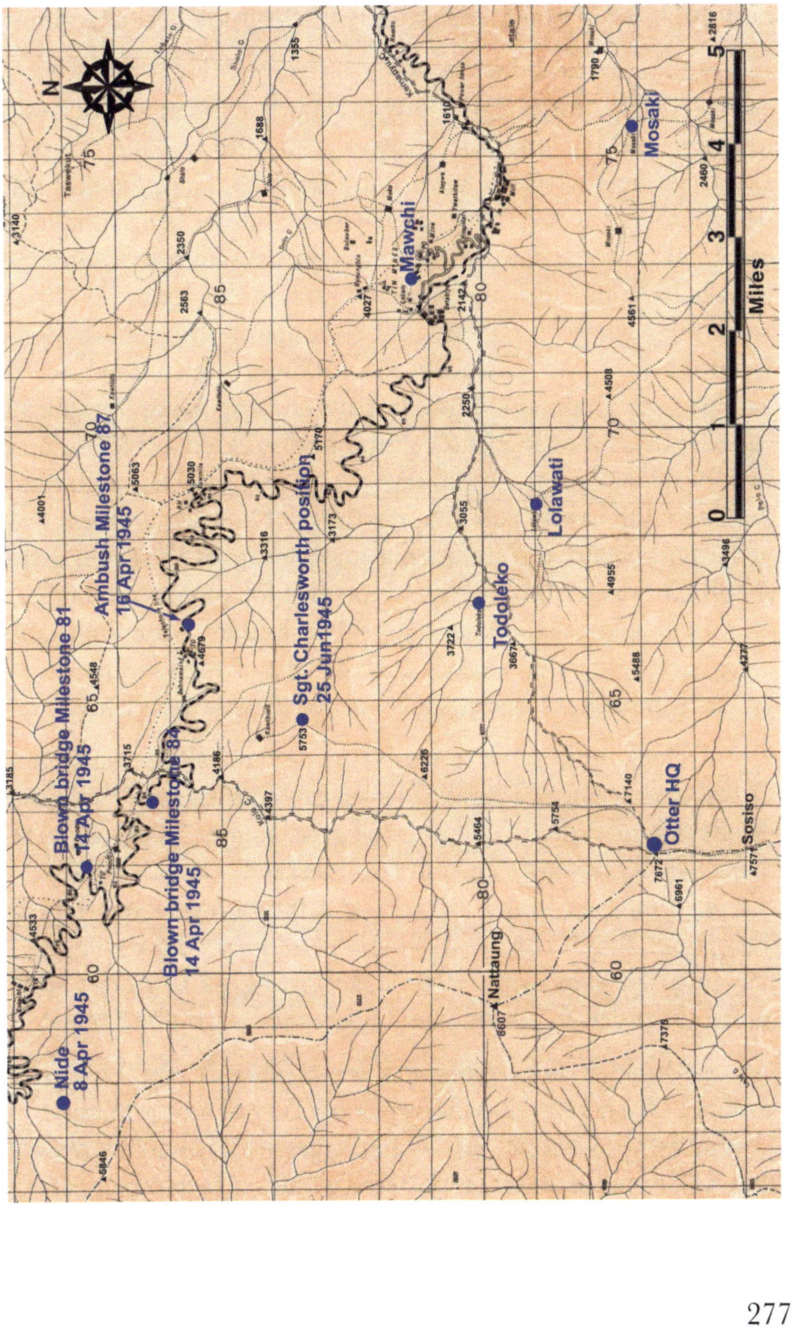
Nide
8 Apr 1945
Blown bridge Milestone 81
14 Apr 1945
Blown bridge Milestone 84
14 Apr 1945
Ambush Milestone 87
16 Apr 1945
Sgt. Charlesworth position
25 Jun 1945
Mawchi
Todoleko
Lolawati
Mosaki
Otter HQ
Sosiso
Nattaung
N
0 1 2 3 4 5
Miles

his personnel file, he remained in the field until 29 July. Edgar was evidently impressed with Captain Macleod, writing that he had displayed a 'splendid example of fortitude and devotion to duty.'

Over a forty-eight-hour period, the Japanese continued to probe and try and push forward, but after making no gains, Edgar wrote that they 'gave it up as a bad job, leaving only snipers to annoy us.' As the Japanese withdrew, levies under the command of Jemadar Saw Tun Sein were sent after them and, with help from static levies on the line of the Japanese retreat, ambushed what remained of the company four times. Edgar reported that the company commander succumbed to his wounds at Thakwiso, his company having been 'practically wiped out.' If Edgar's Otter group had suffered a 'bloody nose' with half a dozen casualties, the Japanese had suffered a devastatingly irreversible haemorrhage. There could have been no better boost to the confidence and morale of the Otter group at this early stage, and a great incentive for others to come and offer their services to Force 136. While Edgar's equanimity may have been somewhat shaken at first sight of the company-sized attack, it must have been quickly restored with this victory.

Back in the Hyena area, Turrall had also been in action. O'Brien described Turrall as 'an impetuous man' who had disobeyed the order to collect intelligence only, and to stay on the defensive. Apparently, Turrall had attacked a 'nearby village' at the beginning of March, driving out the Japanese temporarily. The Japanese returned with a platoon and forced the villagers to flee into the hills with Turrall, according to O'Brien, which 'abruptly ended the disobedient aggressive action by *Character*.'

While it is possible that both Turrall and Lieutenant Colonel Hugh Howell (who replaced Turrall as commander of Hyena) left this action out of their reports, it is equally possible that O'Brien has misrepresented Turrall's attack on the village of Kyaukkyi which came much later on 15 April. Howell wrote in his report that Hyena's operations 'were throughout 'guerrilla' in the strictest sense of the word.' To explain what he meant by this, Howell wrote that 'no action' occurred unless 'all factors' were in their favour, and that on 'only one occasion was an enemy garrison in position attacked'. This can only be a reference to the Kaukkyi action; just ten days after landing, Turrall was not really in a position to go and attack given that he needed to hide casualties and train his recruits. In fact, the Japanese, similar to the attack on Edgar at Sosiso, struck in strength on Turrall's main camp at Chawido. The attack came at 1430 hrs on 11 March, in the middle of a training session for the new recruits.

Turrall had been calling for an RAF strike on Japanese troops concentrating on Pyagawpu for four days prior to their attempt to shut Hyena down. Turrall had messaged Calcutta on 7 March:

> Kindly send fighters or our hand is forced to separate action. Awaiting reply.

To which Calcutta signalled:

> Still hope RAF will attack PYAGAWPU... If small rpt small Jap patrols move northwards and liable guage [sic] information your whereabouts you may arrange ambushes. Make sure that everything is in our favour and also that successful ambush not rpt not taken as signal for general rising.

The RAF never did come, but having been allowed to concentrate their forces, the Japanese did on 11 March. This was a significant action because, not only did it fail, similar to Sosiso, but the Japanese also lost the much-feared Kempeitai Sergeant Karashima and Lieutenant Otakay. These men had led the torture and reprisals in the hunt for Seagrim and the Harlington men, making them ubiquitous personalities throughout the Karen Hills.

Meanwhile, Eustace had been making his way north, 'slipping across the head of a Japanese force which was closing in on PYAGAWPU'. On his way to join Edgar before going on to his Ferret area, Eustace had not been able to communicate with Hyena, who had been pressed by Calcutta to take supply drops for Ferret. Turrall had been unable to do so because of Japanese pressure – but all this was unknown to Eustace, who stumbled on with the one day's rations Edgar was able to spare him at Sosiso on 18 March.

Of the three Character commanders in the field from February and through March, it seems all three needed to possess an abundance of equanimity but maybe some of Edgar's equanimity was restored with the news that he had been promoted to Lieutenant Colonel on 20 March.

57. 'Unswerving loyalty' Part Two

Where the Karen people of Burma are remembered and written about, it is invariably with great fondness and appreciation, as Edgar's full description from which the two words used to title this section illustrates. In a time, however, when the British Empire is much maligned as bringing nothing but subjugation, with attendant misery from an orgy of expropriation and violence, it begs the question: how can the Karen people, presumably the victims of said subjugation, misery, expropriation and violence, have willingly shown 'unswerving loyalty' to the British Empire? Unpacking the answer to this can, perhaps, be adequately found in the following three explanations.

Firstly, the Karen have a tradition of oral history in the form of *hta* song-poems, which are often accompanied by dances known as *dons*. One of the great stories of the beginnings of the Karen people is the story of the Golden Book. It is said that the original father of the peoples of Burma had three sons; a Karen, a Burman and a white boy, who was the youngest. Each son was given a book, but the Burman's book was eaten by white ants, and the youngest son's book was eaten by a pig. The Burman began quarrelling with his older Karen brother for possession of his Golden Book, so he entrusted it to the youngest brother, but he sailed off overseas with it. The Karen believed that one day the white son would return from over the oceans with the Golden Book, and that life would be peaceful and contented once again. In 1813, an American Baptist Missionary, Dr Judson, arrived in Burma. To the Karen, it seemed that the legend of the Golden Book had finally come true, and significant numbers of Karen happily converted to Christianity. Thus, so the narrative goes, many of the Karen people were more willing to accept British colonisation when it started in the 1820s. Before very long, they began serving the Empire, and it was more than likely that it was Karen personnel who saved Edgar after having his head sliced open in the Saya San Rebellion of 1930–32.

This is not to say that all Karen happily accepted foreign rule, of course. History is never that black and white. The Karen are a heterogeneous people, divided into twelve sub-groups. The two main languages are Sgaw Karen and Pwo Karen, accounting for about seventy per cent of the population in the twenty-first century. Besides linguistic divisions, there are important cultural and religious differences. Most Karen are Buddhist, and despite the narrative of the Golden Book as presented above, it is estimated that probably only a sixth are Christian while around two thirds are Buddhist or Buddhist with animist traditions. These differences have contributed to political schisms that Edgar and the men of Operation Character encountered, and which to some extent remain unresolved in 2024. In practical terms, what this meant for Edgar was that not all Karen were willing to fight for the British, which somewhat upsets the applecart of the traditional Anglophile narrative of relations with the Karen; at the very least it provides a caveat when taking the 'Thompson' brothers into consideration.

In 1942, the men of SOE's Oriental Mission encountered Karen villages that belonged to the Thompson Po Min Movement. The movement was named after Thompson Po Min and his brother, Johnson Po Min. It had been around for about a decade and was described as 'semi-political and semi-religious and its followers had the local reputation of being anti-British and pro-Japanese.'[1] An officer seconded to SOE's Oriental Mission reported that they were fired upon from a Thompsonite village in April 1942. Captain Arthur Thompson (his surname is simply a coincidence here) was in charge of a company of Karen serving in the Burma Rifles, retreating along the same road from Toungoo to Mawchi that Edgar and Eustace were preparing to attack in April 1945. Those Thompsonite

---

[1] National Archives, HS 1/27, Report on the Oriental Mission, p.27.

villages hadn't gone anywhere, and Calcutta signalled a warning:

> Good source reports Japs using followers of THOMPSONITE Movement to track down parachutists in MAWCHI area

Further south, Turrall believed that the attack on his base on 11 March had been assisted by 'mistakenly employing individuals either planted or at least ready to inform'. This was based on the observation that in the attack on Chawido, the Japanese 'made a bee-line' for the officers' area, having picked the one possible route to get there. Nevertheless, Poles wrote in his report that:

> The very real loyalty of the Karens cannot be questioned [...] Their welcome was obviously sincere and their faith and trust amazing, and often very touching.

Despite the Thompsonite exception to the rule, then, on the whole, the post-operational reports of all the officers who served on Operation Character praise the loyalty of the Karen. A large measure of this must of course be attributed to the unique bonds forged between men who share combat together, but aside from this and the oral history described in the story of the Golden Book (and the subsequent conversion to Christianity by some Karen communities), there must be more compelling reasons for this narrative of loyalty.

Secondly, then, the Karen people, as far as has been ascertained, migrated south from Tibetan lands around 2500 years ago, settling in the hills between the central plains of Burma and the Siamese/Thai border. Their relations with the Burmans, or Bamar, had been fractious throughout these millennia. Despite both races practising Buddhism, there seems to have been little else in common, and religion wasn't enough to ensure peaceful relations. This had been shown most recently in the massacres of Karen in Myaungmya in 1942, when the Burma Independence Army under Aung San marched into

Burma with the Japanese Imperial Army to 'liberate' colonial Burma. The reprisals in the hunt for the Harlington personnel were also often led by – or at least in cooperation with – Bamar men serving in what was now called the Burma Defence Army. The Karen, so the normal narrative goes, were recruited by the British because they would happily fight the majority Bamar population, their traditional, long-standing enemies.

Again, however, care needs to be taken with such generalized narratives. As has been related here, Edgar recruited Bamar personnel in the Chindwin area. These same men became his Special Groups for Operation Character. The men who dropped into Burma in February 1945 were, therefore, a mix of Karen and Bamar who had already fought together on the Indo-Burmese border. Edgar himself wrote:

> Curiously enough, 80% of the men in these Groups were Burmese whom I had recruited in the CHINDWIN Valley in 1943. In spite of the hereditary antipathy between Karen and Burman these men gained the trust of the Karens and were accepted in most cases as leaders of the Levies. Many people who talk loosely of the character of the Burmese would do well to study their record in CHARACTER Operation and consider whether the nature of the Burman or their own attitude towards him is responsible for many unpleasant incidents during the evacuation of 1942.

During the war and into the post-war period, there were Karen who were willing to work with the Bamar. Not all Karen fought against the government of the new Union of Burma after the country was given independence in January 1948, and indeed it was ex-Burif Karen Rifles units who prevented the communist Bamar rebels from seizing power in Rangoon in 1949, thereby saving the Union government.

So while there is something in the explanation that the Karen looked to the British for protection from their traditional enemies during the 120 years or so of British colonization before the Second World War, and that there were significant recent atrocities which incentivized fighting against both the Bamar and the Japanese, even just Edgar's Special Groups – and Operation Character more widely – demonstrate that explanations of Karen loyalty based on turbulent ethnic relations are not so straightforward.

Lastly, Leslie Glass worked in the Burma Civil Service from 1934 until 1947. In his memoir, *The Changing of the Kings*, he relates how, after 1949, British arms were sent to the government of the Union of Burma. By that year, despite having prevented the communists toppling the fledgling administration, the civil war between Burma's various ethnic communities which continues in 2024 was well under way. Glass wrote that the news that British-supplied arms were being used against the Karen was not well received: 'I have been stopped on the street by men who fought beside the Karens in the war, who have urged this point upon me with tears in their eyes.'

In private collections of documents, various officers from Operation Character continued corresponding with their Karen friends through the decades after the war, despite the difficulties of postage. There was even a conspiracy to help the Karen in their fight against the Bamar government by secretly shipping weapons to them in 1949. The man in charge of this failed endeavour was none other than Lieutenant Colonel Tulloch, the former commander of Operation Character's team Walrus. The point is that there is an abundance of evidence to demonstrate that many of the British who knew the Karen *liked* them. It's not at all too far-fetched to assert that the loyalty under discussion here can be seen to work both ways; it was not simply *for* the colonizer *from* the colonized. Another SOE officer, Major Alex Campbell, who was arrested by the Burma Government for his part in the gun-running plans, lamented the fact that had they had a proper briefing about the people of Karenni before Operation Character, it 'may have prevented some of the officers from treating the Karens as 'wogs"'.

What all this demonstrates is that human relationships are – unsurprisingly – complicated, nuanced, and far from universal in application. Even putting that aside, attempting to explain why a minority population were 'unswerving' in their loyalty to a foreign empire across a gap of eighty years is not without its own challenges. Nonetheless, it is hoped that some idea of who the people are that Edgar spent months behind the lines with can be appreciated, along with the challenges and triumphs of navigating those relationships. And from April 1945, when the Character teams transitioned from a passive intelligence to an overwhelmingly intense combat role, those relationships flourished in a way that only those who have endured such conditions can appreciate.

58. 'The Japs were extremely careless at first'

In order to cut off the Japanese forces in Mandalay facing 14 Army's 33 Corps, a massive deception plan was put into operation. Lieutenant General Frank Messervy's 4 Corps had quietly snuck south from Kalewa to cross the Irrawaddy River to the west of Meiktila. The deception worked to the extent that the Japanese did not believe their own reports and had only days to prepare their defences before 4 Corps fell on the town on 28 February. At the same time, further north, 33 Corps invested the city of Mandalay. By 28 March, the battle for both objectives was over, and the drive south towards Rangoon could continue. The two Corps now crossed paths so that they swapped their flanks. It was now 4 Corps that was racing for Toungoo before the Japanese could regroup there, while on the other side of the Pegu Yomas, 33 Corps made for Prome.

Force 136 had helped to make the capture of Meiktila possible. After Mountbatten's intervention at the beginning of February, eight teams of Operation Nation were dropped behind the lines in February and March, with another three going in during April. Teams codenamed Weasel, Pig, Jackal, Reindeer and Zebra landed on a DZ forty miles south of Toungoo. The Reindeer team, under the command of Major Dave Britton, quickly left for their area of operations and by 12 April had armed and trained 300 men. By that date they were already in action, hitting the Japanese lines of communication – road, river, and rail – smashing reinforcements trying to get to Toungoo. Meanwhile, northeast of Major Britton, Japanese 15 Division were retreating through the Shan States to reach Mawchi. They had to run the gauntlet of three Operation Character teams in order to reach Toungoo; Tulloch's Walrus, Eustace's Ferret, and Edgar's Otter group. SOE teams were thus blocking the two major arteries serving Toungoo.

'THE JAPS WERE EXTREMELY CARELESS AT FIRST'

The Reindeer team were somewhat belatedly ordered by 14 Army to start hitting the Japanese on 19 April. Edgar received the same order on 10 April, which was the day after Reindeer had actually started offensive operations. Edgar had already anticipated this order, having heard that the Army was fighting for Meiktila by early March. Accordingly, he had deployed platoons to five locations along the road from Mawchi towards Toungoo. On 16 April, when 4 Corps reached Pyinmana, Japanese 15 Division reached Mawchi. Pyinmana is about seventy miles north of Toungoo, while Mawchi is about the same distance to the east. There is no doubt that it would have been a very close-run race if Edgar and Force 136 had not been ready to hit 15 Division on the road. It also helped that 'The Japs were extremely careless at first.'

On 16 April, the first truckloads of Japanese troops left Mawch during the night. Two bridges had already been blown by Captain Montague and Jemadar Saw Na Mu, but 'the Japs appeared unaware of the fact.' Not that it would have made any difference, for the first action of Otter ambushed the lead trucks three miles from the first smashed bridge. Edgar recorded that it was Jemadar Maung Po Sein, a Burman, who drew first blood for Otter. Stepping on to the road armed with Gammon grenades, he blew up the lead truck, losing his right eye from a splinter in the process. The rest of the Jemadar's Otter men now sprang into action and the Japanese retreated back to Mawchi. Being 'careless' yet again the next night, the Japanese tried to drive down the road in exactly the same way, and again they were forced to retreat to Mawchi. The Otter teams had already bought 4 Corps two days in the race for Toungoo.

On the third night, the Japanese changed their tactics. Infantry went ahead of the motor transport in strength, forcing the new guerrillas back from the road. The Japanese reached the broken bridges and it took three days to repair them while 'fighting continued in a confused manner'. Once repaired, the

Japanese could continue down the road, but Otter was not done with them yet.

Between milestone 75 and milestone 50, Jemadar Saw Na Mu and Jemadar Tun Sein had been setting Cordtex traps. The Cordtex method had been perfected by P Force during Chindwin patrols and used outside of their defensive box at Palel during the Battle of Imphal. All the recruited levies 'lined up along the road' and with the Cordtex ambush and their small arms, 'the Jap 15th Division had a most unpleasant journey on their way to TOUNGOO.' Japanese vehicles were thrown off the road and down the steep slopes by the Cordtex traps, which 'worked like a charm', while Gammon grenades blew them up on the road, and the levies took their toll with their small arms. The Japanese made futile attempts to chase Edgar's men up the steep slopes, and their mortars – for once – were ineffective. The Otter men had the upper hand, and were firmly in control:

> The levies enjoyed themselves very much during this period. Being far more mobile than the Japs, we were never cut off and hardly one of us was killed. Indeed it is most difficult to kill these hillmen. One of them was shot squarely in the right lung, through the jaw and again through the left hand, and was left for dead. He was, however, very far from dead, and walked up nearly 2,000 ft and 3 miles during the night to our Point Section, where I found him. He eventually recovered.

For their part, being 'extremely careless', the Japanese were easily dispatched. Edgar described them as 'a brave but poor lot' who never seemed to learn from their experiences. Time and again ambushes and booby traps, such as a large rock left on the road, 'would act like a magnet' with the resulting explosion causing casualties.

On 23 April, the tanks of 5 Division of 4 Corps reached Toungoo ahead of the Japanese. It is estimated that Japanese 15

'THE JAPS WERE EXTREMELY CARELESS AT FIRST'

Division was held up for at least a week by the ambushes of Edgar's men, preventing the Japanese from establishing themselves in Toungoo and blocking the advance of 14 Army. This significant achievement was recognized by General Slim who wrote that Force 136's 'greatest achievement was the delaying of the 15th Japanese Division in the Loikaw-Mawchi area, thus enabling IV Corps to reach Toungoo first'.[1] This was because 'levies led by their British officers [...] had a real influence on operations.' That 'influence' contributed a great deal to the recapture of Rangoon by 3 May, because if 14 Army had been held up in central Burma, the Japanese would not have needed to leave the city, and Operation Dracula would have been an opposed landing if indeed it had gone ahead at all.

It had helped that the Japanese were 'extremely careless', but Edgar was where he had worked tirelessly to be, and now he was there, he was making a meaningful contribution to the war in Burma just as he had always known he could. It was only April, with two months behind the lines already behind him, and another six hard months ahead.

---

[1] National Archives CAB 106/48, General Slim, 'Account of operations of Fourteenth Army 1944-1945', p.29.

59. 'Their greatest achievement'

Edgar's post-operational report is divided into sections which he called phases. The phase in which 'the Japanese were extremely careless' was numbered 'PHASE IV' and given the dates 23 March to 23 April. The latter date was when the race for Toungoo had been won; Edgar might have seen this as a decisive moment in his time on Operation Character – but it is more obvious that his phases go from the 23rd of each month because he parachuted in on the night of 23 February. In any case, in preventing the Japanese from reaching Toungoo first, he reckoned that 'During this month we killed approximately 307 Japs and destroyed 30 M.T. [Motor Transport].' Of more significance than the casualties inflicted is of course the time that Japanese 15 Division lost dealing with ambushes, booby traps, smashed bridges and failed attempts to pursue their quarry. This then, was Edgar and Otter's contribution. What of Ferret and Walrus during this phase? What had they done to help prevent the Japanese beating 14 Army into Toungoo?

The short answer to that question for the Ferret team, answered in the report of Major Poles is, perhaps surprisingly, not very much at all. Eustace was clearly an extremely frustrated man who was unable to do very much to help Edgar by way of attacking the road, though he was able to start fulfilling his operational mandate in other ways. Having landed at Pyagawpu, miles from the proposed Ferret area, and with the severe injuries sustained in that parachute drop, the Ferret team's situation didn't improve thereafter. Even aside from finally arriving where they should have been, and the utter confusion caused by having Walrus group dropped on the night of 24 March, several more headaches plagued Eustace for the next month.

The difficulties encountered seem to revolve primarily around three main headaches: communications, relations with the Jedburgh personnel, and supply. All three overlapped, exacerbating each other to the point where Eustace's equanimity was probably more than severely shaken. After sustaining the casualties in the original drop, Flight Lieutenant Breen was the only competent W/T operator, and they only had one B2 radio set and a couple of batteries that they could carry off with them from Pyagawpu. The batteries would need charging, however, and the generator to do so was broken. With this in mind, reinforcements and more W/T equipment were expected when they reached Hoya.

The W/T must have been working for a period of time, for Eustace writes that Breen sent their location to Calcutta every day, and that these signals were acknowledged, but that they received no message in reply. A clue to why this may have been has been added to the report in pen: 'Breen withheld Calcutta's signals'. Whether this is true or not can only be speculated upon from this distance, but it is clear that relations between Eustace and the Jeds were far from satisfactory. His relationship with Calcutta was in the same state, having been ordered back to the Mawchi Road and receiving no urgent supplies. By the end of March, Eustace and his men 'were in rags' and they 'had not had a square meal for many days' added to which their 'boots were all worn out.' Having just persuaded a reluctant headman to support a Karen uprising, he also needed an immediate arms drop to make good on his side of the bargain. Then, on 29 March, the W/T 'batteries had finally given up' and Ferret went off air. A patrol was sent to Edgar to get some communications equipment; it was gone for three weeks.

It then became necessary to send another party to Edgar, because the 'Mk.3 sets intended for intergroup communication had all been dropped to OTTER whereas the crystals and plans were dropped to us.' This provoked another flashpoint between Eustace and Captain Dumont, one of the Jedburgh officers. Dumont refused the order to visit Otter to reunite the signals equipment. As far as Eustace was concerned, since his arrival, Dumont 'took no pains to hide his nature, which was both selfish and undisciplined. It was necessary to reprimand him on several occasions.' The Jeds, including Breen, apparently wanted an independent role, such as they had been told to expect in Calcutta, but which Edgar had very clearly stated would not happen back on 18 February before despatch. In the end, Eustace told the Jed team that they would come under the direct command of Edgar as Otter area commander, rather than him as a group commander, since he 'was powerless to take suitable disciplinary action.'

Meanwhile, the team that had caused much of the Ferret group's hardship had been deployed on a 'hot' DZ by Squadron Leader O'Brien. They were forced on the run immediately on landing, but by the first week in April they were ready to start organizing what was now to be the Walrus area of operations. Tulloch reported that by 18 April he had armed 2000 recruits. By this date, of course, Japanese 15 Division was making its third attempt to break out from Mawchi down the road to Toungoo. Tulloch had therefore missed 15 Division, so Walrus group played no part in delaying the division from reaching Toungoo. There was still action to be had with the 2000 recruits Walrus had raised, however, because Japanese 56 Division was yet to pass south from Loikaw towards Bawlake.

Ultimately, what the Ferret and Walrus reports unambiguously show is that they were not ready to go into action until after 18 April, when it was too late to help Otter in the race for Toungoo. It was the Reindeer team of Operation Nation under Major Britton who ended up supplying the balance of Force 136's assistance to 14 Army. According to Sergeant Brierley, who wrote the post-operation report after Major Britton's death, between 9 and 23 April, Reindeer accounted for 216 Japanese soldiers, twenty trucks, a car, a motorbike, one motor train and two boats. Brierley claimed that no trains were able to reach Toungoo, and that Reindeer provided intelligence disclosing

Japanese positions around Toungoo. Those positions were subjected to air attack which caused 'colossal damage to MT [Motor Transport], and other stores, and destroy[ed] several Jap HQs'.[1]

Reindeer was not in a position to attack Japanese 15 Division, though, so it is reasonable to assert that if it was not for Edgar and his organization of Otter, 15 Division would have reached Toungoo ahead of 14 Army as they would have been unopposed. 'What if' history, as already discussed in the context of the Battle of Imphal, is an inexact game, but at least the question can be asked: what would the impact on Operation Extended Capital have been if the Japanese 15 Army had reinforced Toungoo? The Army commander, General Slim, believed – as already seen above – that for Force 136 it was 'their greatest achievement'.

---

[1] National Archives, HS 1/12, Brierley report, pp.4-5.

60. 'An extremely trying month for all of us'

The tanks of 5 Division did not hang around in Toungoo. Sweeping on south, the race was now to reach Rangoon before the monsoon began. In between 5 Division leaving and 19 Indian Division arriving, the Japanese did momentarily find themselves at liberty in Toungoo before 19 Indian Division drove them back out. Japanese forces were now backed up along the road, and considerable-sized formations were roaming away from the road looking for routes south, but also trying to find food. Food also became the preoccupation of the locals and of the Force 136 teams. It seems it was not so much the Japanese as the food situation which made these weeks 'an extremely trying month for all of us', as Edgar wrote.

Edgar's men in their forward positions were living off the land, while his garrison up on Sosiso were reduced to '¾lb rice per man per day and a little salt.' Edgar reckoned that by the end of April, Otter had two days' worth of food left. It was getting to the point where Edgar faced 'the certainty of having to abandon our base and disperse.' Although a formal document, Edgar's anger and frustration in his report is obvious; in the end, 'in desperation', he petitioned the Army Commander (presumably Slim) directly. He was rewarded with a fortnight's worth of food on 4 May. By then, Rangoon was in Allied hands and the monsoon had started.

If Edgar's anger and frustration is obvious in his report, then Eustace was even blunter. For Ferret:

> This was the most dreadful period during the whole operation. My group was quite literally starved not only of food, but of the sinews of war also. My signals imploring assistance were ignored. Sorties which we were warned to expect did not materialise. We were told that bad weather

prohibited drops on occasions when we could see our aircraft flying over the D.Z. on other missions.

As an example of the 'sinews of war' that Eustace refers to, his ammunition was running short as they had not had a resupply since dropping into Burma ten weeks earlier.

News from the Walrus group was not encouraging either. On 24 April, 800 Japanese attacked Tulloch's HQ at Hoya while he was away seeing about stories of levies deserting.[1] There were no desertions, but with rumours of large bands of Japanese leaving the road, some men had gone to defend their villages from being burned down, as the village of Mohso had been. When he reached Hoya in the evening, the village had been torched and his HQ scattered. The next day he estimated that a further 2000 enemy soldiers arrived in Hoya. Not put off by the numbers, nor by the fact that he only had a single Bren gun and ten rifles at his disposal, the Japanese were engaged 'from advantageous positions'. These Japanese troops were making for Toungoo, but had decided to leave the road after having been ambushed by Major Denning in a more northern part of the Walrus area.

While Tulloch recovered his HQ and moved it closer to the road for better oversight of offensive operations, Edgar began to face a new problem. From early May, starving refugees began arriving at his HQ. They were mostly women and children, and as the days passed towards the end of the month, he had an extra 650 mouths to feed. Messages were sent back to India, asking for 'special relief drops' on 12 and 19 May, but he was told to send the civilians on to Toungoo. With substantial Japanese forces between Otter group and 19 Indian Division, Edgar did not think it feasible to send them off. The inevitable consequence was that the food situation became dire, and impacted upon the main reason Operation Character was in the

---

[1] National Archives, HS 7/106, Report of Lt. Col. Tulloch.

field – to prosecute guerrilla warfare. Edgar simply could not 'understand the failures to assist us to build up reserves of food.'

Despite the food situation, Edgar kept his Otter area tightly controlled and attacks on the Japanese continued during this phase. Welcome reinforcements arrived on 4 and 8 May in the form of seven officers, eight Kachins, and a platoon of Assam Rifles. All were deployed to sub-areas to cover the various southern escape routes that the Japanese could make use of. In the end, Otter ended up with seven sub-areas, all using colours to denote their area of operations. Eustace was in charge of Otter Red; Flight Lieutenant Breen had Otter White, and Otter Green was under the command of Captain Montague, for example. There were plenty of Japanese to attack, with both Japanese 15 and 56 Divisions stuck in the Karen Hills. There were also Indian National Army units to engage. Accordingly, Otter HQ at Sosiso:

> Became the centre of a ring of outposts working from one to two days march from it; but all in mutual support of each other and ready to fall back in defence of the base if an organised attack should be made against it. We had a full platoon of runners in addition to intercom wireless sets, and all posts were in constant touch with the base.

Unable to get to Toungoo, Japanese 15 Division regrouped at Mawchi with the intention of taking the track south towards Papun. Mawchi thus presented a busy target for airstrike, but like the supply aircraft, the fighters never came. Edgar wrote that this was 'One of our major disappointments during this period'. Despite repeated signals and good weather, Mawchi was never hit, which Edgar described as 'heartbreaking'. Edgar was also most miffed about the situation for his friend Eustace; not only was it 'lamentable' that Eustace was unable to hit the road, but Edgar was aware of the 'many privations' he had to suffer during these weeks. That Eustace had been unable to get into action was due to the mess of the Walrus deployment, Edgar reasoned, and had he been informed that this was going to happen, he would have ensured that the area north of the road was ready to commence offensive operations: 'I attribute this failure entirely to the authorities responsible for briefing'. Due to this 'signal failure on the part of the controlling staff' many more Japanese were alive to pose a threat to the Otter guerrillas.

Perhaps, during this period, the greatest achievement of Force 136 was staying alive, evading the remaining troops of two Japanese divisions and, with no supply drops, continuing the fight. It had been hoped that 19 Indian Division would make its way up the road from Toungoo and keep the pressure on the enemy, but like supplies and airstrikes, this proved a forlorn hope too. As it was, Edgar reported that a further 680 Japanese and 45 trucks were accounted for up to 23 May 1945.

61. 'A seething furious mass of dense vapour'

For the Character teams far behind the lines in April, with eyes on grade one targets such as the Japanese concentration at Mawchi and begging for arms and food to be better able to take the war to the enemy, watching empty blue skies for supply aircraft was deeply frustrating. In the post-operational reports of many Character commanders, the Force 136 staff back in India take the brunt of the criticism, but perhaps they were wrong to heap all the blame on officers that Tulloch believed had 'been given a Staff appointment without some experience in the Field.' India Mission was well acquainted with the difficulties of long-range sorties into Burma, as witnessed by the eight months of Harlington failures during 1943. Admittedly, the arrival of Liberators and Dakotas – more than anything – improved the situation, but there were other constants, such as the terrain and the weather, which could and did still confound RAF operations.

Squadron Leader O'Brien, who, after dropping most of the Character teams into Karenni in February continued to pilot supply aircraft, offers some insight from the RAF point of view. As far as he remembered when he wrote *The Moonlight War*, the order to the Character teams to 'launch a full-scale offensive' came 'without any warning'. While it is obvious that he is wrong in that it was not a surprise to the Character teams, perhaps it was for him and his RAF pilots. Where he had been flying by moonlight, now his squadron was expected to fly sorties during the day to up the tempo. There was negligible interference from the Japanese air force, rather; 'our enemy was the weather':

> cumulonimbus start[ed] edging up Burma from mid-March onwards, growing ever more numerous until finally they are no longer individual clouds but just the vast grey turmoil of the monsoon rains. So at this mid-April stage there were days when you had to pick your way carefully over the hills,

when if you stayed under the isolated cumulonimbus the air currents over the rugged terrain would have the aircraft bucking and jolting like a fractious beast, and if instead you stayed above then you had to go swaying and sliding through the great white canyons on a track like Chesterton's drunkard

O'Brien then goes on to specifically describe making drops to Edgar at Sosiso, what he called 'Otter-on-the-Hill'. Making a drop to Edgar's headquarters was 'most demanding' because of its height. During the monsoon, Sosiso at over 7500ft (about 2300m) was 'frequently in cloud or obscured by rain, and almost invariably beset by violent winds.' There were two routes to get there, one of which took eight hours, the other taking eleven, but either way, 'you were always having to weave a route into the site.' These monsoon clouds were extremely dangerous to aircraft; not for nothing did O'Brien describe them as a 'violent turmoil, a seething furious mass of dense vapour; they are the equivalent of great oil fires with their coils of smoke, twisting and turning in awesome power'. In the period up to the Allied capture of Toungoo, O'Brien wrote that three aircraft on sorties for Operation Character were lost to the clouds, with all sixteen aircrew.

The Operational Record book for O'Brien's 357 SD Squadron shows that in the month of April, there were seventy-nine attempted sorties to supply the five Character teams that were in the field by that time, more than doubling the number flown to Character in March:[1]

---

[1] National archives, AIR 27/1761/7, Operations Record Book, 357 SD Squadron.

Team	Sorties	Successful	Unsuccessful	% success
Otter	30	22	8	73%
Walrus	20	15	5	75%
Ferret	10	7	3	70%
Hyena	10	9	1	90%
Mongoose	9	7	2	77%

Since Edgar's was the only team really involved in preventing Japanese 15 Division from reaching Toungoo, the preponderance given to Otter is perhaps justified, but even so, as already described, Edgar's supply situation became critical. What needs to be borne in mind, however, is the total commitments of 357 Squadron. A total of 144 sorties were flown in April for twenty-three operations across Burma, Malaya, and French Indochina. Over half of these sorties went to Character, and almost twenty-one per cent of the total sorties went to Edgar. From the point of view of the RAF – and probably the much maligned Force 136 staff officers in Calcutta – these statistics were ground-breaking and impressive. For the men on the ground, though, however impressive the stats, being desperate for food and ammunition, as well as living in rotting clothes and boots, was their stark reality.

With the entry for each sortie there is often a description of the DZ, and the weather is always described for the flight in and out as well as specifically over the DZ. Comments about the DZ at Sosiso from the various officers in charge of the aircraft who flew sorties to Edgar vary slightly in their appreciation. For example, Squadron Leader Lee commented that the 'DZ is bad being a long narrow ridge on top of a hill almost always in cloud', rather corroborating O'Brien's assessment; others reported it was good for daylight, but 'no use for night'; another officer wrote that the DZ was 'fair' but 'suitable for moon drops only if the area is known'. Flight Lieutenant Smith had a clear DZ which enabled him to record that the 'DZ is very good'.

When all is said and done, the fact is supplies were able to be dropped to Edgar, most with remarkable accuracy, and the DZ was never compromised by the enemy, though it was, once, by a tiger!

While the men on the ground and the men in the air had to contend with their own priorities and problems, Edgar and the other Character officers all recognized and paid homage in their reports to the courage and skill of those who did their best to sustain and protect them – the pilots and crew of the RAF, the RCAF (Canadian), RAAF (Australian) and RNZAF (New Zealand).[2]

---

[2] According to AIR 27/1761/7, 357 Squadron consisted of 631 RAF personnel, 76 Canadians, 22 Australians, and 3 New Zealanders.

62. 'We should have been in excellent shape to kill the Japs'

By 23 May, Edgar reckoned his Otter area had recruited over 2000 levies, divided between the different sub-commands of 'Black', 'Green', 'Red' and 'White'. There were still plenty of Japanese troops in the vicinity, including 113 Regiment, who Edgar considered to be a 'tough proposition'. The Japanese 113 Regiment was part of 56 Division, which, along with 33 Division, was heading south after fighting further north in Burma and over the border in Yunnan Province, China. In the period that Edgar called 'PHASE VI' from 23 May to 23 June, apparently 1147 men of 113 Regiment 'made, presumably, happy reunions with their ancestors.' Yet, if Edgar had been supplied with the 3' mortars and some medium machine guns, as requested, he reported that 'we should have been in excellent shape to kill the Japs.' With refugees to manage and deficient in medical and food stocks, Phase Six continued to be a tough proposition with or without 113 Regiment as the men endured life without food in the monsoon-soaked jungle.

Looking at the operational records of 357 Special Duties Squadron, it is interesting that supply comes in for so much criticism from the Force 136 teams of Operation Character. During May, at least twenty-five sorties were flown to Edgar's Otter group. These flights were not on consecutive days – the 6 and 9 May, for example, had four sorties each – but it does show a concerted effort on the part of Force 136 HQ and the RAF to keep Otter supplied. Of these twenty-five attempts, five were unsuccessful, giving a success rate of eighty per cent. Two of these failed sorties never got beyond the Bay of Bengal due to the wall of cloud confronting the pilots, while just three were due to clouds covering Edgar's HQ.

The tenacity of the RAF crews, who knew that the men on the ground were relying on them, can't be faulted. On 26

'WE SHOULD HAVE BEEN IN EXCELLENT SHAPE TO KILL THE JAPS'

May, for example, the top of Sosiso could be seen, but the DZ couldn't, so they flew off to make a drop at Ferret and then returned to Sosiso. With gaps beginning to appear in the cloud, the 'DZ was visible for limited periods' and these were used to make the drops. Six days earlier, cloud had 'covered all hills and valleys in DZ area', so the pilot made various runs in an attempt to get under the cloud base, but was unsuccessful. The increased time over the DZ meant that the aircraft was low on fuel for the return journey to Jessore, and was forced to refuel at Akyab Island in the Bay of Bengal. Akyab was used for the same reason, again, on 24 May.

While Edgar and his men faced the Japanese and the elements, refugees and supply shortages, on 16 May, Mountbatten had broadcast his 'Order of the Day'. It is recorded in the 357 Squadron records, but it is not known if Edgar would have received it. Certainly none of the Character team reports mention it. The Supremo congratulated his servicemen:

> You have won the race for Rangoon, and beaten the monsoon as well as the Japanese. The fall of the capital 10 days before the rains will be upon you, brings to an end the Battle for Burma, for although isolated pockets of the enemy remain, their doom is now sealed.

A little further on, Mountbatten continued:

> From Kohima to Rangoon, you covered in this great battle 1000 miles of the worst country in the world and under the world's worst climate and conditions.

For the men of Force 136, the 'Battle for Burma' was far from over. In their drive for Rangoon, 14 Army had sliced south past the Pegu Yomas, where an estimated 10,000 Japanese were beginning to collect, now trapped in the interior of the country. These men were trying to make their way to the southeast of

Burma, to regroup with their countrymen east of Rangoon. At the same time, 50,000 Japanese were in the Character area of operations making for the same destination. These enemy forces realized fairly swiftly that 14 Army had settled down to rest and reorganize. There was, therefore, still one hell of a battle left to be fought in Burma, and most of it was to be fought by Edgar and Force 136. This fight was not against 'isolated pockets' of Japanese either, but it definitely was still in rough country 'under the world's worst climate and conditions.'

It must be acknowledged that what the Allied Army had achieved was spectacular. The Japanese had attacked Manipur in March 1944; it was now May 1945. With this in mind, what Eustace had to say in his report seems somewhat more acceptable, even though it put the entire Character operation under a tremendous amount of pressure. On 21 June:

> I discovered depressing news, which was that not only were all Units of 19 Div. greatly depleted by casualties, but so exhausted after their long Burma campaign that the Div. was no longer capable of undertaking an offensive role, and it was unlikely there would be any further advance before the end of the monsoon.

Edgar received the same information in mid-July when he asked after 19 Indian Division's intentions:

> I was advised that 19th Div. was also worn and exhausted and would not press beyond milestone 30 on the road [from Toungoo] unless the Japs withdrew.

For Tulloch in Walrus area, the consequences were clear enough:

> I state categorically that had Army only maintained their presume [sic] up to the end of May or middle of June, the Jap forces in the

'WE SHOULD HAVE BEEN IN EXCELLENT SHAPE TO KILL THE JAPS'

Loikaw-Bawlake area would have disintegrated and the Karen Hills liberated three months earlier than they were. Unfortunately, after the capture of Rangoon, the Army appeared to rest on its laurels.

The reason why Edgar was not 'in excellent shape to kill the Japs' was not due to a lack of effort by the RAF then, but the understandable exhaustion of 14 Army and its consequent inability to maintain a robust offensive capability. Not only that, the focus of the Army had shifted to the next objective: the invasion of Malaya. This, coupled with a lack of the required weapons and the food to sustain them, meant that Edgar's guerrillas were about to face an emboldened enemy.

63. 'His head was lying a few yards from his body'

Phase Seven of Edgar's operation ran from 23 June to 23 July. During this month, his priority appears to have been getting refugees to safety and preventing the Japanese from knocking him off his mountain-top base. Since there was not enough food, Edgar wrote that he was 'obliged' to try and get 'these poor wretches to TOUNGOO as best we could.' On 24 June, Captain Marchant and Sergeant Romain, supported by two platoons of mobile levies, set out with 500 hungry civilians. Using jungle paths to evade the enemy, they made it to their destination by 30 June. On 10 July, another 250 refugees made a similar journey. Two accompanying officers were evacuated to India after shepherding their charges to safety: Captain Buchanan, who had a severe case of dysentery, and Captain Macleod, who had been shot through the shoulder during the Japanese attack on Sosiso at the end of March.

On 25 June, the day after the refugees left, the Japanese decided to have another go at Edgar's HQ. Using a captured Karen levy as a guide, a surprise attack was made on a platoon position on the main spur that led up to the Otter base. The platoon was 'at half strength when attacked':

> Nevertheless, the Gurkha levies who manned it put up a grand fight till all ammunition was exhausted and then retired in good order. To my great regret Sgt. CHARLESWORTH of 'Z' Force was killed in this action.

There is no SOE file for Sergeant Charlesworth because he was on attachment from Z Force, but there is a file for Major Frederick Charlesworth, who was part of Lieutenant Colonel Tulloch's Walrus group. In an example of fortunate yet erroneous filing, there is a page about Sergeant Charlesworth in

'HIS HEAD WAS LYING A FEW YARDS FROM HIS BODY'

Major Charlesworth's personnel file. It is a message that Edgar signalled to Calcutta on 6 July:

> Greatly regret report CHARLESWORTH Z Force missing believed killed in action. When forward platoon overrun by Japs on 25th after a long fight was not among those who withdrew. Had hoped that he had found his way through jungle to some Karen village but extensive inquiry and search has failed to find him. Position still strongly held by Japs and cannot be absolutely sure but think from reports of men with him that there is little doubt he was killed. You will have gathered from Signal 306 dated 20 June how greatly I valued Charlesworth's services.[1]

The Japanese continued their attack after 25 June, and there was more 'stiff fighting' which explains why eleven days later the Japanese were still in control of the outpost where Charlesworth had been killed. Edgar wrote in his report that 'to retake these positions would have been costly' so another approach was put into action:

> I sent parties to hedge them round with grenade and explosive traps, which were duly sprung. A second set of traps was placed on all approaches and was again sprung. The Japs then evacuated the position, and we were able to give Sgt. CHARLESWORTH a decent burial.

The next part of the account reveals yet more of what the Japanese armed forces became infamous for during the Second World War:

> We found the Karen who had been forced to lead the Japs to CHARLESWORTH's position lying

---

[1] National Archives, HS 9/299/1, Personnel file for Major Frederick Charlesworth.

outside the defences; but his head was lying a few yards from his body.

What the document with the signals to Calcutta makes clear, and which Edgar's report doesn't, is that the position was still occupied by the Japanese eleven days after the first attack. Presumably the Japanese were happy to simply coexist with the two corpses for all of that time.

It was not only Edgar that the emboldened Japanese moved against in June. Three weeks before the attack on Edgar's HQ, on 4 June, Eustace wrote that 'the enemy started an organized offensive on our outposts. Their first blow was a full company attack on KUBYAUNG'. In an attack on another outpost, heavy mortars were brought up on ponies, and such was the ferocity of the attack that 'mobile levies deserted' and the 'position was overrun, with the loss of all stores. The enemy suffered no casualties.' On 15 June, Captain Ansell's outpost at Dodo was attacked, and also successfully taken.

The story was the same just north of Eustace, in Tulloch's Walrus area. In early June, it became much harder for the men of Walrus to attack the road because the Japanese began 'well-ordered convoys protected by tankettes and armoured cars.' Like Edgar, Tulloch asked the Army 'for more cooperation' but none was forthcoming. Beginning to think that his position was 'becoming insecure if not, indeed, untenable', Tulloch's mind was made up 'by a Jap attack in great strength' simultaneously on three of his officers' HQs. Tulloch now believed that it was a 'deliberate attempt to liquidate the whole set up in the Karen Hills, possibly as a prelude to some grand counter-offensive envisaged by the Jap High Command.' The next line of Tulloch's report is revealing:

> Our potential value in the hills appears to have been rated much more highly by the Japs than by our own people, judging by the close attention with which we were honoured.

'HIS HEAD WAS LYING A FEW YARDS FROM HIS BODY'

Such was the attention that Tulloch decided to concentrate all his forces at Dawrawhku to avoid having his command 'liquidated in detail.' His orders were acted on in good time, meaning that Major Warren's base was shifted just before an estimated battalion-sized Japanese attack fell upon it.

The 'Battle for Burma' was clearly far from over for Force 136 and its Character teams. Even accepting an expected amount of congratulatory hyperbole intended for the regular forces of 14 Army and the RAF, whose performance since March 1944 had undeniably been spectacular, Edgar and the Character teams were equally undeniably left to more or less fend for themselves. The strain took its toll.

64. 'I had a large abcess [sic] on my back'

Apart from the fact that the Army was, as admitted by officers from 19 Indian Division, 'tired' after a long and successful campaign, sights had been set on the next move in the defeat of Japan. The seaborne invasion of Malaya, codenamed Operation Zipper, required rest and reorganization, and a building up period, before Allied forces could be launched. On 28 May, a little more than three weeks after the fall of Rangoon, the new 12 Army was formed so that 14 Army could be reorganized for Zipper. The 12 Army retained 4 Corps of 14 Army, so 19 Indian Division at Toungoo – as well as 5 and 17 Indian Divisions – remained responsible for Burma. While the Character teams fought for their lives, on 27 June a letter was sent to Brigadier Anstey at Force 136 HQ in Kandy, Ceylon. The authorship is not clear, but their displeasure was:

> For some time I have had the feeling that both you (Kandy HQ) and SACSEA have written Burma off as finished from an SOE and military point of view.

There were five divisions in 12 Army, but they had 'developed a most depressing lack of initiative since taking Rangoon' to the extent that 'we are killing more of the enemy than the entire 12 Army'. The underline is in the original. General Montague Stopford agreed in July, admitting that Force 136 had killed more Japanese than 12 Army had in the past few weeks. In the far south of the Character area, Mongoose felt the pressure just like Otter, Ferret and Walrus. There were concerted drives against Mongoose, with an estimated 2000 enemy troops hunting down Mongoose Red. Further south still, two Operation Nation teams were forced on the run and had to be evacuated from a Mongoose airstrip. Where Edgar had been able to write of his patrols in April that his levies had a 'supremacy over the Jap to an almost unbelievable extent', in June and July most of the Force 136 teams were having a harder time of it.

'I HAD A LARGE ABCESS [SIC] ON MY BACK'

By the middle of July, after five months behind the lines, Edgar wrote that 'Many of my officers and levies were in a strained and exhausted condition.' He also describes the Japanese as 'rather flaccid' about this time in July, but there was a reason for that. The Battle of the Breakout was about to begin. The Japanese trapped in Burma were ready to cross the swollen Sittang, and on 26 July Edgar was warned that around 2000 Japanese would be attempting to transit through his area of operations. Edgar went to join Captain Montague, in command of Otter Green, with two platoons of levies as reinforcements:

> The Japs were severely handled on the SITTANG river, and the broken remnants entered the hills where they were mopped up by the levies in all CHARACTER areas.

As it transpired, this was Edgar and Otter group's last round of serious fighting, as most of the Japanese 28 Army coming from the Pegu Yomas passed to the south, hitting the Hyena and Mongoose areas. The Hyena commander, Lieutenant Colonel Howell, estimated that 9000 Japanese troops came through his area. Edgar was now able to make his way to 19 Indian Division at Toungoo. After visiting the commander in Toungoo, he was going to return to his mountain-top HQ at Sosiso via Flight Lieutenant Breen's White area and Eustace's Red (Ferret) area, but while in Toungoo, he heard about the apparently imminent Japanese surrender. He was therefore asked to remain at Toungoo until there was more news. Edgar had gone to Toungoo specifically to meet replacements who were waiting for his orders so that his 'worn out personnel' could be relieved. There were eight officers and NCOs in total, who Edgar duly sent on to Otters Green, Red and White while he awaited news.

At the same time as Edgar presumably got some rest and saw to his reinforcements, further south, the other Character teams were extremely busy. As the Japanese attempted to reach the safety of the southeast of the country, they had to cross numerous rivers and chaungs. To do this they built rafts out of bamboo to float themselves across the monsoon torrents. Hyena and Mongoose platoons set up positions along the banks opposite crossing points and, put simply, it was a slaughter. Major Milner of Mongoose White described the Japanese attempt to cross the Shwegyin River as 'suicide'.[1] Japanese plans for the breakout had been captured, and many of the Japanese 28 Army had been living off the land since at least April, so they were in a poor state. Airstrikes were called in on concentrations of troops, and levies were confident enough to take boats out on the river to shoot up the rafts, and use 'their dahs in some cases'. All of the Character teams were keeping a body count of how many of the enemy they accounted for, and it was during this period, either side of the Japanese surrender on 15 August, that the Mongoose and Hyena teams saw their tally increase by hundreds. It was as Milner described: 'one-sided killing'.

For Edgar, it was not completely one-sided, as Captain Longmuir lost his life at the beginning of August. The fighting continued after VJ Day (Victory over Japan Day), 15 August, because news of the Japanese surrender took time to be communicated to the Japanese in the field. Even when leaflets were dropped and Force 136 teams sent out emissaries, the news was not believed. In the hunt for food, parties of Japanese continued attacking villages, terrorizing the civilian population, who needed defending. In this way, the fighting went on for weeks after the official cessation of hostilities. Mongoose, for example, recorded that their Battle of the Breakout lasted until 9 September, and only on 17 September did they finally take the surrender of 11,000 Japanese troops.

While Mongoose and Hyena fought on, Edgar had left Toungoo and was visiting his friend Eustace, organizing for Japanese Liaison Officers to come and help persuade their comrades that the war was over. While there, he was summoned back to Toungoo for a conference with 19 Indian Division. When he arrived in Toungoo on 29 August:

---
[1] National Archives, HS 7/106, Report of Major Milner.

'I HAD A LARGE ABCESS [SIC] ON MY BACK'

As I had a large abcess on my back and boils in my ear I was placed in hospital for a week for treatment, but remained in touch with my command by signals through the L.O. [Liaison Officer].

It was the same ulcer, or abscess, that Edgar went to see his doctor about in 1946, after finally arriving back home in Southern Rhodesia. Similar nutritional issues were affecting the other men of Operation Character too. The men in Mongoose group had by now developed skin diseases due to a lack of vegetables, according to Lieutenant Colonel Hood's post-operational report.[2] As far as Eustace was concerned, his team 'had been systematically starved' and were therefore 'very near the limit of endurance'.

The local population were also struggling to survive, and not just because of food shortages: war had deprived them of many of the basics. Material for clothes and kerosene for lamps; oil for cooking; salt which was vital for living in a jungle climate – all were virtually non-existent. The war might have been officially over, but the reality on the ground was something else. There was still much to do in the gap between the defeat of one empire, and the restoration of another.

---

[2] National Archives, HS 7/106, Report of Lt. Col. Hood.

65. 'Polite, amenable and meticulous'

As if dealing with the Japanese wasn't enough, Major Lucas of Mongoose reported that Burmese Nationalists were 'warning villagers to prepare for a second war' after the Japanese were gone.[1] The Burmese Nationalists did not want the Japanese Empire to be swapped back to the British Empire. The country was in a parlous state having been fought over twice in two land campaigns in three years, and although the British Empire was now victorious in Burma, it could never recover its prestige after the disasters of 1942. It was end of days for the British Empire in Asia, not least because the vast majority of the men who fought in 14 Army and recovered Burma were Indian.

The Burmese jungle was still awash with an enemy still determined to fight, but they also needed feeding. Eustace was kept busy 'killing Japs only when they attempted to loot villages.' In an attempt to avoid unnecessary bloodshed, Major Turrall, in an act of folly that nearly cost him his life, tried to tell the Japanese in his area that the war was over on 16 August. He was a confident swimmer, so he decided to brave the Kyaukkyi Chaung. He was captured, bound, and held prisoner, and he was beaten for his efforts. They simply didn't believe him, despite a note he sent ahead of him with a levy – and swimming across with a bottle of whisky in anticipation of toasting the war's end. After a few days, he was shot at when he broke his bonds and ran off into the jungle. He was recaptured and would surely have been killed had the RAF not dropped leaflets specifically naming him as an envoy. Fortunately, the commanding Japanese officer believed the leaflet, so he was escorted back to the chaung for another swim. Nine days after setting out he reached the safety of his own men, but then he then got in trouble with his own superior officers for trying to end the fighting.[2]

[1] National Archives, HS 7/106, Report of Major Lucas.
[2] Richard Duckett, 'VJ Day in Burma: 'I don't believe the Japanese Army has surrendered'' [online] https://soeinburma.com/2019/07/11/vj-day-in-burma-i-dont-believe-the-japanese-army-has-surrendered/

'POLITE, AMENABLE AND METICULOUS'

On 12 September, Edgar flew to Rangoon to meet the Brigadier General Staff (BGS) of 12 Army. They discussed the surrender of Japanese forces who had remained bottled up along the Mawchi Road, and a plan was hatched whereby they would 'leave their arms and equipment in dumps at given places' before moving across to the east bank of the Salween River. After flying back to Toungoo, Edgar decided to drive by jeep all the way to Mawchi on 17 September, trusting 'Jap assurances' that there would be no mines on the road. Making it through to Mawchi in one piece:

> I found my HQ settled in a good house and sitting rather self-consciously on chairs for the first time in seven months.

It would take time for relief to be organized, and for a switch from military to civil personnel to be effected, which necessitated that the men of Character not only stay put, but start taking on a civil affairs role. What this meant in practice was restoring law and order, so levies now transitioned from guerrilla to interim police force to maintain civil order, while others had to deal with the large number of Japanese troops who needed to be induced to surrender.

With this in mind, Edgar went from Mawchi to Kemapyu on 18 September. At Kemapyu he met the 'Jap liaison officers and confirmed orders which had been passed to them by signal.' In his report, Edgar had kind words to say about these Japanese officers, which is perhaps somewhat unexpected after having spent the last two years battling them in some of the most remote and still largely unvisited parts of the Burmese jungle:

> These officers were polite, amenable and meticulous, and later distinguished themselves by the speed with which they went to the assistance of a barge which had overturned in the SALWEEN with certain personnel of the East African Brigade.

This paragraph of the report ends with Edgar confirming he had sent Japanese officers to Eustace and Captain Montague 'to round up parties of Japs'. Eustace, in his own report, wrote how these Japanese officers reached him on 12 September:

> when it was too late to contact the large energy force column [sic] which had crossed West to East along the southern boundary of Walrus area. Capt. Ansell was sent after them with a fighting patrol, but to his great disappointment he was unable to catch up with them owing to the HTU chaung being in full flood. I recalled him, or he would very likely have followed them across the Salween into Siam.

On the Australian War Memorial website there are photos of the Japanese officers about to board a Lysander in Rangoon allegedly to parachute into the Character teams, but these men would have been landed rather than dropped.[3] When Edgar went back to Mawchi at the end of August, he took a camera with him, and he wrote to Geraldine much later mentioning that he had 'taken masses of photographs during this last phase of the war'; another prolific photographer was Major Aubrey Trofimov of Mongoose Green. Both men took several photos of these Japanese Liaison Officers, which gives us a 'face' for the enemy all these years later.[4]

As September flowed into October, apart from rounding up Japanese troops, across the Character area commanders such as Edgar were concerned 'almost entirely with relief work for the

---

[3] Australian War Memorial, 'Rangoon, Burma, c. 1945-08. Three Japanese soldiers stand beside Westland Lysander IIIA V9303 of No. 357 Special Duties (SD) Squadron RAF' [online] https://www.awm.gov.au/collection/C304849

[4] An amazing number of Trofimov's photos have been published: Aubrey Trofimov, *A Most Irregular War: SOE Burma, Major Trofimov's Diary, 1944-45* (Devon Press, 2023).

'POLITE, AMENABLE AND METICULOUS'

Karens and in paying off and disbanding our levies.' Instead of weapons, the priority was rice. Edgar organized Dakotas to fly in and free drop rice at four locations at a rate of seven sorties and 35,000lbs of rice per week – about 17.5 tons. A ton of food per day was supplied by road to feed Otter's levies by the trucks of 19 Indian Division. On 21 September and 7 October, a total of 670,000 Rupees were dropped to pay off the levies, and by 20 October this task was done. The levies were also disarmed, although 50 were kept on strength 'for local defence against dacoits'.

On 21 October, Edgar and his HQ left Mawchi for Toungoo. He was happy that the relief measures left in place were 'adequate' and 'well in hand' by this date. Eustace had already arrived in Toungoo the day before him, and was already back in Calcutta by the time Edgar made it to Rangoon on 24 October. In Rangoon, Edgar continued wrapping up affairs until 5 November, writing his post-operational report and dealing 'with many matters concerning the future of the P Force Groups and Karen Levies.'

Eight months of intense work behind the lines was finally over. The world war was finally over, but for many of the peoples across Southeast Asia a new war for independence from their European colonial masters was about to start. The humiliations of 1942 had destroyed any residual ideas of British or French or Dutch supremacy, and nationalist movements now renewed their battles for independence from India to Indonesia. Indians won their independence from Britain in 1947, with Burma soon after in 1948. Edgar was to take no part in this process of decolonization. For him it was time to decompress, to recover and to reflect on what he had achieved, and start thinking about home and Geraldine.

66. 'I am dog tired'

In February, just before emplaning for Operation Character, Edgar had written to Geraldine to warn her not to expect any regular post from him. During his eight months behind the lines he had only managed to get one letter to Southern Rhodesia, four months post deployment. By then, sometime in June, he had been awarded an immediate Bar to his MC. The Bar was in recognition of preventing Japanese 15 Division from beating 5 Division to Toungoo in April. Edgar had told Geraldine that:

> he was in the midst of a great adventure, and that he was well and fit, and that the worst dangers were over.

In her private memoir, Geraldine continued, now quoting Edgar's letter:

> Everybody is celebrating Victory, but I have a war still on my hands and security must be observed. Tell Joy the North West Passage is a poor thing to my adventure.

Geraldine was obviously 'glad and relieved' to know that Edgar was 'alive and well' having not heard from him for so long. His next letter to her was sent another four months or so later, dated 10 November 1945. Edgar had left Rangoon:

> I am now in Calcutta finishing things off, getting operational reports written up, accounts settled and my boys disbanded and paid off.

This is somewhat curious given that his operational report is signed off in Rangoon and dated 3 November, and that therein, Edgar makes it clear that all the levies were paid off in the field. Perhaps the anomaly can be explained quite simply, though. Just as soldiers post 2006 were given time in Cyprus to decompress after six-month tours of Afghanistan, so Edgar needed time.

'I AM DOG TIRED'

Edgar was not ready to go home, he needed to decompress too. His letter continued:

> Hope to be ready for leave in three or four days. I am dog tired and if I did not get leave I would have to go into hospital. In any case it will be some time before a booking can be arranged for me in a troop ship, so I might as well spend the time on leave. I shall go to Darjeeling where it should be very cold and there I hope to renew my wasted nerves and sinews.

While Edgar's report is invaluable in providing us with his official, on the record, account of his part in Operation Character, his words 'off the record' are just as important. In his letters to Geraldine, even though there can be anomalies such as the one exposed above, it is here that the man, the husband, the war-shattered father can be seen. Even taking into consideration the likelihood of censorship, and the selective reproduction by Geraldine for public consumption in *The Life of a Jungle Walla*, and that he was writing for his wife, who he had not seen for the best part of six years, the following summation of Edgar, by Edgar, is instructive:

> You appear not to understand what a strain and responsibility of these months behind the Jap lines has been.
>
> My Burmese and Karen guerrilla force that I raised in the Chindwin was the spearhead of the invasion of Burma. I raised an Army in the Karen Hills behind the Japs and had three thousand riflemen under my command with over twenty officers. My groups spread out, and cut off the lines of communication of the Japs between Burma and Siam, other groups followed after. I gave the lead and the operation was one of the most successful in this campaign, and the people responsible were

> 'Peacock's Force'. Four groups of my Force led the assault, and with the Levies that gathered round them they became a great Army which killed over 12,000 Japs east of the Sittang River. I was in the Central Group which cut the main line of communication.
>
> The road from Toungoo into Siam, here we killed 3,000 Japs, when the Japs 15th Division was racing for Toungoo to reinforce it before our troops arrived. I stopped it on the road for nearly a week so that our Army was able to capture Toungoo before ever the Jap reinforcements arrived. For this I was given the Bar to my M.C. It is a very long story of hardships and privations for eight months.

The next part of this letter did not make it into the book, unsurprisingly given the tension that it reveals between Edgar and Geraldine:

> It is a very long story of hardship and privation for eight months, but there is not a man now in the army here, who does not know my name, and the majority wonder why I am not dead, or in hospital or on leave, and yet you, who should understand, say nasty things to me, because I just wanted to get away somewhere among strangers, and lie back and forget and let my wretched body and mind recover, before I start the business of post war adjustment and journey home. I am damn tired and you are not fair to me, my mind is sick, and I have to fight myself to prevent myself from going flop. Honours have been thrown at me etc. etc., but all I am craving for is rest for a month.
>
> Now do you understand? Well for goodness sake do not start quarrelling with me and trying to make me do what you think is good for me.

'I AM DOG TIRED'

From Geraldine's point of view, she just wanted her man home, and, as she wrote, how could she and the girls have realized what he had been through when they had been 'told so little about it all'? Many men had already returned to Southern Rhodesia, and here she was facing yet another Christmas without Edgar, having probably expected him home fairly soon after 15 August when Japan surrendered.

For the men who fight in them, the conflicts of the 21st century are not so different to Edgar's experience sixty odd years previously. Just like Edgar, Scots Guards Captain Leo Docherty wrote that at the end of his tour he 'revel[ed] in the fresh fruit and salads. The crunchy iceberg lettuce is a delectable treat after the monotony of bland MREs and Afghan rice.'[1] Food was, perhaps, the easy part. Readjusting to family life after high intensity conflict could be much more fraught for many soldiers. At least there is some support in place now, but for Royal Irish Captain Doug Beattie MC, he knew who he needed support from after returning from his second tour of Afghanistan. After his first tour, he wrote:

> I eventually told her [...] things I feared would repulse her and make her hate me as a person. But in the end it had been OK. Back then I should have had more faith in my wife. This time I would.[2]

---

[1] Leo Docherty, *Desert of Death: A Soldier's Journey From Iraq to Afghanistan* (London: Faber & Faber, 2007), p.171.
[2] Doug Beattie, *Task Force Helmand: A Soldier's Story of Life, Death and Combat on the Afghan Front Line* (London: Simon & Schuster, 2009), p.313.

67. 'I am full of eagerness to be home'

Edgar's next letter to his wife arrived from Darjeeling. He stayed at a Planter's Club which he apparently found 'most select and comfortable.' One of the nurses who had treated his appendicitis back in May 1944 was there with a friend, and the three of them – and possibly others – went out in the evenings together. Their argument about his not going home immediately was still on Edgar's mind:

> When I left Calcutta for leave, I had not had one single day off for nearly nine months and was dead beat. I know you will not understand, or will you? Why I did not rush home at once.

The letter continued, and Edgar was quite candid:

> To carry on in Calcutta, fighting for a place on a troopship, and arriving home in my then state, would not have been fair to you or me. Mentally I am still sick, and I suppose my experiences have changed me to some extent. You must try to bear in mind and be tolerant, or else we will just get on each other's nerves. You, too, have had a pretty grim time, and I have to bear that in mind. So for Heaven's sake don't let us have misunderstandings etc. about nothing.

As someone who 'despised weakness in himself or in others', Edgar's admission here that he was mentally unwell, and that his experiences had changed him, could be interpreted as surprising. His daughter did also describe him as 'courageous, uncompromising and outspoken' too, however, so perhaps this is an example of that. In any event, he did seem able to reveal himself to Geraldine in his letters to her, if not in person.

Before going on Operation Character, Edgar and Geraldine had discussed post-war possibilities, and Edgar

'I AM FULL OF EAGERNESS TO BE HOME'

returned to 'our ideas of caravanning, and wandering about taking photos and writing.' He wanted Joy to be his paid secretary so that he could 'write seriously', as he considered it 'essential to have a thoroughly efficient stenographer.' Geraldine wished that he would ask her to have a go at this job as she 'longed to have the chance of being all in all to him.' In the event, neither Edgar's wife nor his daughter filled this role, and Edgar never got around to writing up his war. Later in the letter, he wrote:

> I am full of eagerness to be back home, and to see you all again, and the changes on the farm. I shall probably be moody and difficult, but you will have to overlook that darling, these years have set their mark on me no doubt, as they have done to others.

Another admission from Edgar that the war had taken its toll on him. It is, after all, the soldier's burden:

> The fighting had been hard on minds as well as bodies. The damage was not obvious in the euphoria of survival and home-coming. But over the months, a number of cases of post-traumatic stress disorder were diagnosed among battle group soldiers. Though this number was in single figures, no one was immune. Almost a year after the events, one of the bravest and most optimistic of the senior NCOs could not bear to fall asleep for fear of the flashbacks and the faces of his dead friends that haunted his dreams.
>
> Homecoming was weird for everyone. The ordinariness of [...] life was startling and unsettling after what the men had been through.[1]

This could very well describe the return to 'normal' life for Edgar, or any soldier of the Second World War, but in fact it

---

[1] Patrick Bishop, *3 Para* (London: Harper, 2007), p.268.

comes from Patrick Bishop's book on 3 Parachute Regiment in Afghanistan.

It was at this point when Geraldine was full of hope and trepidation for Edgar's final homecoming that she learned of her mother's death in Britain. Alicia's 'regular letters' had stopped, and though she knew that her mother had been ill, nonetheless her passing came as a 'great shock'. She hoped, however, that having lost her mum, Edgar would 'return to give me sympathy and companionship'. It was with this in mind that Geraldine wrote a final wartime letter to Edgar in which she hoped to 'clear up any misunderstandings, so there would be nothing between us when he finally arrived.'

Two paragraphs of Geraldine's private memoir relate what happened next, and it is difficult reading, tragic even. After all the hardships of the war, similar to many returning Second World War soldiers, the reunion of Mr and Mrs Peacock was not to be a happy one:

> Oh what a fatal letter that proved to be. It certainly did not have the reaction I had meant it to have, but quite the reverse.

After telling Edgar how much she longed to be in his arms and how she was looking forward to helping him repair from his experiences, Geraldine asked for reassurance of his wartime fidelity:

> I thought he would say, as he had done before, 'of course not silly, of course I love you, and only you.' Instead of which it had a most disastrous effect upon Edgar, and whether it was the war or the letter I don't know, but Edgar was never the same after receiving it. He said his first reaction after receiving it, was to walk clean out of my life and never come home at all, but he realised I was just being foolish.

'I AM FULL OF EAGERNESS TO BE HOME'

From her point of view, Geraldine 'was merely longing to be loved and to hear him say so. But I verily believe it killed his love for me'. As he was on the verge of leaving India then, Edgar was no longer 'full of eagerness to be home.'

68. 'An old beret and the uniform of a colonel'

Edgar and Eustace travelled home to Southern Rhodesia together, arriving in February 1946. Edgar had signed up and started his Sergeant's course in July 1940, more than half a decade earlier. He had been home once on leave, for ten days in November 1941 just after he had been commissioned a Second Lieutenant. It was not only the returning soldiers who were anxious about homecomings. Geraldine wrote that she and the girls went to meet Edgar 'with mixed feelings':

> What would he be like after all these years? What changes would we see in him, and he in us? Joy had become a sophisticated young lady, now, and Wendy a big schoolgirl of fourteen, and I, I suppose I must have changed too, though far less than the girls as they were still growing. We sat in the little waiting room thinking our own thoughts, till we heard the plane arrive.

In 1995, a book entitled *When Daddy Came Home* was first published.[1] A call had gone out for people to share their memories of when their serviceman father or husband had come home. The call was answered, and a book filled with the testimonies of British families was the result. Although the book is specifically about soldiers returning to Britain, Edgar's homecoming, and the homecoming of thousands of Commonwealth veterans from across the Empire, would not be dissimilar to the sorrowful tales told within the book's pages:

> Men who'd danced so closely with death found the normality of family life not a haven but a torture. They couldn't forget and they couldn't move on, and in a world desperate to look forward instead of backwards, many were lost souls.

---
[1] Barry Turner & Tony Rennell, *When Daddy Came Home: How War Changed Family Life Forever* (London: Arrow, 2014).

'AN OLD BERET AND THE UNIFORM OF A COLONEL'

Interestingly, Geraldine mentions how they had heard on the wireless that families needed to 'make allowances' for their returning menfolk. Edgar's letters to Geraldine had said the same. It was therefore a 'shy' trio of girls who watched as Edgar climbed down out of the aircraft

> so worn and thin, wearing an old beret and the uniform of a Colonel, a very different Edgar to the young Lieutenant who had come home so eagerly on those earlier ten days of leave.

It didn't help that, on his way home, Edgar had called in to see his brother, and his brother was dying. Even at this hour, his brother's wife, Rene, refused to allow Edgar in the house. Geraldine hoped that with her recent loss and Edgar now experiencing his, the two of them might be drawn 'closer together'. It was not to be, though, and similar to the stories in *When Daddy Came Home*, 'The smallest of grievances became mountains impossible to climb.' For Geraldine, her 'mountain' was her hunt for reassurance in her final letter sent to India, a letter sent with her best intentions. Yet she recognized that those who had been far from the horrors of war needed to be patient, so wanted to 'let the first move come from him.'

For Eustace too, the long-awaited family reunion was tough. He wrote:

> Returning home after six years absence to a country whose civilian population had not heard a shot fired in anger nor experienced privations of any sort, was an anti-climax. I felt aware that my personality had changed and it was soon evident that my wife and I were no longer compatible.

Eustace applied for a job as Game Warden in Mpika, Northern Rhodesia, and by late 1946 he was back in the wild, appreciating the vibrant ecology where southern and central Africa meet. From there, he and Edgar corresponded regularly, while Edgar tried to settle back into family life.

For many men, their return to family life came with the expectation of picking up from where the war had interrupted, a time when the man ran the household. In the absence of their menfolk, though, wives and children had had to get on with life, and had grown used to the home being theirs, as illustrated in *When Daddy Came Home:*

> Families had got on well enough without a man in the house. Now he was back, if he thought he could just take over where he had left off, he had another think coming. There were consequences, summed up by the sadness of the girl who was ten when her father came home. As a grown woman, she told us: 'Things were never the same. My parents had changed. Life had changed them. They had missed so much of each other. My father had an enemy to fight. My mother had the constant struggle to keep the home fire burning. I don't know who had suffered most'.

Geraldine wrote that Edgar was 'afraid that he had lost his authority in his long absence'. This fear became manifest when Geraldine forgot to serve him cabbage for breakfast and he shouted furiously 'I am master of this house'.

'This house' was not one that the newly reunited family were to stay in for much longer. While up in Salisbury for army medical board and demobilization, Edgar went looking for a new home, as he had accepted a job in a timber exploration company and would be working out of Umtali. Seven miles outside of the town he had found a farm for sale, and similar to nearly a decade before, he had bought it on the spot. He wrote home to say it was ten times the size of their farm in South Africa, and that Geraldine 'would have to live up to that standard, and think in pounds now, and not in pennies.' The purchase of this latest farm was, plausibly, one way in which Edgar can be seen to have reasserted the authority he imagined he had lost.

'AN OLD BERET AND THE UNIFORM OF A COLONEL'

While 'Many men came home with changed personalities, particularly those who had seen action', the purchase of Fern Valley was not without precedent, and nor indeed was Edgar disappearing for weeks to oversee subsequent affairs. This time, it meant that Edgar did not go to Joy's graduation in Grahamstown while he saw to the sale and started his new job. He also argued with the medical board to try and get more than a month's leave, but apparently ended up with no leave at all. Shortly after that, his new job fell through, and he was also back in hospital for the abscess on his back to be treated.

With Edgar away, it was back to letters, and the excerpts Geraldine placed in her memoir are thoroughly optimistic. Edgar wanted Geraldine to enjoy her month away with the girls; the sale of their farm had gone through; he had passed the medical board; the abscess on his back was 'quite well' and he felt fit; and he sounded excited for Geraldine's return so they could start their 'new adventure'. Geraldine 'felt everything was all right'; a promising post-war life stretched ahead of them.

69. 'Starting from scratch'

Edgar wasn't fazed that his job with the Rhodesian Teak Company had terminated more or less before it even began. The purchase of Fern Valley would keep him occupied. Set in 2500 acres of land with excellent views and access to the facilities of Umtali nearby, Edgar was excited about this next chapter in his life. Geraldine left the old farm with 'mixed feelings'. She had kept it afloat by herself all those years Edgar had been away, a time of drought and a time in which she nearly died after her emergency operation to remove a lump. She had certainly faced her own struggles to 'keep the home fire burning', and now she was suddenly being upped and made to leave it all behind.

On arrival at Fern Valley, Geraldine and Wendy discovered that they were 'starting from scratch once more.' There was no electricity, water had to be fetched from the river, there was 'no attempt at a garden', and the house was 'bare and empty'. That first night the three of them sat on boxes eating sandwiches for supper and watched the sun set over their new kingdom before building their beds and settling down for the night in their new home.

In her memoir, Geraldine comments that one of the people they employed on the farm later on was not much of a 'pioneer'. In 1946, Southern Rhodesia was a colony with just over fifty years behind it since Cecil Rhodes' columns had marched into Matabeleland. Umtali was founded as Fort Umtali in 1897, and has been known since 1982 as Mutare. Situated on Zimbabwe's eastern border with Mozambique, it is known for its trading links with the Indian Ocean dating back through the centuries. When the Peacocks moved there in 1946, the town had a population of around 10,000 so it was still quite a pioneer town with much to be developed. In the coming years, Edgar and Geraldine played a significant part in that development, constructing a dam for water supply, and building an entire

'STARTING FROM SCRATCH'

township for locals to live in. By 1971, Umtali had attained city status, and today has a population of over 200,000.

Before playing their part in the growth of Umtali, Edgar and Geraldine needed to attend to their new property. The house was 'old and rambling', with a small kitchen which relied on a wood fire for cooking. There wasn't even a sink in the beginning. In any case, all water came from the river, 'carried back to the house by native boys, who poured it into a small drum which was connected by pipes to the kitchen and bathroom'. An outside fire was used to heat water in old paraffin tins. The water works were solved by Edgar laying six miles of pipe and building a reservoir. Taps were fitted and some semblance of modernity established. Even so, humans are subject to the vagaries of weather, and a drought in 1947 dried up the mountain spring which fed the miles of pipes. Edgar wrote to Eustace about this time describing how his crops were all shrivelled up and dead, and his fear that there would be a famine.

With crops dying and the drought enduring, Edgar resorted to a skill he had learned on their first farm in South Africa: brickmaking. This was the start of the township, for before very long, Edgar had fifty-four workers with fifteen wives and twenty-five children living on the farm. Just as Edgar turned to brickmaking to continue making a living in 1947–48, in 2013 there was brickmaking in Fern Valley for the same reason. In 2019, concerns that the brick moulding business was a leading cause of deforestation in Zimbabwe, as fire is needed to set the bricks, led to a ban on any buildings being constructed with anything other than cement bricks. A company called Manicaland Bricks is now the main brick supplier in Mutare. Mutare is the provincial capital of Manicaland. Maybe this brick business is part of Edgar's legacy to this region of Zimbabwe...

With money running low, the decision was made that plots of land needed to be sold. Government rules did not allow land to just be sold any old how, and if land was to be sold to build a township, then it must have a water supply. Never one to be put off by a big project, Edgar got to work building a dam:

> He was working furiously, with dam scoops and oxen, and his own lorry, and his determination was rewarded, for it was completed before the rains came.

The resulting dam became something of a local marvel, a place of leisure attracting picnickers and swimmers, campers and fishing. Edgar even made a boat for the reservoir he had created. Pipes were laid to bring water into the plots where houses were built and before too long a township had been created. In a book about Manicaland, Chapter 15 is about those who 'took part in the growth' of the province. Part of the entry for Lieutenant Colonel Peacock reads:

> After demobilisation in 1946 he found a farm at Umtali - Fern Valley - where, with only his African boys he built what was considered an impossibility - a dam on the Dora River. As the dam was more than sufficient for his own use, he surveyed about six hundred acres of his farm and plans were drawn up, dividing this into two acre plots. So it was that the suburb now known as Fern Valley was started.[1]

If Edgar's legacy of bricks and a suburb are not enough, a third less tangible one from the Southern Rhodesian newspaper *The Herald*, dated 7 November 1963, might make a brace into a hat trick:

> Standing on a hillside looking across a bush-filled valley not far from Umtali is a typical Rhodesian farmhouse. It is big and rambling, with passages

---

[1] Hulley, Cecil, 'Memories of Manicaland', 20 October 2010 [online] https://memoriesofmanicaland.blogspot.com/2010/10/

and long verandas. But it is deserted, for locals say the house is haunted.

An Umtali man who visited the farmhouse recently, heard footsteps and smelled smoke in the empty rooms. But he could find no sign of life.

Talking about this later, he was told 'that house is haunted. Old man Peacock walks about there, smoking his pipe'.[2]

---

[2] 'Footsteps riddle in 'ghost' farmhouse', *The Rhodesia Herald*, 7 November 1963 [online] https://www.herald.co.zw/footsteps-riddle-in-ghost-farmhouse/

70. 'He must be ill in some way'

'Old man Peacock' was not very old when he died on 4 March 1955, aged 62. Geraldine had been worried for some time that 'he must be ill in some way', but she was never able to find out what it was. She did try, but not by asking him.

Judging by her memoir, these were not the happy, adventurous post-war years that Geraldine had hoped for when they set off for Fern Valley in 1946, shortly after Edgar's return. The wartime dream of caravanning and writing and painting and exploring southern Africa together never happened. Everything that she hoped would bring them together and provide a basis for the companionship she craved, didn't. It would be easy to blame Edgar's wartime experiences entirely, just as so tragically related in the pages of *When Daddy Came Home*, but Geraldine had experienced Edgar's severance from her through the 1930s. Whether it was that fateful letter, or a whole host of points of tension that Geraldine set out in her memoir, will never be known for sure: Edgar's voice in his marriage is missing. Geraldine chose to believe he was ill, for she was at a loss to explain why he continued 'to punish me for past offences after all these years.'

Apart from his mental health and his abscess, Geraldine wrote that Edgar's eye had been damaged by explosives while on Operation Character. As a result, for his war pension, he had to go for regular check-ups with the doctor. Geraldine would go with him, but stayed in the car while he saw the doctor. Eager to find out if there was anything else wrong, one day she fabricated some story to get herself an audience with the doctor, and asked him what was wrong with Edgar. She left none the wiser, but with the advice to do nothing which would upset or anger Edgar, as he had high blood pressure. She didn't rate her chances of success with this, for 'everything I did was wrong.'

'He must be ill in some way'

It is quite heartbreaking to read how these nine years after the war played out for Geraldine, but whether they provide more insight into Edgar's character or Geraldine's is a difficult measurement to make, if indeed it should be measured. Married lives are often complicated, but whereas Eustace and his wife went their separate ways, Edgar and Geraldine didn't, for whatever reason.

There were still, of course, shared 'big life' moments such as Joy's wedding, and the King's tour of Southern Rhodesia in April 1947. These memories are tinged with sadness for Geraldine, however, as she 'wondered what Edgar's feelings were as he proudly escorted his beautiful daughter up the aisle'; and she 'felt embarrassed' when they went to see the King, 'as if she ought not to be there, so estranged had we become.'

One Sunday in 1952, the dam burst. It is fortunate that nobody was killed, and that the only casualty was the boat Edgar had made. Geraldine was worried for Edgar's health, knowing that he was already ill, but Edgar simply said the dam would need to be built again, and so he did.

The busted dam that year was not the only flood, if the physical water can be taken as a metaphor for emotions. One morning, Geraldine plucked up the courage to ask Edgar if he still loved her. At his reply, her 'heart nearly stopped beating. I felt paralysed and unable to speak.'

He replied 'I did once.'

For the last six years, Geraldine had supposed that 'he must be ill in some way', or that it was down to 'the after effects of the war'. He went on to explain that they should stay together for the children, that there was nobody else, and that he did not want her to go away or take a job elsewhere.

But Edgar really was ill. Despite the knowledge that he no longer loved her, Geraldine remained faithful to her wedding vows and nursed him through the final sick weeks of his life. One morning in March 1955, Edgar was delirious, so Geraldine sent for an ambulance. His first night in hospital, he fell out of his bed and banged his head, so Geraldine stayed with him on the second night. As she sat holding his hand in the early hours of 4 March, Edgar said her name just once and he 'slipped away so peacefully'. She gave her husband one last kiss on the brow and went to tell the nurse of his passing.

71. 'With God's help I determined to do it'

Geraldine was collected from the hospital by Wendy and her fiancé at around 2 am. Joy and her husband Roddy, with their two children, drove all night to get to Umtali. Roddy took everything in hand, organizing Edgar's funeral, for which Geraldine was ever so grateful. Afterwards, Geraldine went to stay with Wendy until she was ready to face the world once again. Despite the anguish of the post-war years, Geraldine 'could not believe that Edgar would never come back' and found it tough.

It was decided to wind up the farm, but before it was even sold off, Geraldine moved into a flat in Umtali with Wendy. The next four months were spent distracted by preparing for Wendy's wedding so that Geraldine 'had no time to think over my own grief.' After the wedding, Joy and Roddy took her away on a month's holiday so she could cope with 'losing' her youngest daughter too.

For the first time in thirty years, Geraldine was her own boss, with nobody to look after, and no Edgar to tiptoe around. She started running art classes one day a week and tried to get a job in Umtali to fill the rest of the week. There were no jobs for a lady of her age, however, so she resolved to do something else, something that Edgar had never got around to:

> Then it suddenly came to me, that I must write the book that Edgar had always intended to write when he came home, about his war experiences, and had always been prevented from doing so by hard work, and later ill health. I felt guilty and afraid at meddling with his papers and war reports, and fancied I could hear Edgar's scorn at such an idea of me trying to write a book at all, much less one about a war that I knew nothing about. But I had his letters, which were so descriptive, and

many notes and reports, and so with God's help I determined to do it, and the amazing thing was it eventually turned out a great success, and many were the congratulations I received on what they said was a very fine effort.

The Life of a Jungle Walla was written and then published in 1958. The book somehow beat the security which still shrouded SOE in the 1950s. Since Edgar had reports, Geraldine reproduced them in full, beating the official declassification of SOE files by just under forty years. Other books, too, beat the Public Records Act of 1958, books such as Duncan Guthrie's *Jungle Diary* (1946), and the story of Major Seagrim published as *Grandfather Longlegs* (1947).

By writing up Edgar's war, Geraldine was finally able to understand so much more of what her husband had done between 1943 and 1945, and to grieve the man she had met all those years before on the boat, as a 'ship-board affair', as predicted by the fortune-teller in a hall on a rainy English afternoon. It had been quite a journey.

Photos 3

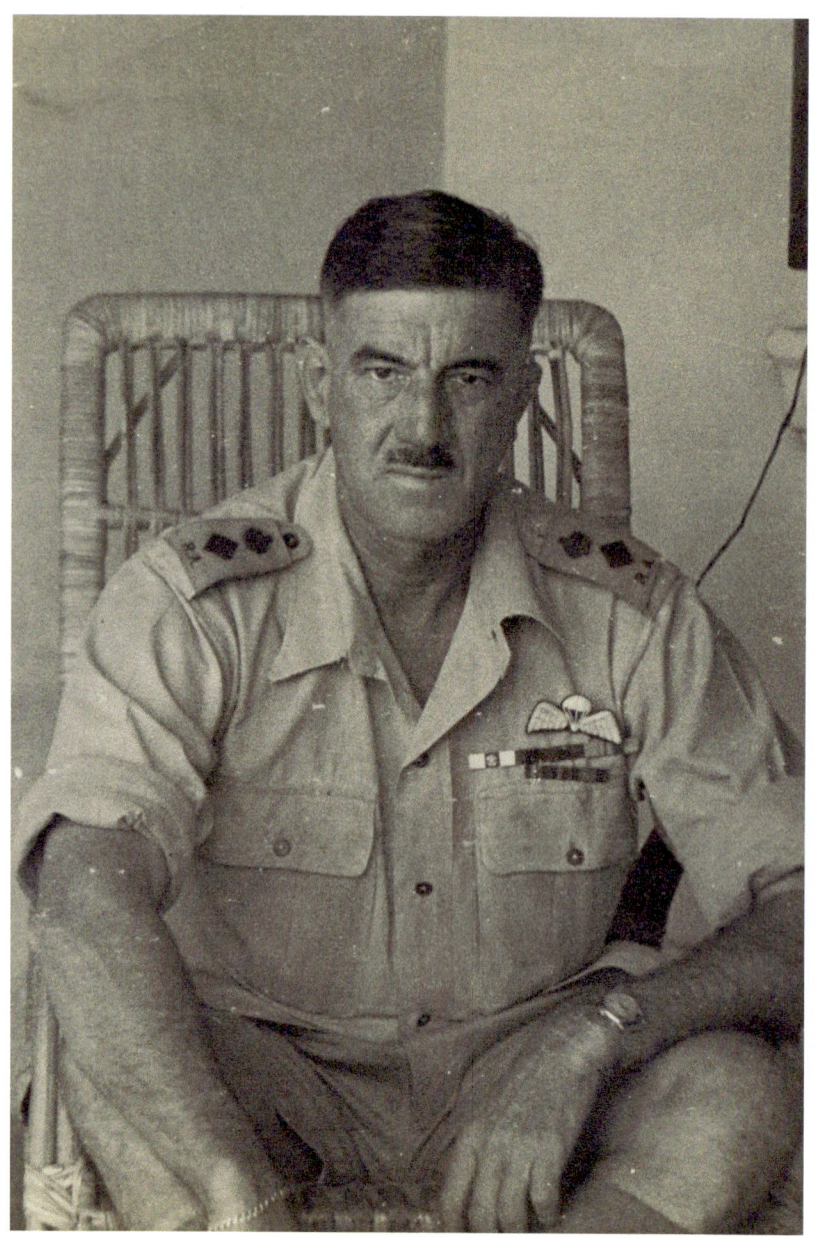

Edgar Peacock in 1947, aged 55

Edgar Peacock with wife, Geraldine, after receiving his DSO and the Bar to his MC in Rhodesia, 1947

Photos 3

Edgar Peacock on Fern Valley Farm, Umtali circa 1953. In the background can be seen his youngest daughter, Wendy who tried hard to be the son he never had.

Geraldine, Edgar & Wendy Peacock at Fern Valley, in December 1954.
Taken 3 months before Edgar's death on 4 March 1955

The dam built by Edgar Peacock at Fern Valley, Umtali under construction circa 1950

Fern Valley Dam, 1951

72. Jungle Warrior: Britain's Greatest SOE Commander

After the war, and while he was busy establishing his new home at Fern Valley, Edgar still had a battle to fight. Surviving correspondence between Edgar and Eustace reveals that, in their opinion, their frank and vocal criticisms of certain Force 136 staff officers had resulted in most of the recommendations made by Edgar for men under his command being left out of the honours and awards published in the *London Gazette* in 1946. This included not only Edgar's British officers and NCOs, but many of the Karens, Burmans and other Burmese who had proved so steadfast and gallant in their wartime service. Eustace was very angry in his letters, writing things of certain officers that probably shouldn't be repeated here because relations of such people couldn't fail to be offended. Edgar was much more restrained than Eustace, but the fact does remain, and it was an extremely stark fact, that the men of P Force who went in first and established Character, enabling it to be the great success it became, did not receive their DSOs and their MCs, their BGMs or their knighthoods. It was the opinion of many of the officers, even those who joined Character later and got their recognition, that the situation stank. The War Office found itself lobbied from all sides, including by the former head of Force 136, Colin Mackenzie:

> There are several mishaps among the Burma recommendations - one of the outstanding ones is that Peacock's DSO has been written down to a M.I.D [Mention in Dispatches].[1]

Mackenzie, along with many Force 136 officers besides Eustace and Edgar, were most concerned that 'a considerable injustice' to the Burmese men of Operation Character, and particularly the Karen, didn't go unchallenged. In the end of course, Edgar

---
[1] Major Eustace Poles, Private Papers.

got his DSO, and men whom Edgar fretted about such as Major Saw Butler also received his DSO, but the amount of work that went into restoring this particular apple cart to its correct position took up a considerable amount of Edgar's energy – all the while he was struggling with drought, an impending famine, and his ill-health. Edgar was never anything but busy. He always seemed to be fighting a battle of some sort.

It is his proactive 'will do' attitude that is possibly most responsible for making Edgar's life as remarkable and extraordinary as it was. He knew what he wanted and he pursued everything he wanted in life with utter fearlessness. As a result, he was either held in very high regard, a leader to be followed, a man whose grand plans were to be supported; or he was not liked. Being outspoken in his pursuit of what he thought right is surely why the DSO was originally downgraded to an MiD; one staff officer is supposed to have been heard to say on the subject of awards that 'They had fixed Otter area, who would get nothing out of it.'[1]

Medals, however, do not necessarily maketh the man. As Edgar wrote to Eustace, at his age in 1946 he did not have a career ahead of him, he didn't need the DSO. He was now a farmer in a remote part of the British Empire, but he was 'very distressed' about the treatment of the younger officers under his command and he wanted them to know that he still had their interests at heart. He was also burning with a sense of injustice that had to be rectified; due recognition and promises had to be kept to the scores of Karen who had served the Empire so selflessly. In taking on the 'fortunate and powerful' Edgar, those who allegedly sought to block the awards should have known that they were unlikely to prevail.

Despite coming home a Colonel, a highly decorated Colonel who had had an outstanding war in one of the most

---

[1] Edgar Peacock to Eustace Poles, letter dated 15 January 1947. Private papers of Eustace Poles.

demanding of theatres, Edgar largely remains today an unknown colonial from the wild places. He might have been known in Burma as the great Peacock of Burma, the saviour of the villagers, someone who knew all those jungles better than anyone else, but these pre-war reputations were not so much lasting as contributory, by their tangible truth, to the wartime reputation he was able to earn later. This wartime reputation, however, was only known to a few people because of the nature of the Special Operations Executive. Enveloped in secrecy, with security that many found exceedingly frustrating, men and women throughout the global branches of SOE were kept in the shadows for decades after the Second World War. When at last it was decided that news of the exploits of SOE could trickle into the public domain, the focus of the subsequent interest was almost exclusively Eurocentric. What had SOE done to prevent Hitler from developing the atom bomb? What had SOE done to support the D-Day landings? There was no great clamour to find out what SOE had done in the Far East, and to a large extent there still isn't. The story of the men in Force 136, such as Edgar Peacock, therefore, remains relatively unexplored. Medals and rank alone are not enough to gather the attention that might be considered deserved for these men.

Does Edgar deserve any attention, then? Does he deserve this biography? Should he be remembered as a hero of the Second World War? Should he be placed alongside Wingate or even Slim as one of the most famous men to serve in Burma? What are the criteria for answering these questions if rank and medals are to be considered merely a pointer to extraordinary things? What happens to the perception of a man once he is humanized beyond his often dehumanizing wartime experiences? Can or should the 'hero' status of men for their actions in war be compromised by their peacetime lives? So many subjective yet somewhat ethical questions – who deserves to be remembered and how? What marks Edgar out as any more special, extraordinary, interesting, heroic or worthy than scores of other men or women of his time?

It could be argued that Edgar served his time, just like many men, making a career in far-flung, unheard of places of the British Empire. Maybe he did things a little differently, such as taking his wife and children out on tour in the Burmese jungle, but his core job was one that others did before him, and after. Equally, hundreds of thousands of men and women served their country during the war, and while fewer ended up in Special Forces, Edgar was still one man among many thousands of men and women who did. And yet.

Edgar was not like the majority of these. By any measurement, Edgar had a remarkable war. From signing up as a private when he took five years off his age, to completing a course in parachute instruction at over fifty years of age; from his dogged determination to get to Burma, which took him – via training one of the Burma campaign's best known Indian Divisions – to being the principle reason the Army came to value Force 136 by his attachment to another Indian Division; from the forging of a multi-ethnic force of guerrillas which was thought to be impossible, to being the brainchild of SOE's most successful military operation of the entire Second World War.[2] No other SOE or indeed any other Special Forces officer spent as long behind the lines commanding operations as well as achieving such stunning results at both a tactical and strategic level. Edgar is therefore, surely, one of the Second World War's best kept secrets – at least up until now.

---

[2] Operation Character was recognized by Richard Aldrich as one of SOE's 'most spectacularly successful military operations of the war' in his *Intelligence and the War Against Japan* (Cambridge University Press, 2000), p.336.

Afterword
by
General Sir Douglas D. Gracey, KCB, KCIE, CBE, MC,

Officer Commanding 20th Indian Division, Burma 1944–45

(Foreword To *The Life Of A Jungle Walla*)

It would have been a pleasure as well as an honour to have written this foreword to Edgar Peacock's autobiography. It was a shock to me that one so young in heart, so full of energy and initiative had died. I am glad, however, to pay this small tribute to a very gallant soldier, who, as Eustace Poles says, was a prince among guerilla leaders.

I met him first when he was working in my area in the Kabaw Valley in 1943, and though not under my command at that time, he and his band of guerrillas were of the greatest value to my troops in giving them the latest information about Japanese movements. In the book will be found an account of his epic rescue of Capt. Gibson in the early days of the Japanese advance. When he came to me and insisted that I must help him to go out and get Gibson back, I thought he was mad, but if loyalty without thought of self is madness, give me madness every time. His stark courage and obstinate persistence got him there and back, when very few would have started. Later, his small group was a valuable addition to my division during the early and most critical days of the: Japanese attack on Imphal, but I lost him far too soon. He left to train and plan for his greatest adventure on the Mawchi road in the Karen Hills - Operation "Character". There is a full account of this wonderful operation in the pages that follow, which made such an outstanding contribution to the brilliant success of IV Corp's advance to Toungoo, Pegu and Rangoon. I cannot do better than quote from Field Marshal Sir William Slim's book, Defeat into Victory, pages 499-500.

Kimura was driving his men as hard as Messervy and I were driving ours. He had ordered all troops in the Shan Hills to get to Toungoo with sleepless speed. Their roads were the fair-weather hill tracks that ran roughly parallel to our route, sixty or seventy miles to the east. Opposite Toungoo and about seventy miles from it, this track turned abruptly west, and joined the Rangoon road in the town, and it looked as if they might beat us to it. But I still had a shot in my locker for them. As they drew south, their way led them through the country of the Karens, a race which had remained staunchly loyal to us even in the bleakest days of Japanese occupation and they had suffered accordingly. Over a long period, in preparation for this day, we had organised a secret force, the Karen guerillas, based on ex-soldiers of the Burma Army, for whom British officers and arms had been parachuted into the hills. It was not at all difficult to get the Karens to rise against the hated Japanese: the problem was to restrain them from rising too soon. But now the time had come, and I gave the word, 'Up the Karens!' Japanese, driving hard through the night down jungle roads for Toungoo, ran into ambush after ambush; bridges were blown ahead of them, their foraging parties massacred, their sentries stalked, their staff cars shot up. Air strikes, directed by British officers, watching from the ground the fall of each stick of bombs, inflicted great damage. The galled Japanese fought their way slowly forward, losing men and vehicles, until about Mawchi, fifty miles east of Toungoo. They were held up for several days by road-blocks, demolitions, and ambuscades. They lost the race for Toungoo.

The life and soul of this party was Edgar Peacock.

Afterword

I hope this biography will have a wide circulation amongst serving soldiers, as there is much in it for them to learn in the art of warfare, when the odds seem against them, as they so often will be, and the shattering effect that well trained and boldly-led "guerrillas" will always have, in suitable terrain, on more stereotyped formations. I especially commend the offensive employment of explosives, in the use of which "P Force" under Peacock were masters.

I have tried in this brief foreword to pay my sincere tribute to Edgar Peacock, not only for his great courage, but also for his outstanding leadership.

Those of us who served with him will know that what I have written is totally inadequate to do him full justice.

Douglas GRACEY
24th May 1958.

Glossary

Honours & Awards

BGM - Burma Gallantry Medal
CBE - Commander of the British Empire
DSO - Distinguished Service Order
GCB - Most Honourable Order of the Bath; Grand Cross
KCB - Most Honourable Order of the Bath; Knight Commander
KCIE - Knight Commander of the Indian Empire
MC - Military Cross
MiD - Mention in Dispatches
VC - Victoria Cross

- Basha - a short-term shelter built in the jungle
- Chaung - dry river bed, but a torrent in the rainy season
- Chital - a species of antelope
- Dacoit - a robber or bandit in Burma; they perform dacoity
- *Dons* - a traditional Karen dance
- Durbar - a huge military parade held on special occasions in India
- Garry - horse carriage
- Golden Book - a Karen legend about the beginning of their people

Glossary

- GSI(K) - General Service Intelligence. The K didn't mean anything. This was the purposefully non-descript name for SOE in India given for security reasons
- *Hta* - in Karen culture, a song-poem used as oral history
- Impi - a regiment of African military, e.g. a Zulu impi
- Longyi - Burmese name for a sarong
- Mahout - elephant rider/trainer/carer
- Nullah - dry river bed, an Indian word for Chaung (see above)
- Rinderpest - a cattle disease which decimated herds in Southern Rhodesia
- Sambhur - a species of antelope
- SEAC - Southeast Asia Command
- Stoep - verandah
- Veldt - the open African grasslands/plains

Appendix One

Timeline of Edgar's Life:

11 February 1893 - Born Nagpur, India

1914 - Edgar posted to Burma to work in forestry

January 1922 - King Edward's Royal Tour reached Burma

1922 - Edgar took leave in the UK, travelling to find a wife and invest some earnings

October 1922 - Met Geraldine aboard the SS *Walmer Castle*

22 April 1924 - Edgar married Geraldine in Rangoon Cathedral

April 1924 - First posting of their marriage: Pyinmana

1924 - Second posting of married life: Mawlaik

20 July 1925 - First daughter, Joy, born Mandalay

1926 - Epic floods in Burma

1928 - Geraldine, Joy, and Edgar visit the UK

1928 - Returning to work, Edgar posted to Mergui, southern Burma

1930-1931 - Edgar posted to Maymyo

1930-1932 - Saya San Rebellion. Edgar nearly murdered 1931

February 1932 - Edgar retired from Burma Forestry employment

24 June 1932 - Edgar followed Geraldine to the UK to take charge of the laundry

10 February 1934 - Edgar left the UK for South Africa to build their new home, Kleinwonder

APPENDIX ONE

5 March 1935 - Geraldine and the children followed Edgar out to South Africa

1939 - The Peacocks moved to Southern Rhodesia

3 September 1939 - Britain declared war on Germany, and Southern Rhodesia, as a 'quasi-dominion' (self-governing since 1923) was thereby also at war

July 1940 - Edgar enlisted

October 1940 - Edgar finished his instructor's course and passed out as a Sergeant.

5 July-25 October 1941 - Officer training at Njoro, Kenya. Passed out Second Lieutenant

25 October - 31 December 1941 - Artillery training at Larkhill in Kenya

31 December 1941 - Posted to 54th (Nyasaland) Field Artillery

9 March 1942 - Embarked Mombasa bound for Colombo, Ceylon

22 March 1942 - Disembarked Colombo

25 April 1942 - promoted Lieutenant

March to October 1942 - Defence of Ceylon

19 October 1942 - Posted to Intelligence School, Karachi

October to November 1942 - Edgar completed Intelligence Course No.15

30 November 1942 - Instructor Class 'C', Intelligence School, Karachi. Promoted Acting Captain.

30 December to March 1943 - At HQ Eastern Army lecturing 7 Indian Division in jungle warfare and touring the Indian jungles, including where he grew up as a boy in Nagpur.

4 March 1943 - Joined the Special Operations Executive

JUNGLE WARRIOR

18 March 1943 - Promoted Temporary Captain

1 November 1943 - Promoted Acting Major and in command of 'P Force' in the Upper Chindwin area, attached to 20 Indian Division

1 February 1944 - Promoted Temporary Major, War Substantive Captain

March 1944 - Caught behind the lines as the main army retreated in the face of the Japanese attack on India. Rescue of Captain Gibson for which Edgar was awarded the Military Cross

April to May 1944 - In action in a defensive box in Palel to defend Imphal

May 1944 - Evacuated to hospital with appendicitis

June 1944 - P Force extracted from the Battle of Imphal and sent to Camp Tweed to rest

August (?) 1944 - Return to Ceylon, this time for training for a big SOE operation

23 February 1945 - Deployed on Operation Character, Karen Hills, Burma

20 March 1945 - Promoted Acting Lieutenant Colonel

10 April 1945 - Character teams ordered to begin offensive operations by General Slim

13 April 1945 - Otter group received the order to prevent Japanese 15 Division from reaching Toungoo

16 April 1945 - A week of intense fighting on the Mawchi-Toungoo Road, with Otter group relentlessly ambushing the Japanese

22 April 1945 - 5 Division's tanks beat the Japanese into Toungoo, leaving 19 Indian Division to hold the town after they pressed on south towards Rangoon

APPENDIX ONE

20 June 1945 - Promoted Temporary Lieutenant Colonel, War Substantive Major

October 1945 - Left Operation Character

November 1945 -Edgar in Calcutta

December 1945 - Edgar on leave in Darjeeling, recovering

February 1946 - Edgar returned to Southern Rhodesia

1946 - Fern Valley bought and family moved north to Umtali

1952 - The dam on Fern Valley Farm burst

4 March 1955 - Died in Umtali hospital

Appendix Two

Military Identifiers / Designations

Often, units in the British Army and of the British Empire will be recorded thus: '1/2 King's African Rifles'. The first number is the battalion, the second is the regiment. Here, then, it is identifying the 1st Battalion of the 2nd Regiment of the KAR.

British Army Formations in the Second World War

- **Section** - usually 10–12 men
- **Platoon/Troop** - three or four sections, usually 30–40 men
- **Company** - three platoons, usually around 120 men
- **Battalion** - usually three companies and an HQ company, around 500–1000 men
- **Brigade** - usually three battalions, around 3500–4000 men
- **Division** - usually three brigades, 12–16,000 men
- **Corps** - two or three divisions, up to 50,000 men
- **Army** - two or three corps, up to 150,000 men

Specifically for Burma in 1944, Louis Allen set out the following:

Section - 8

Platoon - 32

Company - 127

Battalion - 800

APPENDIX TWO

Brigade - 2500
Division - 13,700
Corps - 30–50,000
Army - 60–100,000

For illustration, IV Corps under General Scoones consisted of:
17, 20 and 23 Indian Divisions
50 Indian Parachute Brigade
254 Indian Tank Brigade
+ Corps Infantry

17 Indian Division had two brigades, while 20 and 23 had three each. Edgar worked with 100 Brigade of 20 Indian Division. 100 Brigade consisted of three battalions: 4/10 Gurkha Rifles, 14/13 Frontier Force Rifles and 2 Border

For comparison with the Japanese Army:
Division - 12–22,000
Infantry Brigade Group, formed of three regiments - 8000
Infantry Regiment - 2600
Battalion - 800

Bibliography

Private Collections
- Peacock family documents
- Poles family documents
- Gardiner family documents

Archives
The National Archives
- AIR 23: Air Ministry and Ministry of Defence: Royal Air Force Overseas Commands: Reports and Correspondence
- AIR 27: Air Ministry and successors: Operations Record Books, Squadrons
- AIR 28: Air Ministry and Ministry of Defence: Operations Record Books, Royal Air Force Stations
- BT 26: Board of Trade: Commercial and Statistical Department and successors: Inwards Passenger Lists
- CAB 79: War Cabinet and Cabinet: Chiefs of Staff Committee: Minutes
- CAB 106: War Cabinet and Cabinet Office: Historical Section: Archivist and Librarian Files: (AL Series)
- CAB 121: Cabinet Office: Special Secret Information Centre: Files

BIBLIOGRAPHY

- CO 968: Colonial Office and Commonwealth Office: Defence Department and successors: Original Correspondence
- FO 371: Foreign Office: Political Departments: General Correspondence from 1906–1966
- FO 643: Foreign Office: Burma Office, Burma Secretariat, and Foreign Office, Embassy, Rangoon, Burma: General Correspondence
- HS 1: SOE Far Eastern files
- HS 7: SOE Histories and War Diaries
- HS 9: SOE Personnel files
- WO 95: War Office: First World War and Army of Occupation War Diaries
- WO 106: War Office: Directorate of Military Operations and Military Intelligence, and predecessors: Correspondence and Papers
- WO 169: War Office: British Forces, Middle East: War Diaries, Second World War
- WO 172: War Office: British and Allied Land Forces, South East Asia: War Diaries, Second World War
- WO 203: War Office: South East Asia Command: Military Headquarters Papers, Second World War
- WO 208: War Office: Directorate of Military Operations and Intelligence, and Directorate of Military Intelligence; Ministry of Defence, Defence Intelligence Staff
- WO 308: War Office: British and Commonwealth Forces: Historical Records and Reports, Korean War

- WO 373: War Office and Ministry of Defence: Military Secretary's Department: Recommendations for Honours and Awards for Gallant and Distinguished Service (Army)

The British Library

India Office Records

- Records of the Military Department (IOR L/MIL)
- Burma Office Records (IOR M)
- Official Publications (IOR V)

Bibliography

Books & Articles

Aldrich, Richard, *Intelligence and the War Against Japan* (Cambridge University Press, 2000).

Allen, Louis, *Burma: The Longest War* (London: Phoenix, 1998).

Barnard, Jack MC, *The Hump* (London: Four Square, 1966).

Beattie, Doug, *Task Force Helmand: A Soldier's Story of Life, Death and Combat on the Afghan Front Line* (London: Simon & Schuster, 2009).

Bishop, Patrick, *3 Para* (London: Harper, 2007).

Bryant, Raymond, 'Fighting over the Forests: Political Reform, Peasant Resistance and the Transformation of Forest Management in Late Colonial Burma', *Journal of Commonwealth and Comparative Politics* 32: 2, 1994, pp. 244–60.

Cruickshank, Charles, *SOE in the Far East* (Oxford: OUP, 1986).

Davies, Philip, *Lost Warriors* (Croxley Green: Atlantic Publishing, 2017).

Docherty, Leo, *Desert of Death: A Soldier's Journey from Iraq to Afghanistan* (London: Faber & Faber, 2007).

Duckett, Richard, *The Special Operations Executive in Burma: Jungle Warfare and Intelligence Gathering in World War Two* (London: IB Tauris, 2017).

Duckett, Richard, *The Diary of Major Alfred Trutwein: Psychological Warfare in Burma* (Privately published, 2021).

Duckett, Richard, *Serving the Empire: The Karen of Burma* (Devon Press, 2023).

Dun, Smith, *Memoirs of a Four-Foot Colonel* (New York: Cornell University, 1980).

Ghosh, Parimal, *Brave Men of the Hills: Resistance and Rebellion in Burma, 1825–1932* (London: Hurst, 2000).

Glass, Leslie, *The Changing of the Kings* (London: Peter Owen, 1985).

Guthrie, Duncan, *Jungle Diary* (London: Macmillan, 1946).

Jackson, Ashley, *War & Empire in Mauritius & the Indian Ocean* (Basingstoke: Palgrave, 2001).

Kirby, S.W., *The War Against Japan*, Vols. I–IV (Uckfield: Military & Naval Press, 2004).

Lunt, James, *A Hell of a Licking: The Retreat From Burma 1941–42* (London: Collins, 1986).

Lyman, Robert, *A War of Empires: Japan, India, Burma & Britain 1941–1945* (Oxford: Osprey, 2021).

Maung Maung, U, *Burmese Nationalist Movements 1940–1948* (Edinburgh: Kiscadale, 1989).

McEnery, John H., *Epilogue in Burma 1945–48* (Tunbridge Wells: Spellmount, 1990).

Morrison, Ian, *Grandfather Longlegs* (London: Faber, 1947).

O'Brien, Terrence, *The Moonlight War* (London: Collins, 1987).

Peacock, Geraldine, *The Life of a Jungle Walla: Reminiscences in the life of Lieutenant-Colonel E.M. Peacock* (Ilfracombe: Arthur Stockwell Ltd, 1958).

Richards, Frank, *Old Soldier Sahib* (Uckfield: Naval & Military Press, 2003.

Short, Stanley, *On Burma's Easter Frontier* (London: Marshall, Morgan & Scott, 1945)

Slim, Field Marshal Sir William, *Defeat into Victory* (London: Pan, 1989).

The Prince of Wales' Eastern Book: A Pictorial Record of the Voyages of H.M.S. 'Renown' 1921–1922 (London: Hodder & Stoughton, 1922). Also available online https://commons.wikimedia.org/wiki/File:The_Prince_of_Wales%27_Eastern_book,_a_

BIBLIOGRAPHY

pictorial_record_of_the_voyages_of_H.M.S._
%22Renown%22,_1921-1922_(IA_cu31924098820289).pdf

Tinker, Hugh, *Burma: The Struggle for Independence, 1944–1948, Vol. 1 From Military Occupation to Civil Government* (London: HMSO, 1983).

Trofimov, Aubrey, *A Most Irregular War: SOE Burma, Major Trofimov's Diary, 1944–45* (Devon Press, 2023).

Turner, Barry, & Rennell, Tony, *When Daddy Came Home: How War Changed Family Life Forever* (London: Arrow, 2014).

Tydd, Bill, *Peacock Dreams* (London: BACSA, 1986).

Verlander, Harry, *My War in SOE* (Bromley: Independent Books, 2010).

Wohlers, David, 'Prome, Burma – How a Village in Colonial Burma Became the Global Epicenter of Scientific Forestry and Impacted the Founding of the United States Forest Service', *Journal of Forestry* 117: 5, 2019, pp. 515–24.

Woodburn-Kirby, Major General S., *The War Against Japan Vol. 2: India's Most Dangerous Hour* (Uckfield: Military & Naval Press, 2007).

Websites

- 'About Myanmar', *Sampan Travel* [online] https://www.sampantravel.com/about-myanmar/

- Arboriculture: 'A History of State Forestry in Burma', December 2014 [online] https://arboriculture.wordpress.com/2016/12/24/a-history-of-state-forestry-in-burma/

- Australian War Memorial, Japanese Soldiers at Mingaladon boarding a Lysander [online] https://www.awm.gov.au/collection/C304856

- Brain, Jessica, 'Edgar the Peaceful', *Historic UK* [online] https://www.historic-uk.com/HistoryUK/HistoryofEngland/Edgar-the-Peaceful/

- 'Burma Riderless Horse Mystery', *Aberdeen Press and Journal*, 18 May 1931 [online] https://www.newspapers.com/

- Chilvers, Hedley, *The Seven Lost Trails of Africa: Being a Record of Sundry Expeditions, New and Old, in Search of Buried Treasure* (London: Cassell, 1930) [online] https://erroluys.com/biography3.html

- Dattani, Saloni, 'What were the death tolls from pandemics in history?' *OurWorldInData* [online] https://ourworldindata.org/historical-pandemics

- Duckett, Richard, 'The Special Operations Executive in Burma' [online] https://soeinburma.com/

BIBLIOGRAPHY

- Evans, Richard, "What if' is a waste of time', *The Guardian* [online] 13 March 2014, https://www.theguardian.com/books/2014/mar/13/counterfactual-history-what-if-waste-of-time

- 'Fighting in Burma', *Portsmouth Evening News*, 26 March 1931 [online] https://www.newspapers.com/

- Fobar, Rachel, 'China promotes bear bile as coronavirus treatment, alarming wildlife advocates', *National Geographic*, 25 March 2020 [online] https://www.nationalgeographic.com/animals/article/chinese-government-promotes-bear-bile-as-coronavirus-covid19-treatment

- 'Footsteps riddle in 'ghost' farmhouse', *The Rhodesia Herald*, 7 November 1963 [online] https://www.herald.co.zw/footsteps-riddle-in-ghost-farmhouse/

- Holledge, James, 'Black King's Buried Loot', *The Sydney Morning Herald*, 4 August 1954 [online] https://trove.nla.gov.au/newspaper/article/29607652

- Hulley, Cecil, 'Memories of Manicaland', 20 October 2010 [online] https://memoriesofmanicaland.blogspot.com/2010/10/

- Loi Thi Ngoc Nguyen, Protecting the Human Rights of Refugees in Camps in Thailand: The Complementary Role of International Law on Indigenous Peoples, *Laws* 12:57, 14 June 2023 [online] https://pure.strath.ac.uk/ws/portalfiles/portal/167577483/Nguyen_Laws_

2023_Protecting_the_human_rights_of_refugees_in_camps_in_Thailand.pdf

- Mehta, R.D., 'Cholera in Hyderabad State', *The Indian Medical Gazette*, December 1950 [online] https://pdfs.semanticscholar.org/4978/da57190724dc9e2a08eb43f282c42d8262dc.pdf

- Montclair University, 'The Little Red God' [online] https://msuweb.montclair.edu/~furrg/int/lredgod.html

- Mori, Emiliano et al, 'Reclassification of the serows and gorals: the end of a neverending story?', *Mammal Review*, April 2019, 49:pp.256-262 [online] https://www.researchgate.net/publication/332752477_Reclassification_of_the_serows_and_gorals_the_end_of_a_neverending_story

- Nanisetti, Serish , 'Epidemic was a seasonal terror in Hyderabad, *The Hindu*, 27 March 2020 [online] https://www.thehindu.com/news/cities/Hyderabad/epidemic-was-a-seasonal-terror-in-hyderabad/article31185071.ece

- O'Brien, Sam, 'Bird's Nest Soup', *Gastro Obscura* [online] https://www.atlasobscura.com/foods/birds-nest-soup

- Report on the Administration of Burma 1926 - 1927 (Superintendent, Government Printing & Stationery, Rangoon, 1928) [online] https://www.myanmar-law-library.org/law-library/legal-journal/reports-on-the-administration-of-british-burma/nouvel-article-no-402.html

BIBLIOGRAPHY

- Schlich, W. 'Sir Dietrich Brandis, K.C.I.E., F.R.S.' *Nature* 76, 131-132 (1907) [online] https://www.nature.com/articles/076131a0

- 'The Last Post of Dunluce Castle', *Hostilities Only*, 1st April 1921

- 'The Prince of Wales' arrival at Calcutta: Edward, Prince of Wales. Royal Tour of India, 1921-1922', *Royal Collection Trust* [online] https://www.rct.uk/collection/2702482/the-prince-of-wales-arrivalnbspat-calcutta-edward-prince-of-wales-royal

- Who are these red gods that call from nature?, *Farm Progress*, 18 April 2008 [online] https://www.farmprogress.com/farm-business/who-are-these-red-gods-that-call-from-nature-

INDEX

Note: Formations and units of the British and Colonial military forces are indexed under 'British Armed Forces'; those of the Japanese Army are indexed under 'Japanese Army'.

A
Abyssinia, North Africa •22, 108, 123–124
Ansell, Capt Frank •15, 245, 255, 309, 317
Arakan •150, 151, 193, 199, 228, 241, 274

B
Battle of Imphal. See Imphal, Battle of
Battle of Kohima. See Kohima, Battle of
Battle of the Admin Box •150
Battle of the Breakout •312–313
bird's nest soup •96
Boyt, Maj. Noel •184, 185–186, 189, 193
Breen, Flt. Lt. Arthur •292–293, 312
brickmaking •109, 115, 135, 332
British Armed Forces
   3/8 Gurkhas •178, 182, 207
   7 Indian Division •149–150, 151, 156, 193, 199, 354
   14 Army •216, 287–288, 290, 293, 311, 315
      intelligence •146, 167, 273
         Imphal •212
         P Force •183, 217
         Operation Character •253, 290, 291, 293–294, 304–306, 310
   15 Corps •193, 274
   19 Indian Division •305, 311
      Imphal •194
      Toungoo •295–296, 298, 305, 311–313, 318, 355
   20 Indian Division •194, 199, 201
      Imphal - P Force •212, 213
      P Force •167, 170, 171, 182, 188, 191, 193, 197, 199, 204, 217, 355
   21 East African Brigade •126–127
   357 Squadron, RAF Special Duties •231, 235, 239, 300–301, 303–304
   Burma Rifles •97, 227–228, 250, 282
   Northamptons •178, 181
   Royal Artillery •122, 124, 136, 162
      54 Nyasaland Field Battery •124, 136, 142, 146
Buchanan, Capt. Frank •261, 307
Bulawayo, Rhodesia •112–113, 121, 122
Burma Independence Army (BIA) •165, 172, 283
Burma National Army (BNA) •232
Butler, Maj. Saw •261, 345
Butler, Sir Harcourt •44, 46

C
Camp Tweed, India •213, 217, 218, 222–223, 355
Cape Town, South Africa •41, 54–55, 58, 60–61, 63, 71
Carey, Sgt. Neville •260–261
Carver, Sgt. Eric •261

369

INDEX

Ceylon (now Sri Lanka) •125, 126–129, 130–131, 136–139, 140–142, 143–146, 223, 228, 229–230, 231, 234, 276, 311, 354–355
Chaklala parachute training camp, India (now Pakistan) •223, 231
Charlesworth, Sgt. •261, 307–308
Chin •68, 218, 227
Chin Hills •92, 193
Chindit(s) •12, 22, 151, 157–158, 175, 228, 241, 243
Chindwin River (Upper)
　Forestry Service •87, 91, 115, 138, 146
　P Force •7, 149, 151, 157–158, 160–161, 162, 167–170, 171, 173–174, 176–177, 180, 182, 185, 188, 189, 191, 193, 194, 196, 201, 202–203, 212, 217, 221, 228, 284, 289, 320, 355. See Also P Force (Peacock Force)
cholera •6, 23, 91, 143–144
Cordtex traps •196, 215, 289
Craddock, Sir Reginald •44
Critchley, Lt. Col. Ronald •235
Cumming, Lt. Col. Mount Stephen •162–166, 170, 273, 274

D
dacoits •20, 318
Dakota aircraft (C47) •5, 21, 221, 231–232, 239, 240, 243, 246, 275, 299, 318
Dawna Mountains •101, 115
Denning, Maj. Arthur •235, 296
Dimapur •151, 193, 212
drought (1947) •332, 345
Dumont, Capt. Albert •292–293

E
Edwardian scam, England •37
Eureka Diamond, South Africa •32, 112
EWS(C)), Eastern Warfare School, Ceylon •223

F
Fern Valley •330, 331–333, 335, 343, 344, 356
　dam •331, 333, 336, 343
Force 136 •1–3, 148, 170, 211, 221, 222–224, 232–233, 237, 239, 244, 272–273, 274, 278, 287–288, 290, 293–294, 295, 298, 299, 301, 303–305, 310, 311, 313, 344, 346–347. See Also GSI(K), SOE
Forest Research Institute College, Dehra Dun •29

G
Gammon grenades •288–289
Gardiner •156, 164, 235–236, 245
Gibson, Capt. John •173, 185–186, 194–196, 217
　rescue of •7, 197, 198–200, 202–204, 206–208, 210–211, 213, 348, 355
Godwin, Alicia (née Orpen) •33–35, 36–39, 61, 82, 91, 94, 98, 103, 325
Godwin, Rev. Robert •33–35
Gracey, Gen. Sir Douglas •176, 182, 201, 204, 208, 217, 232, 348
Grenade trap. See Cordtex traps
GSI(K) •148, 156, 194, 221. See Also Force 136, SOE
Guthrie, Capt. Duncan •247, 252, 339

H
Ha Go, Japanese operation, Arakan •193, 199
Hemphill, Capt. •261
Horana, Ceylon •223, 227
Howell, Lt. Col. Hugh •278–279, 312
Hudson, aircraft •164, 231

I
IFBU. See Indian Field Broadcasting Unit (IFBU)
Imphal •151, 156, 174, 185
Imphal, Battle of •7, 193, 194, 197, 199, 201, 203, 211–212, 213, 215, 221, 222, 294

20 Indian Division •212, 213
Kabaw Valley •212
P Force (Peacock Force) •211, 213, 215–217, 289, 355
Palel •213–215
SOE •213, 215–216
India, invasion of •189, 193, 217. See Also March on Delhi
Indian Field Broadcasting Unit (IFBU) •69, 167, 217
Irrawaddy River •138, 165, 174, 184, 221, 232, 287

J

Japanese Army (IJA)
  15 Army •193, 212, 221, 253, 294
  15 Division •253, 287–290, 291, 293–294, 297, 301, 319, 355
  28 Army •193, 312–313
  56 Division •293, 297, 303
Japanese surrender •312–313, 316, 322
Jedburghs •223, 228, 233, 236–237, 238, 244, 292–293
Jessore, India •231, 233, 236–237, 239, 240, 244, 304
Johannesburg •36, 109
Jungle tours, forestry •89, 116

K

Kabaw Valley
  Battle of Imphal •193, 196, 201, 212
  P Force •171, 177, 215, 348
  rescue of Capt. Gibson •199, 201, 210
Kachin •92, 164, 218, 227, 274, 297
Kachin Hills •92
Karen •68, 101
  history of •232–233, 274, 281–286
  Operation Character •5, 22, 217, 222, 227, 236, 248, 250, 252, 274–275, 283, 292, 307–308, 318, 320, 344, 345, 349
  Operation Harlington •69, 163–165, 248
  P Force •156, 178, 181, 184, 188, 194, 207, 210, 213
Karen Hills •232, 256
  Operation Character •5, 7, 224, 227, 233, 243, 248, 250, 275, 297, 306, 309, 320, 348, 355
  Operation Harlington (Seagrim) •163–165, 227, 231, 279
Kemball, Capt. Arnold •175
Kimberley, South Africa •32, 112
Kin Scouts •171–172, 174, 176, 178
Kohima •304
Kohima, Battle of •212, 216, 221
Kyauk Kyaw, Battle for •171, 177, 178, 180–182, 184, 185–186, 188, 189, 191, 196

L

La Martinière College, Lucknow •6, 26
Liberator aircraft (B24) •221, 231, 246, 299
Life of a Jungle Walla •15, 172, 208, 320, 339, 348
Lobengula, Matabele King •112
Longmuir, Capt. •313
Loosmore, Sgt. Glyn •234
Lourenco Marques (now Maputo) •108–109
Lucas, Maj. John •315
Lysander aircraft •253, 317

M

Mackenzie, Colin •155, 167, 274, 344
Macleod, Capt. John •261, 276, 278, 307
malaria •96, 110, 115, 117, 145, 221, 222–223
Mandalay •88, 184, 253,

INDEX

275, 287, 353
Manipur, India •157–158, 193, 212, 217, 221, 222, 227, 305
March on Delhi •90, 189, 212, 216. See Also India, invasion of
Marchant, Capt. John •307
Mawlaik •139, 151, 156, 201
  pre-1945 •87, 89, 92, 94, 95, 115, 353
Maymyo (now Pyin Oo Lwin) •20, 21, 97–98, 99, 353
McCrindle, Maj. Eric •164, 227, 248
ME25 (Military Establishment 25) •223, 228, 229, 239, 276
Medals, denial of •344, 345
Meiktila •233, 287–288
Mergui (now Myeik) •94, 95–97, 115, 125, 353
Messervy, Lt. Gen. Frank •287, 349
Milner, Maj. Frederick •313
Moluku Saw •262
Montague, Capt. John •288, 297, 312, 317
Moreh
  Battle of Imphal •199, 212, 213
  rescue of Capt. Gibson •201, 202, 206–208, 210
Morshead, Lt. Col. Henry •21
Moulmein (now Mawlamyine) •99–101
Mountbatten, Admiral Lord Louis •222–223, 233, 274, 304

N

Na Mu, Havildar Saw •203, 206, 288–289
Nimmo, Maj. James •164, 227, 248, 255
Noronha, Capt. •178, 180

O

O'Brien, Sqn. Ldr. Terence •21–22, 235, 239, 240–241, 243, 245–247, 274, 278, 293, 299–300

Operation Capital •221
Operation Extended Capital •222, 224, 233, 294
Operation Character •16, 165, 224, 256, 287, 305
  ambush technique •215
  ambushes •215, 290, 296
  attack on Otter area HQ •276, 278, 307
  briefing •235–237, 241, 298
  drop zone •236, 241, 243–244, 247
  Ferret area •280, 291
  Ferret team •246, 252, 254, 291
  Hyena area •245–247, 252, 278–279, 312–313
  Japanese surrender •266, 312–313
  launch •240, 246
  Mawchi Road •253, 264–265, 292, 316
  Mongoose area •311–314, 315, 317
  Otter area •245, 250, 254, 278, 287, 292, 297, 300–301, 303, 345
  places:Chawido •252, 279, 283
  places:Hoya •292, 296
  places:Kemapyu •267, 316
  places:Khebu •253, 258, 263, 280
  places:Kyaukkyi •278
  places:Loikaw •253, 290, 293, 306
  places:Mawchi •253, 259, 276, 287–288, 290, 297, 299, 316, 318
  places:Nattaung •253, 259
  places:Pyagawpu •244, 245–246, 248, 250, 252, 257, 279–280, 291–292
  places:Sosiso (Otter HQ) •253–254, 276, 295, 297, 300–301, 304, 312
  places:Toungoo •253, 287–290, 291, 294, 297, 307, 312–313

372

refugees •296, 303, 307
starvation •295–296, 301, 303, 314
Walrus area •253–254, 287, 291, 293, 296, 305, 309
Operation Corton •96
Operation Dracula •290
Operation Harlington •163, 165, 227
Operation Longcloth •157
Operation Nation •287, 293, 311
Operation Zipper •311
Orpen, Francis •32–33

P

P Force (Peacock Force) •7, 151, 159, 162, 165–166, 167–170, 171–174, 175, 177, 178, 181–184, 185–188, 189, 193, 196–197, 198–201, 202–204, 206, 211–212, 213–215, 217, 218, 221, 227, 230, 232–235, 237, 240, 244, 261, 267, 270–272, 289, 305, 318, 321, 344, 350, 355
    ambushes •214–215
    Imphal, Battle of •215
Palel •201, 203, 213–215, 217, 289
Papun •252, 297
Peacock, Charles •6
Peacock, Edward •24
Peacock, Gerald •6, 24, 52–53
Peacock, Geraldine (née Godwin) •33, 74–75, 77, 82, 325, 338, 341–342
    breast cancer •146
    dengue fever •85–86
    erysipelas •160
    wedding •63, 66–69, 71–72, 87, 336
Peacock, Irene (née Bowder) •49–50, 52–53, 58
Peacock, James •24, 26
Peacock, Joy •11, 26, 42, 81–83, 89, 91, 93–94, 95–96, 99–101, 104, 109–110, 115–118, 135, 147–148, 319, 324, 327, 338, 353
    1st visit to England •91
    Birth •89
    memories of her father •116
Peacock, Lt. Col. Edgar •12, 16, 76, 79, 82–83, 241, 255, 261, 270, 340–342
    'The Great Peacock of Burma' •44, 46
    abscess •10, 29, 314, 330, 335
    appendicitis •151, 217, 219, 323, 355
    exhaustion •321
    injuries, eye damage •335
    Military Cross, citation •208
    post conflict •319
    post war, return home •327
    promotion:Captain •147
    promotion:Major •160
    promotion:Second Lieutenant •123
    promotion:Sergeant •121, 255
    PTSD •323, 327
    Royal Hunt •44
    trainer, jungle warfare •149–150, 156, 191, 354
Peacock, Percy •6, 12, 24, 26
Peacock, Thomas •23–24
Peacock, Wendy •6, 21, 26, 105, 111, 113, 116, 118, 147–148, 327, 331, 338, 342
Pearson, Sgt. Leonard •255
Phoenix Laundry, East Grinstead •101, 103–104, 106
Pietersburg (now Polokwane) •109
Po Sein, Jemadar Maung •288
Poles, Eustace •7, 15, 117, 121, 122–124, 127, 130–131, 141, 143–144, 151, 156–158, 170, 175–176, 178, 186, 193, 194, 199, 204, 206, 213–215, 217, 227, 246, 255, 270–271, 283, 291, 348
    broken rib •204, 205, 252
    broken rib, #2 •247
    post war, return home

INDEX

•327–328
Prince of Wales •30, 44–45
PTSD (Post Traumatic Stress Disorder) •327, 329
Pyin Oo Lwin •97
Pyinmana •61, 71, 78, 87, 288, 353

R

Rangoon (now Yangon) •5, 16, 45, 63–64, 66–68, 71, 87, 93, 95, 125, 126, 129, 165, 216, 222, 224, 253, 275, 284, 287, 290, 295, 304–306, 311, 316–318, 319, 349, 353, 355
Rebecca-Eureka system •238
Rhodes, Cecil •32–33, 36, 112, 331
Romain, Sgt. •307

S

S-Phone •238
Saya San Rebellion •20, 98, 100, 118, 241, 282, 353
Scoones, Lt. Gen. Geoffrey •166, 167, 201, 217
Seagrim •12, 15, 68, 163–165, 227, 231, 248, 250, 255, 279, 339
Ships
    HMS Cornwall •130
    HMS Dorsetshire •130
    HMS Hermes •130
    HMS Holyhock •130
    HMS Newcastle •231
    HMS Teredos •130
    HMS Vampire •130
    SS City of Exeter •108
    SS Dunluce Castle •41
    SS Walmer Castle •42, 48, 52, 55, 77, 353
Shwebo Plain •221
Sibong •207, 210
Sittang River •253, 312, 321
Slim, Gen William •150, 167, 177, 183, 193, 197, 199–200, 221, 222, 232–233, 273, 274–275, 290, 294, 295, 346, 349, 355
SOE •7, 12, 14–16, 22, 69, 92, 96, 100, 121, 143, 148, 150, 151–155, 156–158, 162–164, 166, 167, 169–170, 171, 174, 175, 177, 178, 184, 191, 212, 213–217, 218, 221, 222–224, 227–228, 231–233, 237, 272–273, 276, 285, 287, 307, 311, 339, 344, 346–347, 352, 355. See Also Force 136, GSI(K)
    Force 136 •241
    Imphal, Battle of •215
Southern Rhodesia (now Zimbabwe) •29, 33, 111, 113, 121, 135, 146, 159, 170, 229, 314, 319, 322, 327, 331, 333, 336, 354, 356
Special Forces •1, 5, 16, 347
Special Groups, SOE •5, 7, 22, 223, 227–228, 230, 232–234, 237, 239, 274, 284–285
Special Operations Executive (SOE). See SOE
Stopford, Gen. Montague •311
Swan, Flt. Lt. John •166, 167, 173, 185–186

T

Tamu •171, 177, 185, 194, 196, 199, 201, 206–208, 210, 212
Taschereau, Capt. •267
Thompson, Capt. Arthur •282
Thompsonite Movement •283
Toungoo, Burma •253, 287, 289, 295–296, 313
Transvaal, South Africa •33, 36, 60, 112
Trofimov, Maj. Aubrey •234, 317
Tulloch, Lt. Col. John •253–254, 260, 285, 293, 296, 299, 305, 309–310
Tun Sein, Jemadar Saw •195–196, 278, 289
Turrall, Maj. Rupert Guy •22, 240, 245–246, 250, 252, 278–280, 283, 315

U

U Go, Japanese operation •200

Umtali (now Mutare) •329, 331–334, 338, 342–343, 356

V
V Force •218
Verlander, Sgt. Harry •239
Vivian, Capt. •262, 267

W
Weather, affecting RAF Ops •299, 301
White, Capt. Stanley •174
Wingate, Maj. Gen. Orde •12, 22, 157–158, 175, 346
World War One (The Great War) •12, 19, 39, 42, 44, 46, 68

Y
Ya-Nan •207
Yangon •16, 67, 95, 253
Young, Maj. James •260–261
Yu River •193
Yuwa •178, 180, 185, 194, 196

Z
Z Force •218, 274, 307–308

BV - #0076 - 300425 - C13 - 229/152/18 - CC - 9781916556843 - Gloss Lamination